# BEYOND
# SELLING
# VALUE

## A PROVEN PROCESS TO AVOID THE
## VENDOR TRAP

## MARK SHONKA
## DAN KOSCH

**Dearborn**™
Trade Publishing
A **Kaplan Professional** Company

This publication is designed to provide accurate and authoritative information in regard to the subject matter covered. It is sold with the understanding that the publisher is not engaged in rendering legal, accounting, or other professional service. If legal advice or other expert assistance is required, the services of a competent professional should be sought.

Vice President and Publisher: Cynthia A. Zigmund
Acquisitions Editor: Mary B. Good
Senior Project Editor: Trey Thoelcke
Interior Design: Lucy Jenkins
Cover Design: Design Solutions
Typesetting: Elizabeth Pitts

IMPAX is a registered trademark of the IMPAX Corporation.

Published by Dearborn Trade Publishing, a Kaplan Professional Company

Printed in the United States of America

06  10  9  8  7

**Library of Congress Cataloging-in-Publication Data**

Shonka, Mark.
  Beyond selling value : a proven process to avoid the vendor trap / Mark Shonka, Dan Kosch.
     p.  cm.
Includes index.
  ISBN 0-7931-5470-7
  1. Selling. 2. Value. 3. Customer relations.   I. Kosch, Dan. II. Title.
  HF5438.25 .S53 2002
  658.8′1—dc21

                                    2002006508

Dearborn Trade books are available at special quantity discounts to use for sales promotions, employee premiums, or educational purposes. Please call our Special Sales Department to order or for more information at 800-245-2665, e-mail trade@dearborn.com, or write to Dearborn Trade Publishing, 30 South Wacker Drive, Suite 2500, Chicago, IL 60606-7481.

# ADVANCE PRAISE FOR *BEYOND SELLING VALUE*

"This book is destined to be a sales classic—the next must-read selling book! Shonka and Kosch really get it. The stakes are higher and selling value is more important than ever before. This is a great read that won't just tell you what to do; it will tell you how to do it!"
　　—Larry Wilson, Founder of Wilson Learning and Pecos River Learning Center, and best-selling author

"This book is essential reading for anyone in sales today. *Beyond Selling Value* has taken the things that the best value-oriented sales professionals do by instinct and put them into a system so they can be done by design."
　　—Joe Demharter, President and Chief Executive Officer, Pitman Company

"In a day when providing value is the baseline, Shonka and Kosch redefine the competitive edge in selling by going *Beyond Selling Value*. Employ these tools and you will create real adversity for your competitors. This book is worth booking a slightly longer flight just to read it twice!"
　　—Paul G. Stoltz, Ph.D., President of PEAK Learning, Inc. Author of the *Wall Street Journal*, *Business Week* bestseller, *Adversity Quotient: Turning Obstacles into Opportunities*

"Most salespeople consider themselves professionals and would like to sell higher, faster . . . and beat the Vendor Trap. Unfortunately many have not been taught how. This book is as good a step-by-step guide as I've come across. It should be required reading."
　　—James J. Ryan, President and CEO, Carlson Marketing Group

"A *must* read for anyone in sales and marketing. Mark and Dan have hit a grand slam home run with their approach on how to secure a new account and successfully grow with them. A real eye opener on the art of selling and making customer presentations."
　　—Jim Miller, Former CEO, Miller Business Systems, and author of the best-selling books, *Corporate Coach* and *Best Boss, Worst Boss*

"Today's salespeople don't need a book to tell us that it's tougher to sell value than ever before. What we need is a roadmap with signs to help us take advantage of the opportunities that are out there. That's what this book delivers. The process and approach in *Beyond Selling Value* is the best I've seen for helping sales professionals triumph again and again."
　　—Dan Servos, Vice President and General Manager, AOL Telecom Vertical Group, America Online, Inc.

"The strategies and tactics discussed in *Beyond Selling Value* work! I have seen a measurable effect on our close ratio as a result."
　　—Chris Matzke, Senior Vice President, American Express Retirement Services

"*Beyond Selling Value* provides good insight into the sales channel in our dynamic economy. Shonka and Kosch clarify the sophistication that is needed in the contemporary environment, and the steps that are needed to confront current challenges. I particularly like the focus on value, which provides direction to avoid being treated like a commodity."
   —Max H. Bazerman, Jesse Isador Straus Professor of Business Administration, Harvard Business School

"This book presents a powerful paradigm shift in selling value."
   —Jim Loehr, CEO and best-selling author

"I have only been introduced to the sales approach in *Beyond Selling Value* for a short time and am already a big believer. The approach is logical, efficient, and the way I like people to sell to me. In a short period, I have watched our people make some very impressive sales utilizing the tools and skills taught by IMPAX. Organic growth is critical to the success of Hub International, and IMPAX will play a very important role in helping us achieve our sales goals."
   —Martin P. Hughes, Chairman and CEO, Hub International

"This book is like a Swiss Army knife, giving people the tools required for selling success in the new work world. *Beyond Selling Value* should take its rightful place in every thinking salesperson's briefcase!"
   —Richard J. Leider, Founder, The Inventure Group, and author, *Repacking Your Bags and Whistle while You Work*

"I am a believer in the premises behind *Beyond Selling Value* and have seen the process work firsthand. While pressure on margins will never go away, the strategies and tactics presented in *Beyond Selling Value* provide a proven process to do just what the book says—go beyond selling value."
   —John Rowe, Director of Retirement Sales, Merrill Lynch Retirement Group

"Most companies are under incredible pressure to join the herd, and 'your product is a commodity' is a mantra on the lips of many of our customers. *Beyond Selling Value* delivers the tools and processes that your company needs to set it apart from the crowd. Chock-full of stories that illustrate each key concept, this book lays out a step-by-step roadmap that will help you win customers for all the right reasons."
   —Robert W. Bradford, Coauthor of *Simplified Strategic Planning: A No-Nonsense Guide for Busy People Who Want Results Fast,* and CEO of the Center for Simplified Strategic Planning

"It's a brave new sales world characterized by extremes—relentless Web-based commoditization on the one hand, and interdependent value-driven relationships on the other. There's no question where you need to be focusing if you want to be successful. *Beyond Selling Value* provides you the process and tools for building critical value-based relationships."
   —Lisa Napolitano, CEO, Strategic Account Management Association (SAMA)

"ADC has embraced this process as a critical part of our go-to-market strategy. It has been essential to shifting us to a more customer-driven approach to how we build and sustain customer relationships. If you are concerned with differentiating yourself, this is a must read."
   —Rick Roscitt, Chairman and CEO, ADC

"To gain competitive advantage in today's dog-eat-dog business environment, you must not only work to get better than you have ever been, you must also get different. *Beyond Selling Value* will help you do both. Ignore it at your own peril."
   —Jim Ericson, Managing Partner and Program Director, The Masters Forum

"Kosch and Shonka have stripped the topic of selling value down to the no-nonsense why's and how's, and transfused it with the juice it really deserves. In addition to great reminders of the basics that work, they provide real techniques, in detail, to work them. They pull no punches about the realities of a lean-and-mean business environment while providing fresh and important perspectives about how to navigate it successfully. A must-read for creating and leveraging productive client relationships!"
   —David Allen, President, the David Allen Company, and author of the best-selling: *Getting Things Done: The Art of Stress-Free Productivity*

## DEDICATION

This book is dedicated to David S. Matlow, the creator of the IMPAX®
Process and the founder of the IMPAX Corporation

# ACKNOWLEDGMENTS

We gratefully acknowledge and express deep appreciation to the many people who have made this book possible.

To Malcolm Fleschner, whose talents, humor, and insight have helped make this book what it is. The late nights and the laughs are what made the experience of writing this book enjoyable. We couldn't have asked for a better, more talented writer to work with. And also to Malcolm's wife, Kristin, for her patience and understanding.

To the team who worked on this book, especially:

- Mary Good and the rest of the Dearborn Trade team: Cynthia Zigmund, Don Hull, Paul Mallon, Leslie Banks, Elizabeth Bacher, Terri Joseph, Sandy Thomas, and Trey Thoelcke
- Jonathon Lazear and Christi Cardenas from the Lazear Agency
- John Roth and Jeff Ringhoffer
- Our virtual book title team

To two key leaders in our business, Scott Anderson and Chip Kudrle, and to our outstanding teammates, who have built this business and delighted our clients, including: Christopher Smith, Pete O'Brien, Mike Webb, Tammy Ubl, Mike Brown, Jeff Vint, Jay Carthaus, Dave Lynn, Jim Ninivaggi, Marilynn Gregory, Carol Arce, Johnna Krantz, Karl Busch, Kathy Bolton, Ira Kasden, Paul Boucherle, Bill Larner, Barry LaValley, Deb Peters, Heidi Armstrong, Gerry Spencer, Todd Hendries, Doug Lyons, Rick Bowlby, and Jeff Barovich.

To our clients, who have trusted us with their most valuable asset, their sales force. In particular: Joe Demharter, John Rowe, John Bruder, Bill Klanderman, Dave Fraser, Gary Jarosz, Martha Richardson, Ed Kilroy, Dan Servos, Bruce Hanley, Greg McCamus, Tim Eichorst, John Cobb, Phil Styrlund, Kevin Hrusovsky, Bill Olin, George Harris IV, Frank Jerd, Dave Knorr, Errol Schoenfish, John Temple, Dick Johnson, Charlie Burnham, Jim Harvin, Jim Ryan, Regan Hutton, Rob Abele, Karen Kracher, Ken Lowden, Bob Briggs,

Cathy Barthel, Bill Siefkin, Greg Demming, Robert Vulpis, Dolores Wilverding, Sarah Brown, Dave Oulighan, Tom Moberly, Gene Duncan, Dave Roy, Tom Mezera, Fred Spero, John Caron, Mike Higgins, Tony Giorgio, Paul Oberhaus, Tom Beddow, John McCarthy, Larry McBride, Jim Nelson, Craig Carson, Jimmy Watts, Terry White, and Rich Blakeman.

To our friends, advisors, and mentors, who helped us prepare for this opportunity, including: David McKane, Narayan Ramachandran, Brian Dietmeyer, Lisa Napolitano, Libby Cannon and the team at SAMA, John Wagner, Jay Zack, Mike Hogan, Charlie Cooper, Tom Thomas, LoAnn Mockler, Jim Miller, Sally Casper, and former IBM colleagues, including Grant Farquhar, Pat Warner, Larry Wood, Woody Shakleton, Phil Soran, John Wright, and John Vanderheyden.

From Mark:

- To Taylor, Brittany, and Derek—my inspiration, purpose, and joy
- To my heroes, Mom and Dad, for your encouragement and faith
- To my family: Chelle, Drew, J. Scott, Geri, John, Sister Marie Madeleine, Ted, Shelly, Mike, Gina, Earl, and Jan

From Dan:

- To my wife and best friend, Therese, thank you for all of your love and support
- To my children, Kristina, Laura, and Jason, you each give me inspiration and perspective
- To my Dad, gone but not forgotten
- To my Mom, for always being there
- To my family, Debbie, Donna, Deann, Farrell, Paal, Scott, Jim, Maureen, Kathy, Trish, Dan, and Mark

To all of our friends and family members, who have always been there to support us.

To God, in thanks for our friendship, partnership, and this opportunity.

# C O N T E N T S

# The Power of Presentation

# Implementing the Process

# FOREWORD

What makes selling value so difficult today? Salespeople—even those who are trained to ask the right questions, probe for critical needs, and apply solutions to customers' long-term business challenges—frequently find themselves confronted with buyers who only want to talk about price. Salespeople are told to sell to true decision makers, but are never given the tools to reach the corner offices where these key executives are located. They're told to become sales consultants, only to find that prospects aren't particularly interested in being consulted with.

As publisher of the nation's top sales magazine, I hear a familiar refrain over and over again from salespeople in nearly every field, as well as sales managers, VPs of sales, and even CEOs. They tell me that so many buyers are focused on this one issue—price—that salespeople are forced to choose between two unappealing options: lose the deal or abandon selling value. Selling in this environment means that even when you win, you lose.

As Shonka and Kosch point out, however, there is another path. Confronted with this lose-lose scenario, the sales professional's role itself is responding by dividing into two separate tiers. Slowly becoming obsolete are those at the bottom who persist in trying to compete with little more than price, features, and a winning personality to recommend them. At the top are the salespeople willing to fight the tide and break out of the "Vendor Trap" by refusing to sell to buyers who only care about price, by elevating their selling efforts, and by moving beyond traditional notions of what it means to sell value. This path, they argue persuasively, is the future of selling.

Admittedly some top sales performers have the innate instincts, ability, and eloquence to rise above the pack and get in front of prospects who are empowered to buy value and close on mutually beneficial business relationships. In this book, the authors clearly demonstrate that what these top performers do by instinct can be systematized into a reproducible process that nearly anyone can follow. I was intrigued to read as the authors provided a master-blueprint to help salespeople:

- Conduct penetrating information-gathering research meetings with key players.
- Cultivate a strong network of coaches who want you to win.
- Go over, around, or through the gatekeepers and "ankle-biters," such as product evaluators and purchasing managers who don't understand the value you offer.
- Gain regular access to the decision makers who are not only able to but also eager to buy into truly value-based solutions.
- Deliver blow-'em-away business presentations to executives you once might have been intimidated even to meet.

And unlike so many sales guides I've read, this is not some academic textbook you can only get through with the help of multiple cups of coffee. The authors are not professors—they're as hands-on as they come. Not only are they operating within breathing distance of top sales professionals, consulting in today's selling trenches with some of the most admired sales organizations in the world, they're also out there on the front lines themselves, successfully selling in the same price-obsessed marketplace the rest of us face.

I was also impressed by the authors' unique approach to the professional selling challenge. Every year I'm confronted with thousands of ideas to help sales professionals improve, yet so much of what passes for new sales ideas are merely the same old tools repackaged. But here you'll find something genuinely different—a perspective and process that take selling value to a new level. This is the level where price objections, controlling gatekeepers, restrictive RFPs, and all the other exasperations of the Vendor Trap fall away until you're allowed to deliver the kind of value solutions that make being a sales professional so rewarding.

In addition to showing you how to raise the level of your game, the authors also provide a series of real-life case studies that drive home the critical lessons in an unforgettable way. This book is an enjoyable and fast read. With each page of the manuscript, I became more determined that my own sales team never be caught in the Vendor Trap.

Ultimately, 21st-century sales professionals will have to decide whether to be leaders or followers in selling's next generation. Both for individual sales professionals eager to strike out with a fresh plan for attacking the new challenges they face and for managers with sales teams to reinvigorate and redirect, this book offers a detailed, street-smart roadmap to help you leverage your strengths, elevate your selling game, and achieve long-term sales success.

—Gerhard Gschwandtner, Founder and Publisher, *Selling Power* magazine

# PREFACE

Unless you missed the headlines, you've probably heard that the role of the direct sales professional is dying. The experts tell us that the walls are coming down; since the advent of the new, frictionless economy, barriers between suppliers and customers have been falling, eliminating the need for salespeople and other middlemen who merely gum up the works of commerce.

Naturally, all the hype over selling's imminent demise has inspired a lot of fear. As buyer-seller transactions slowly abandon the customer's office and conference room in favor of streamlined avenues like the Internet and telechannels, sales traditionalists are left with fewer buyers to glad hand, shoulder-clap, and call by their first names.

Now let's be clear. Sales channels are changing, but in many cases the change is for the better. Unquestionably, inside sales and the Internet have driven efficiencies and improved communication. In fact, we spend a great deal of time helping our clients take advantage of these alternative sales channels.

But the existence of additional channel options is no more killing direct sales than VCRs killed the film industry. As Mark Twain might have put it, were he a business professional today, the reports of direct selling's death have been greatly exaggerated. But only partly. As a salesperson, if how you sell can be commoditized, consolidated into a simple questionnaire, and farmed out to the Internet or to telemarketers operating out of a minimum-security prison, then you should be afraid. You're a vendor, and your days are numbered.

During the vendors' heyday, salespeople could ask a few cursory questions, compare features and benefits, and then close like crazy. But today's customers are not so easily swayed. In response, many salespeople have tried to break out of the Vendor Trap in favor of an alternative path: selling value. Instead of talking their way through sales calls by hammering away on product features and then closing hard, the value sellers have begun to ask penetrating questions, listen to their customers, talk about long-term benefits, and look to solve customer problems.

But along the way the value sellers have encountered a formidable obstacle: gatekeepers. Gatekeepers, going by misleading titles like "product evaluator" or "purchasing agent," missed the memo about the shift to value selling. Used to dealing with vendors, they continue to focus on features, side-by-side product comparisons, and their favorite topic of all, price.

Gatekeepers view salespeople as vendors competing on a grid. They're willing to hear about value, but only to the extent that your value-added services can be broken apart and placed on the grid somewhere. As a result, so-called value merely becomes another item on the gatekeepers' commoditization checklist. At this point, many salespeople with the best intentions of selling value run into a brick wall and revert to old habits. As a result, selling value has become glorified product selling—selling products in the form of solutions to people who buy products to solve operational problems. In reality, it's only vendor selling—all dressed up perhaps, but still with nowhere to go. This commoditization of value is bleeding the life out of direct sales.

Understandably, many value-minded salespeople have responded by grousing about gatekeepers. "How can we sell value to people who only want to beat us up on price and kill our margins?" they've been heard to wail. The simple answer: you can't. And you shouldn't even try. It's not the gatekeepers' fault that they aren't interested in buying value. That's not their job. The fact is, in today's marketplace, selling value and selling to gatekeepers are not compatible.

So what's a sales professional to do? To stop the bleeding and start winning today, you must rethink your selling efforts and go beyond—beyond vendor-based selling and beyond what you may think selling value means. Beyond selling value means breaking out of the Vendor Trap and undermining the gatekeepers' influence; it means moving up in the customer organization and selling to the individuals who are empowered to buy value. These are the true decision makers—the executives who can say yes when everyone else says no and can say no when everyone else says yes.

And this is precisely where the future of professional selling lies. With *Beyond Selling Value,* we're taking a stand. We're saying that the direct sales channel can flourish, it needs to flourish, and it will flourish. Unlike the naysayers, we're optimistic about the future. We believe that those of us in the direct sales profession should be hopeful, as long as we're ready to take that step beyond the Vendor Trap and beyond commoditized value selling.

We have to say, "We're not going to be vendors any more; we won't be commoditized; we refuse to compete exclusively on price." Instead of focusing on features and price, or selling to gatekeepers who insist on contorting value onto a grid, we must proactively understand how our customers do business, find ways to address pressing business issues, and recommend strategic solutions that improve the way our customers do business. It means stepping away from a limited focus on departmental solutions in favor of big picture business value. It means presenting business fit, not product fit.

And it's not enough just to want to do things differently. We have to make change and take our customers along with us. Remember the saying, "If you always do what you've always done, you'll always get what you've always got?" It's not enough to set your sights on the decision maker—but then settle for selling product to an evaluator. It's not enough to want to present your company's value to the executive who can buy value but then to let a gatekeeper block your path. It's not enough to dream about making a value-based business presentation to a high-level executive—while you're busy scribbling out an RFP response. You have to rethink the opportunities you pursue, how you create your plans, what you choose to learn about your customers, the level of people you are willing to sell to, and the way you present your value. As the German philosopher Goethe said, "Knowing is not enough. We must apply. Willing is not enough. We must do."

What business you're in doesn't matter, either. Whether you sell technology solutions, professional and corporate services, consumer products, telecommunications, transportation, software, coal, electricity, grease, portable toilets, or shoelace tips, some buyers are insidious—they prove every day that they can turn anyone's products and services into a commodity. But only if you let them.

If you allow customers to commoditize you and trap you with the straitjacketing *vendor* label, then you better watch out. Watch out for buying consortiums and consultants coaching your customers on how to buy. Watch out for gatekeepers who put you on the grid and beat you up on price. Watch out for all the doors slamming in your face. And watch out for job listings, because soon enough no one's going to need you anymore.

Ultimately, the reason most sales professionals today don't sell value and wind up on the grid is because they lack the skills and strategies necessary to go beyond traditional selling tactics. A big part of the problem is that sales professionals have been misled by the existing literature. There's no shortage of books dedicated to being customer centered or customer intimate. So why isn't everyone doing it? Because despite all the talk, no one actually delivers the tools that sales professionals need. Sure, they'll talk about understanding the customer's business or selling higher in the client organization, but that's where the lesson ends.

Beyond the talk, rethinking the conventional wisdom on selling value requires tools—specific, step-by-step strategies for gathering the right kind of information about a customer account; for bypassing or working through gatekeepers; for gaining access to the senior-level decision makers who can appreciate your value; and for making presentations that simply blow away those decision makers with your professionalism and understanding of their business.

This book delivers those tools.

So, if you're ready to rethink how you sell value and to begin viewing yourself as a business professional, not merely a sales rep, then you're ready for *Beyond Selling Value*. This book will help you understand the customer's business better than ever. You'll learn how your solutions can positively impact your customer's critical concerns. You'll stop worrying about how to differentiate your products from your competitor's and start focusing on helping your customers differentiate themselves from their competitors. If you do these things, you will always have a home and make a good living selling.

Direct selling is dying? Not on our watch, it's not.

# CHAPTER ONE

# It's a Jungle Out There
## TODAY'S SELLING CHALLENGES

How do you sell?

Are you a vendor selling products or services in an increasingly crowded marketplace? Then you're probably working hard all the time, handling price objections, and struggling to differentiate yourself and your products in the face of some tough competition. As a vendor, you probably deal with a parade of product evaluators including purchasing agents, many of whom are gatekeepers intent on limiting your access to the true decision makers in upper-level management. Your focus is on closing this sale today rather than on building long-term relationships. This is what being a vendor means in today's selling environment.

But maybe you're not just a vendor. Instead of simply selling products or services, do you proactively engage customers to identify additional needs beyond the narrow scope of a request for proposal (RFP) or a buyer's immediate concerns? If so, you're probably effective at resolving specific client issues that crop up after you've established a relationship. One step removed from the vendor, you sell solutions to customers' operational problems in addition to products. You are a problem solver.

The professional selling food chain has two more steps, however. Do you identify customers' critical business issues and devise targeted solutions to

FIGURE 1.1    Perceptions Pyramid

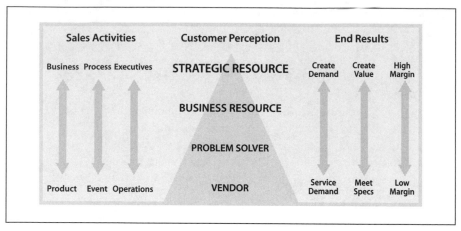

solve these core concerns? Do you form partnerships between your organization and customers' organizations to strategically advance both businesses and develop mutually beneficial, long-term business strategies? If so, rather than being a vendor or a problem solver, you may be a business resource or even a strategic resource.

Figure 1.1 describes the ascending levels of value sales organizations offer their customers. The more time you spend focusing on product, events, operational issues, and meeting with technical individuals and product evaluators, the lower you and your company are perceived on the pyramid.

But the more your time is driven by a process that focuses on both the customer's business as well as product needs and you meet with senior-level management as well as technical and operations people, the higher you and your company will be perceived on the pyramid. You create demand because executives value you as an integral part of their business and processes.

## PERCEPTIONS

- If you are perceived as a *vendor,* you may be reacting to service demand and spending your time focusing on product and price.
- If you are perceived as a *problem solver,* you are good at resolving specific client issues.
- If you are perceived as a *business resource,* you are assisting the customer to solve real business issues. You help customers increase market share, drive down costs, and enhance customer satisfaction. You efficiently manage the relationship at all levels, focusing on the customer's

business and business issues and positioning your solutions in this context.

- If you are perceived as a *strategic resource,* you are involved in mission-critical applications or functions and engaged in mutually strategic activities. Working at the executive level in activities such as joint strategic planning, you and your customers are helping, on a company-to-company basis, to advance each other's businesses.

Realistically, few professional salespeople fit into one category all the time. Depending on the individual sales situation, at different times you may find yourself at opposite levels of the pyramid. When you're at your best, you're selling business solutions to individuals who are empowered to make long-term strategic buying decisions. But more often than you would probably like, you're also in front of product evaluators, getting beat up on price and struggling to stand out from a crowd of similar products or services. This is the situation we call the Vendor Trap.

So what can you do to break out of the Vendor Trap? It requires nothing less than revolutionizing the way you sell. Traditional selling activities simply will not do the job. Don't think that you can react to the customer's buying process with the hope that maybe this evaluator will be different and this time you'll be able to sell value. You won't. You'll wind up losing the deal, or if you do win it, you'll win it at a price that shreds your margins.

As Ben Franklin put it, "The definition of insanity is doing the same thing over and over and expecting different results."

Avoiding the Vendor Trap means more than falling back on a combination of traditional tactics and strategies, however. Wanting to infuse a customer-focused strategic process simply isn't enough. It requires committing to a whole new approach to the professional sales function—what we call Beyond Selling Value.

So what does going beyond selling value and avoiding the Vendor Trap mean in the real world? Let's look at how one IMPAX client, a small petroleum company, benefited from applying this process. The company's specific product is grease—oil in barrels. They compete against some of the top, tough companies like Sunoco and ExxonMobil.

They also compete in an aggressive marketplace without the benefit of low prices. Added to this scenario, they enjoyed nearly no product differentiation. You can imagine the struggle they faced. Customers were commoditizing their grease, and the only way to respond was to sell product below acceptable margin. Yet the CEO committed to winning—not by what kind of grease they sold, but by how they sold it.

Changing their orientation completely, the company redefined themselves, going from a mere grease supplier to a lubrication management services company. They also decided they would no longer sell primarily to purchasing agents. Instead, the targets of their efforts would be VPs of manufacturing and plant managers—the people who lie awake at night worrying about the plant's health. By tying themselves to lubrication management, an issue plant executives faced every day, the company knew it could help the managers get more product through the plants, improve product quality, and strengthen safety capabilities. As a result, they would help improve the margin of the product coming out of the plant.

One example of how their selling efforts changed was reflected in their sale to Eaton Corporation. In this opportunity, the sales rep faced a host of challenges:

- The company was perceived by Eaton Corporation as one of a number of grease vendors in a crowded field.
- Eaton Corporation had commoditized grease and recognized no product differentiation between different competitors.
- Eaton Corporation stated that their primary factor in the buying decision would be price.
- The rep's product carried a higher price tag than most of the competing firms.
- The rep was dealing with Purchasing and an evaluator in Plant Operations.

The rep had to follow his CEO's lead—he had to rethink the way he sold grease. In fact, he had to stop selling grease altogether and start selling lubrication management services. Because he knew that he faced long odds of winning this business through traditional selling practices, he took a shot.

After conducting the right research, he worked with his coaches to gain access and present to Eaton Corporation's VP of manufacturing. Instead of positioning his product to address the evaluator's need for grease, he presented a lubrication management solution that impacted the plant's throughput, quality, and margins—his research told him these issues concerned the VP. Price fell away as a compelling factor in the face of such a value-oriented solution, and the rep won the business.

This rep experienced firsthand the power of rethinking the way you sell value. So did his bank account.

## SELLING CHALLENGES

Because the first step in the process is research, we'll begin by asking you to do a little research on yourself. Take a moment to consider the toughest obstacles you face out there in the field. What selling issues keep you awake at night?

Based on our work with hundreds of clients selling a broad assortment of products and services in all types of business-to-business environments, we have identified some of the greatest selling challenges in today's market-place:

- Competition is increasingly aggressive.
- You have greater difficulty differentiating your company's products and services from the competition's.
- Customers and prospects only look for the lowest price and ignore value.
- Sales cycles are longer and more complex.
- Gatekeepers, who keep you from meeting with senior-level decision makers, are increasingly prevalent.
- Customers and prospects perceive you as a vendor and not as a business resource.
- Customers are more knowledgeable and more demanding than before.
- In many industries, mergers, acquisitions, and consolidation of entire industries have fueled a trend toward larger opportunities, but fewer of them.

This list is daunting. Factor in the emergence of inside sales and the Internet, as well as the general uncertainty facing the sales profession, and today's sales professionals clearly face a ton of pressure—pressure to make margins and pressure to differentiate themselves from increasingly cutthroat competition. Bob Briggs, EVP Business Development of Carlson Wagonlit Travel, reflects on this when he says, "It really is tough out there. A lot of companies are struggling with competition and the challenging economic environment. When that happens, sometimes you have no choice, you just have to sell your way out of trouble."

If you're like most sales professionals, you probably see your situation in almost every item on that list, regardless of the company you represent, how big your company is, or the industry you work in.

Competition, however, is nothing new. In Prohibition-era San Francisco, a surprise police raid netted 25 of the city's top bootleggers. As they were arraigned, the judge motioned each of them forward one at a time and asked, "What is your name?" and "What is your occupation?" To the second question, each man answered, "I am a Realtor."

Finally, the judge came to the last defendant. "And what is your profession?" the judge asked.

"Your honor, I'm a bootlegger," he responded.

Surprised, the judge laughed, asking, "So how's business?"

"It would be a lot better," the defendant answered, "if there were not so many Realtors around."

No matter what name it goes by, competition will always force you to make every effort count.

## THE VALUE SELLING CHALLENGE

The issues listed above create what we call the Value Selling Challenge, which consists of four key points:

1. *Selling value today is tougher than ever.* If selling value were easy, nearly everyone would be doing it. But no matter how hard we try, today's customers seem more determined than ever to beat us up on price; force us to respond to RFPs; and tear down, compartmentalize, and commoditize everything we have to offer.
2. *Fewer people can buy value.* Despite the current corporate emphasis on empowerment and committee decision making, which involve more people in buying decisions, in fact fewer people than ever are capable of investing in value. An increased number of product evaluators—or gatekeepers—are encouraged to cut costs and focus on price.
3. *The people who can buy value are located higher and higher in an organization.* Just as fewer people can buy value, the ones who do wield that power are higher up the corporate hierarchy, more isolated from the front-line professional salespeople who can deliver value-added business solutions.
4. *To sell value to senior-level decision makers, you have to understand what makes them tick.* You have to understand their business and what they value. Keep in mind that when you're selling to lower levels, those customers want to learn more about your company. Senior levels only want to learn more about their company.

## CONCLUSION

No question: it's tough out there. Just as moving beyond traditional value selling has become almost essential to sales success, breaking out of the Vendor Trap has also become harder than ever. But it's not impossible. If your objectives are to identify opportunities, move beyond gatekeepers, and present strategic business solutions to senior-level decision makers, you must find a sales process that addresses each of these goals. As you will see, that's exactly what this process was designed to accomplish.

# CHAPTER TWO

# Bare Bones and Brass Tacks
## THE IMPAX® PROCESS

We've talked a great deal about all the challenges out there facing sales-people intent on selling value in an increasingly commoditized market-place. Now let's turn things around and start talking about solutions.

> *"We cannot become what we need to be by remaining what we are."*
> *—Max De Pree*

Our solution is the IMPAX® Process. This is the sales process that we implement with our clients as they rethink the way they sell value.

So what is the IMPAX Process? A senior-level executive at DuPont once commented, "The IMPAX Process takes the things that the most successful value-oriented salespeople do by instinct and puts them into a system so they're done by design." Divided into three sections—research, communication, and presentation—the following chapters will show you step-by-step how to gather critical insider information about a target account or opportunity, then develop and work with coaches to understand the potent business fit between your two companies. Next you'll learn strategies for gaining access to the executive-level decision makers who are empowered to buy the value you have to offer, along the way handling and disarming any gate-keepers who crop up to try to block or control you. Finally, you'll learn how to develop and deliver high-impact business presentations that blow away decision makers with the depth of your understanding of their business and excite them about entering into a business relationship with you.

With these elements in mind, let's begin this brief overview with the first section of the process—research.

# RESEARCH

In this case, research doesn't mean stodgy, boring, academic research in a library. To us, research means understanding the customer's business from their perspective to give you the tools to develop credibility with senior-level decision makers. This requires gaining a business perspective—not only an understanding of where your service or product fits but where the customer's organization is going as a business.

> *"An investment in knowledge always pays the best interest."*
> *—Benjamin Franklin*

We break down research into four areas:

1. *Data.* This section tackles a topic that salespeople know they should make a priority but probably neglect too frequently—gathering and utilizing data on the account. Data is the publicly available facts and figures about an account, generally accessible through quarterly, annual, and 10K reports (U.S. companies only), *D&B Reports,* magazine articles, the company Web site, and a variety of other sources. We'll talk about what data sources are, the tactics to get them, and different ways to leverage them in the sales process.
2. *Information.* Gathering data isn't enough to get a complete picture on the customer—you need information as well. Moving beyond traditional "needs analysis," you need to understand the customer's business as well as where your product fits. Information can only be obtained from people who have an insider's perspective on the business. We'll show you exactly what information you need to elicit and how to leverage it.
3. *The coach network.* Most sales professionals would probably agree—you can't make a big sale or keep an important customer without coaches. Coaches are the knowledgeable individuals, whether inside or outside the target company, who want you to win. Coaches can be found in many places—in the customer's organization, as former employees of the customers, as associates in related fields, as individuals within your own company, and in many other locations. We'll show you how to build an effective coach relationship or, when you need to, a coach network.
4. *The research meeting.* Understanding what you need to learn isn't enough; we'll show you how to get that information. Specifically, we'll show you how to conduct effective and efficient research meet-

ings focused on gaining a better understanding of your prospect's or customer's business. The research meeting is how you gain that insider's perspective that's crucial to selling value.

## COMMUNICATION

Communication means different things to different people. In our world, communication is all about leveraging the research we do to gain access to the right levels. If your goal is to be customer focused and to sell value, then you need to sell to the level that can truly buy value. As an IMPAX client once told us, "Being customer focused is a waste of time if your customer doesn't pay you for it." And that's true. The question is, how do you leverage customer focus? How do you leverage research? That's where communication comes in. You leverage research in two ways:

1. *To gain access to true decision makers.* We'll identify the right buying influences and share a series of strategies and tactics on how to get to decision makers. These tactics work whether you're with a well-known *Fortune* 100 company or an unknown upstart. As a part of the process, you have to gain access and present to the people who can really buy value, and this section will show you how.
2. *To deal with gatekeepers along the way.* This is the topic that, more than any other, keeps salespeople awake at night. It's also the topic that, more than any other, most sales books avoid. We'll introduce a four-step process, complete with a series of strategies for successfully dealing with gatekeepers who want to block your access and limit your success. You have to get to the people who can buy value, and that means not taking no for an answer until you reach them.

> Remember: Being customer focused is a waste of time if your customer doesn't pay you for it. You need to translate your understanding of the customer's business into a compelling reason to want to work with you. That's what we call "business fit."

## PRESENTATION

At this point in the process, you've gathered the right knowledge and leveraged it to gain an audience with the true decision maker. So now what? How do you make such a strong impression on this person that you compel him or her to invest in your effort and actually pay more for the value that your company can bring? You do it by delivering the kind of presentation the decision maker won't see from any of your competitors.

The business presentation you make will be different. Unlike the typical "show up and throw up" sales presentation, this presentation focuses first on what you've learned about the customer's business and then places your recommendations in context with those business issues and objectives. Visually, it helps the decision maker understand that you're not just another vendor. With this presentation you differentiate yourself, not just based on what you sell but on how you sell it.

> Beyond Selling Value means delivering more than a "show up and throw up" presentation to the decision maker.

If you're nervous about even the thought of standing in front of a senior-level decision maker and presenting a story about his or her business and the fit between your two companies, don't be. We'll show you how to develop and deliver such high-impact business presentations that presenting will become one of your most rewarding and enjoyable sales activities.

Decision makers who buy value can be impressed and compelled if you sell to them the right way. After presenting to a senior-level decision maker, a salesperson at a large chemicals company that's also an IMPAX client received the following letter, which illustrates the power of this kind of business presentation:

> Dear Jim,
> I felt very positive about our business session Tuesday afternoon and evening. The attention of Dick and his leadership team was noticed and appreciated. The plant tour was enlightening. But the guts of the presentation provided by your team was the key to us taking the next step in our total supply relationship. I was very impressed with your penetration and understanding of our business.
> I look forward to a continued opportunity to improve each other's businesses.
> Yours truly,
> Scott Pike
> Managing Director

It's important to note that this decision maker was very successful and accomplished. In fact, he had just appeared on the cover of a national business magazine. Yet he still took the time to write a letter to a sales rep who had impressed him. It wasn't the typical sales activities, like the plant tour, that struck him—it was the rep's presentation.

## PREMISES

There we have the bare bones of the IMPAX Process—Research, Communication, and Presentation. As you read this book, we also want you to keep in mind some of the underlying premises that drive the strategies and tactics of the process. In fact, this process was born out of a frustration that even good sales training doesn't always get implemented. We get all fired up to be more effective with the new techniques we've learned, but then we get back to the office and we're swamped with voice mail and e-mail, and we never quite get around to implementing the new training. How many of us have credenzas or bookshelves filled with good books on selling that we never consult anymore? What a waste! That's why implementation is built into every step of this process. Here are the underlying premises of the IMPAX Process:

**Premise 1: Senior-level decision makers are more likely to buy from you based on what you know about them and their business rather than what they know about you and your products.** Today, fewer people within an organization can truly buy value. These individuals are also located higher in the organizational structure. And what are these people most interested in? Typically not your product or your service, but rather what's important to them. It's their objectives, it's the issues that keep them up at night. It's how their performance is being measured. It's their MBOs.

A VP of Sales once told us a cautionary tale about his company's CEO calling on the CEO of their largest customer. During the call, the selling CEO really got on a roll as he talked about the great things going on in his business, how the stock was growing, and how they were acquiring companies and adding services left and right. He was just enthused about everything the company was doing.

At some point the CEO listening to all this leaned back in his chair and, with an uninterested stare, pointed his index finger in the air, began to twirl it in small circles, and deadpanned, "Whoopee." Has this ever happened to you? Probably not. But how many times do you think this same thought has run through a customer's mind while you droned on through your pitch? They were probably just too polite to open their mouths (except maybe to yawn).

**Premise 2: No single event in the process is as important as a meeting with the decision maker.** Every stage in this process is critical, and effective salespeople know that skipping steps early in the sales cycle will come back to haunt them later on. That said, everything you do in the preliminary stages is focused on one key event: your business presentation to the decision maker—the one person who is empowered to buy the value you offer. So, as you gather data and information, conduct your research meetings, and build the groundswell of support along the way, remember to keep your eye on the prize: the opportunity to stand up in front of the decision maker and present the critical business fit between your two companies.

One software client told us about a presentation he made before learning this process. He was meeting with a senior-level VP, so he made the flat-out best product pitch he could. About ten minutes into the presentation, the VP stopped him cold, saying, "I know you have to do your spiel, but when do we get to talk about my company?" That's when the rep realized he should have taken the time to do his research.

**Premise 3: You only get one chance to make a good first impression.** When you have the opportunity to be in front of a senior-level decision maker, what do you do to make sure your presentation goes as smoothly as possible? Keep this in mind: you only get one chance to make a good first impression, so doing your homework will give you the best chance to shine in that first meeting. Consider ahead of time what kind of impression you want to make, and tailor your presentation to fit that image.

> If you think it's tough to make a good first impression, just try changing a negative perception.

As a separate but equally important point, we all know that lasting impressions are critical, too. Changing a lasting impression can often be difficult. For example, when you think of Gerald Ford, what do you think about? What comes to mind? Tripping and falling down? We've posed that question to thousands of people, and rare indeed is the person who responds with "President of the United States." He was the most powerful man in the world at one point, and the first thing we think about is his falling down. He tripped a few times, and that first impression just hangs in our minds. Chevy Chase and *Saturday Night Live* probably contributed, too, but the point remains that lasting impressions are important. As your organization changes, grows, and evolves, you may find you're not necessarily who you were three or four years ago, yet customers may still perceive you that way. Although difficult, changing lasting impressions is possible.

**Premise 4: Early and continued access to the decision maker is critical to success.** In many cases, getting there once isn't enough, is it? You need to get to the decision maker again and again. You need to be so good, you get invited back. One of the challenges we hear all the time is, "What do you talk about with a senior-level executive?" If you just go in and have a product discussion, you will probably lose their interest right away and won't get back on this person's calendar. Instead, you want to focus on their issues and be perceived as a business resource who can make an impact on those issues. This will get you invited back.

An IMPAX client, a high-level executive at a customs brokerage house, likes to tell the following story about an eager young sales rep:

> This guy came on like gangbusters, telling me how he was going to solve all my problems. He's standing there in his Armani suit and tie telling me how he can help me with this and he can help me with that. About 20 minutes into the call, I stopped him mid-sentence and said, "I'm sorry, but I have to stop you. Tell me something. Do you even know what business we're in? Do you know what we do? Do you know where we're going as an organization?" He couldn't provide a satisfactory answer to any of the questions. So I told him, "Let me give you some advice. Next time you have the opportunity to meet with someone at my level, do your homework." And with that I ended the call.

By doing your homework and getting to know the customer's business inside and out, you dramatically increase your chances of being invited back.

**Premise 5: For effective positioning, the power of a presentation exceeds the power of a product demonstration or a discussion.** To illustrate, we had an opportunity to present at a large airline's sales management conference. As you would expect, prior to that speaking engagement we did some research and learned something about their selling issues, challenges, opportunities, critical success factors, business direction and issues, etc. As we were getting ready to present, another person was still in the room working. In conversation with him, we did a little additional research, asking how the meeting was going, what were the highlights so far, and if there were any particular concerns to watch out for.

Soon after meeting him, we gave our speech on Selling Value, which was very well received. In return, the airline agreed to give us the opportunity to meet with Rob Barrett, the Senior Vice President of Sales. After the speech, we were introduced to Rob. He said he was very pleased with the speech and the message. We said to him, "Rob, we have one question for you." We were going to ask for an hour of his time so that we could present to him. Before we could ask, however, he interrupted and said, "Yes, but it had better be a damned good presentation." We agreed to call his administrator, Laura, and set up a one-hour meeting to talk about how our two companies might continue working together.

The meeting was set up for a few weeks later. Several days before the presentation, we called Laura to confirm the logistics of the meeting. We asked if she had a conference room available. She asked why we needed a conference room, and soon after we began positioning the meeting to her, she stopped us and interjected, "Wait a minute; this sounds like a presentation!" We said, "Yes, that's exactly what it is, a presentation." She said, "Oh, no, you can't do that. You can't present." Not understanding her meaning, we asked why. "Because Rob hates presentations," she said.

We knew better than to argue with her, so we simply asked what she suggested we do. She said, "I think you should come in and have a chat." Our reaction to this message was immediate. After landing the opportunity to meet with a decision maker at the level of Senior Vice President of Sales for a multinational corporation, you never want to risk just "chatting." We knew we couldn't possibly make the right impression or have any real impact with a chat. We had to present, so then and there we resolved that, despite Laura's warning, we were going to make a presentation, with or without the conference room.

> Beyond Selling Value means passing on the opportunity to chat with a decision maker. With decision makers, your goal is to stand up and deliver a professional business presentation, not to sit down and chat.

In preparation for the presentation, we called Paul Hunter, the gentleman we had met before our presentation. It turned out that he was a Regional Vice President of Sales, working directly for Rob, and had a major influence on his boss's decisions. As a result of a research meeting we conducted with him and subsequent conversations, Paul quickly became a very strong coach for us. He was committed to us for several reasons, foremost among them that he believed IMPAX could make a powerful impact on his sales organization, improving the way his people positioned themselves and the airline as a value provider for their customers.

On the day of the presentation, we arrived early and set up in Rob's office. When he and Paul were grabbing a cup of coffee in the cafeteria, Rob turned to Paul and asked, "Okay, how quick?" Paul didn't understand and asked, "What do you mean?" Rob said, "How quickly do you think I can get rid of them?" Paul still didn't understand. Rob said, "This presentation, how quickly do you think we can end it—how about ten minutes? I'll bet you I can end this meeting in ten minutes or less." Paul said he wasn't sure why Rob would want to do that and provided support for what we were trying to accomplish. Nonetheless, Rob was determined to end our meeting quickly.

Arriving in his office, however, Rob was immediately struck by his company's logo prominently displayed on our flip chart. This initial surprise set the tone for our entire meeting. The tone, of course, was that the whole presentation would focus on Rob and his business and his objectives instead of IMPAX and our services. As is typical, this approach was very effective, and instead of shuffling us out in less than ten minutes, Rob gave us an hour-and-a-half, 30 minutes more than scheduled. We agreed on the spot to begin a business relationship between our two companies.

In Rob's words, "IMPAX wouldn't be here today if they had just chatted. It would have been a ten-minute meeting, and they would have been out. It's the presentation that sets them apart!"

**Premise 6: You must prove the business fit before you prove the product fit.** In later chapters, we will talk a great deal about this concept of the business fit. Business fit is all about answering some critical questions:

- How can our two companies, working together, build a relationship that helps you accomplish your business goals?
- How can I help accomplish your objectives?
- How can I help with the strategies that are important to you?
- How can I help you deal with the market issues that are your top priority?
- How do our two companies complement each other?

> Beyond Selling Value means not spending time comparing your product with the competitor's, but helping your customers strengthen their own competitive advantages.

Too often, salespeople focus exclusively on why their products are better than the competition's, which results in a discussion of which features provide the best fit for the customer's needs. Of course, there is an appropriate time to discuss product fit. You do have to position the benefits of the products or services you're actually selling, and there's a right time to do that. But this needs to come after you've made a strong case for a business fit between your two organizations. We'll talk more about this later in the book.

After going through this process, a manager at a client company that sells business-to-business insurance said this to us:

I did a business presentation to my target account, a large New England bank, last week. I did the research, determined the product fit and business fit, and gave a presentation, and it all went great. I think it worked because I stopped talking about product and started talking about business fit. I talked about their marketing challenges for mortgages and how our program could assist in addressing the issues of the bank. It was not product-related, and that's an important part of why it went so well.

## STRATEGY

The strategy behind the IMPAX Process has three key elements:

**Strategy 1: Research from the bottom up to help you gain support and access.** What does it mean to research from the bottom up? It means most of the best research can be done at middle-level management and supervisory levels. That's because these people have a broad perspective, but they're also close enough to the field to know what's really going on.

A fundamental challenge in doing research from the bottom up is to avoid making any assumptions, especially when you're calling on a long-time customer. To illustrate what we mean, here's a question for you. From your perspective, who is American Express's biggest competitor? If you're like most people, you probably think of Visa and MasterCard. But it's not. It's cash. Surprising, but true.

We had a client who was selling to American Express, and he tells this story. He was doing what we call a coach review—reviewing his presentation with a coach in the company—and when he got to the point about a competitive marketplace, he said something about "your top competitors, Visa and MasterCard." The coach stopped him and said, "Actually, that's not true. Be careful. This is a very important point. Only 17 percent of all financial transactions are made on credit. Our top competitor is not Visa or MasterCard. It's cash."

That's one example of an assumption that we might make, especially if we've been working with a customer for a while, or even if we haven't. Watch out for such assumptions as you're doing your research. Can you imagine what a difference it made for that sales rep when he presented, knowing that he wouldn't make this simple but critical error?

**Strategy 2: Sell from the top down and at all levels.** Selling from the top down doesn't mean that's all we do. We need to sell effectively at all levels and work all the right strategies at all levels. But again, if we're selling value, and fewer and fewer people can buy value, and they tend to be at a high level, we need to include them in our process.

Critical to selling value is selling to the people who can buy value.

The following real-world story illustrates the importance of selling to the right people.

A few years ago at a conference, a colleague introduced us to another attendee who had expressed an interest in hearing about our consulting business. As always, we were eager to dive right into talking about IMPAX, but we remembered to practice what we preach. Instead, we first asked him a few questions so that we could then describe our company in the best possible light. We asked what he did for a living, and he responded that he was the vice president of sales for a small manufacturing company. This was great to hear, because we knew we could use manufacturing company clients as examples when we talked about ourselves.

We kept on talking or, more precisely, we continued doing research, asking questions and learning more about his business, his position, and his interests. At one point, he said, "You know, I have a sales philosophy." Whenever someone has dedicated enough thought to an issue to develop a full-blown philosophy, it's bound to be good, so we paid close attention. When we asked what the philosophy was, he said, "Whenever I hire new sales professionals, on their first day of work I invite them into my office and present them with a big magnet. I tell them to put the magnet into their pockets and take it on all of their sales calls. Why? I tell them that if the magnet sticks to the desk of the person they're calling on, then they're calling too low in the organization!"

More seriously, he went on to say, "Most salespeople are very good at calling on traditional levels, like purchasing agents with metal desks. As we focus on selling value, we need to get better at selling to all levels, including the decision makers on Mahogany Row."

**Strategy 3: Focus on the business fit, not just the product fit.**  To sell value, you need to sell at all levels, including senior levels. Again, the focus of this process is on business fit as well as product fit.

Beyond Selling Value is all about the business fit.

Here's another example. A client of ours had targeted a multibillion-dollar industrial company and was selling in an RFP environment. The RFP was for business process reengineering services. Our client was competing with three other well-known companies. Looking at it honestly, this sales rep felt he didn't have a prayer: his company was fourth out of four, there's no way they were perceived as being in that business, they were high priced, and they didn't have the best service. So in the month he had remaining to respond to the RFP, the rep decided to use the IMPAX Process. He had some relationships in the business, which he leveraged to gain a presentation meeting with the president and the president's executive committee.

In their presentations, the competitors simply talked about their own products and services. By contrast, in his presentation our client talked about the customer's business (which no one else did), his products and services and the strength of the product fit, and the strong potential business fit between the two companies. In presenting the business fit, the rep talked about how his company could help address the issues that were important to the customer's business. He talked about the fact that the two companies shared a similar business philosophy, including a commitment to customer service and value. He said that by working together his company could support some of the customer's key objectives, particularly the goal to increase market share by a few percentage points. In the roundtable discussion that followed the presentation, the president commented to the committee, "We had three consulting companies come in today and act like vendors, and we had one vendor come in today and act like a consulting company."

The sales rep ended up closing the presentation with no negotiation on price. The customer executive even wrote a letter to our client saying, "Although we haven't started working together yet, I feel like we already have a strong business relationship."

We'll talk more about the business fit in Chapter 4. But remember that when you're avoiding the Vendor Trap and moving beyond traditional value selling, the focus has to be on the business fit between the two companies, not just the product fit.

## BEYOND SELLING VALUE AND YOU

The bar has been raised for those of us who sell value. What does moving beyond the traditional notions of selling value mean? To us, Beyond Selling Value means that you, the sales professional:

- Assume an attitude that says, regardless of your product or service, "I deserve to sell at a very high level, because I help my customers achieve their long-term business goals."
- View selling value not through the limited lens of short-term departmental issues but through a larger lens offering a perspective into the customer's broad-based business objectives.
- Plan accounts and opportunities as if you were a part of the customer's senior management team and not a sales rep selling solutions.

- Consider the research process an opportunity to ask differentiating questions that focus on the customer's business rather than the traditional cursory questions addressing departmental needs or application requirements.
- Are perceived as understanding the customer's business even better than many of the customer's employees do and as knowing how to leverage that understanding to sell value.
- Don't settle for selling to evaluators who think they can buy value. Instead, you insist on selling to decision makers who truly can buy value.
- Refuse to accept being trapped by gatekeepers, and know a range of strategies and tactics to work with, through, or around anyone who tries to block you.
- Have the skills and confidence to be compelling and maximize the opportunity when you're in front of senior-level decision makers.
- Deliver powerful presentations to decision makers, highlighting the value of a business fit between your two companies, not just a low-level departmental product or solution fit.
- Are perceived by your executive-level customers more as a strategic resource than a simple solutions provider.
- Proactively sell and promote your value at senior levels of your customer's organization.

It's been said that trust building is the number one business skill of the future. How you sell can have a dramatic impact on the degree to which your customers trust you.

In the past, selling often involved a product-focused process in which you approached product evaluators who judged you on your product, price, company strength, etc., and then decided if and when to introduce you into their decision-making process. This process is different because it allows you to control the process while remaining focused on what's most important to your customer.

## WARNING SIGNS

As you think about selling value in a crowded, competitive marketplace, what are some warning signs that cause you to consider changing your sales tactics? Many different red flags have triggered our clients to rethink how they sell. From the sales rep's perspective, these include:

- "I'm currently perceived as a vendor. The customer doesn't even look upon me as a key supplier, let alone a partner."

- "There's a ton of focus on price. All I run into is, 'Okay, how low can you get?'"
- "I'm only calling on one person at the account."
- "I don't have a coach."
- "I'm blocked by a gatekeeper."
- "I have no relationship with the senior-level decision maker."
- "I have limited or no understanding of senior-level management's priorities."
- "I'm not able to get in front of senior-level management in the right time frame."
- "I'm not able to close efficiently."
- "My sales cycles are too long."
- "This account has been on my forecast forever."
- "I'm having trouble differentiating myself from the competition."

These statements are some of the most common we hear from frontline sales reps who feel that they need to do something different.

Managers tend to face a separate but related set of challenges. They include:

- "The forecast continues to slip."
- "We're always dealing with low-level contacts."
- "When we do get in front of a decision maker, we don't make a powerful impact."
- "It's always, 'How deep of a discount can I get for this prospect?'"
- "Are we perceived as businesspeople bringing value or salespeople hawking products?"
- "When I ask my reps what the customer does, they answer 'About $100,000 in sales.'"
- "Why are we always trapped by gatekeepers?"
- "Why are we always behind the eight ball, reacting to our customer instead of proactively driving new opportunities?"

## BENEFITS TO MOVING BEYOND TRADITIONAL VALUE SELLING

This brings us to the primary benefits of using this process. The process will help you:

**Shorten the sales cycle.**  Some people who learn about the process initially worry that it will lengthen the sales cycle. One recent client who shared that initial apprehension had this to say: "When I first learned about the process, I thought it would lengthen the sales cycle. Implementing it, I realized that, while I did expend more effort up front in the research phase, the effort proved valuable when I raced through the close much more quickly."

In fact, our clients frequently tell us that because the salesperson has more control and does not get stalled or hindered by gatekeepers, this process actually shortens the sales cycle. Nothing drives a fast sales cycle like the commitment and involvement of a senior-level decision maker.

**Assess the probability of the sale early on in the sales process.** Using this process, you will be able to establish whether an opportunity is viable early in the sales cycle. Efficient research and a presentation to the decision maker are strong qualifying steps, especially if the decision maker is excited and supportive of the opportunity.

It's also possible that in using the process, you will assess and qualify an opportunity out, saving yourself valuable time, energy, and money spent on lunches and golf games. Certainly the best result is to get a "yes," but if you're eventually going to get a "no" from the decision maker, it's best to get it quickly.

**Become a true resource to a customer or prospect.** Critical to the process is gathering the right information about the customer's business, which will allow you to impress the eventual decision maker with your knowledge of his or her business. In countless situations, our clients have heard customers respond, "You know more about our business than a lot of the people who work here." It's this positioning that lays the foundation for you to be perceived as a true business resource well into the future.

**Manage customer expectations.** In your customer relationships, how many times have expectations gotten a little out of whack? With this process, when you get in front of senior-level management to talk about the relationship and your knowledge of the business, you become able to manage those expectations more effectively.

**Differentiate yourself from the competition.** The two steps that help differentiate users of the process are research and presentation. We hear this all the time. One Fortune 50 client of ours was conducting a research call on a customer in a lucrative but highly competitive sale, when in the middle of the call the contact said, "No one's ever come in here and asked me questions like that before. Other people just talk about products and services. I really appreciate that."

Another IMPAX client in the desktop publishing business used the process to prevent a low-priced competitor from stealing a key piece of multimedia business. Hearing that the competitor had all but closed the business, the rep hastily scheduled three research meetings. He then won a meeting with the company president. After presenting his understanding of the customer's business, the rep asked if he had demonstrated a fair understanding of the challenges facing the president's company. The customer responded, "Definitely. The problem with your competitor is that they don't understand the big picture." At the conclusion of the presentation, the customer added, "Everybody talks about partnering, but nobody knows how to do it. You guys separate the wheat from the chaff. Why shouldn't we put as much business as possible into your hands?" Turning to the other members of his organization, the president asked, "Can anyone tell me why we don't want to move forward with this proposal?"

When you're looking to differentiate yourself from the competition, your most powerful tool is the sales process you use.

**Elevate the priority of a project.** How many times have your projects floundered, dead in the water? Customers have many projects on their plates and only so many ways to spend their time, efforts, and capital. This process gains commitment from upper-level management, elevating your project closer to the top of the priority list.

**Continue to improve customer relationships.** With the coach network you establish, as well as the value you demonstrate to the decision maker, you can reapply the process to develop and manage the relationship.

**Close value efficiently.** Many of our clients who are looking to develop new business want to close efficiently and effectively. They find the process helps them quickly drive to a closing forum with the right decision maker.

One sales rep with a telecommunications firm used the process on an opportunity for a bookstore chain's long-distance business. With only two weeks to act before the decision was to be made and in a crowded field of 13 vendors, the rep needed to act fast. She conducted three research calls—two over the phone—obtaining many otherwise unavailable insights into this privately held company's business. Of the 13 competitors, she was one of only two who presented directly to the decision maker and the only one to talk primarily about the customer's business and the business fit between the two companies. A week later, she won the business with no negotiation on price, despite having a premium more than 20 percent greater than other bidders.

## SELECTING TARGETS

Based on the information presented so far, which of your accounts or opportunities do you think make good candidates for using the process?

Experience shows that this process works with any type of account, especially if you're really focused on selling value in ways your competitors aren't.

Admittedly, some sales representatives don't particularly care about selling value. They prefer to fire off a response to an RFP and be done with it. That's up to them. Most reps, however, want to do more—they want to sell value, and they want to differentiate themselves and stand out from the pack.

Here are some examples of customer situations where the process has proven effective:

**Established customers.** With your existing customer base, you can use the process to identify and close additional opportunities, create the right first impression with new executives, change inaccurate perceptions of you and your company, manage priorities and expectations, and help address customer satisfaction problems.

**Prospects.** With new opportunities you achieve an immediate leg up on the competition, helping you stand out from the start, giving you the inside track to winning the business, and turning prospects into solid customers.

**Competitive situations.** Differentiation is key to anyone selling value. There are a variety of ways, however, to look different. You can differentiate yourself on price, on service, or on how you do business, how you sell, and how you understand the customer's business. You can use the process to differentiate yourself not just on what you sell and on your price but on how you sell and how you do business.

One of our customers was a manager operating in an industry where formal presentations were not the norm. He wasn't sure whether his people would be able to present effectively, but he was confident about the impact. At one point he said, "If we just stand up and present, even if we suck, we'll still blow away the competition." Of course they didn't suck—they were terrific, and they ignited a revolution in selling in their industry.

**Former customers.** If you have a former customer who won't work with you because of past problems, you can use this process to say, "Hey, that's water under the bridge. There's potential value in our proposed relationship. Let's move forward."

**Old and new customers.** Whether you've had an account for 20 years or you just got the account, this process can help you leverage all the information you've built up over time and make a seamless transition to a new approach. Alternately, the process can help you get a fresh start, leveraging the fact that you're new. You can say, point blank, "I want to be of service to you; I want to provide value, but to do that I've got to learn more."

**Small and large companies.** The size of the target customer doesn't matter. This process has been used to sell to some of the largest companies in the world and also to some of the smallest. In fact, one client told us he wanted to use the process to sell to Brad Richards. And we asked him, "Is that a company, Brad Richards, Inc. or Brad Richards Corp.?" "No," he said, "it's just Brad Richards. He's working for a firm now, but he may start his own company, and if he does, I want to be the person he turns to." He used the process, and as a result of his presentation, when Brad Richards did leave his company and strike out on his own, he looked to this rep and said, "You know where I'm headed; help me get there."

**Any time in the sales process.** This process can be used at any point in the cycle, whether you've already received the RFP, you're proactively recognizing that someone's going to come out with one and want to be there first, you have to present an RFP response a week from tomorrow, or you're just proactively trying to sell value. In each of these cases, you can plug the IMPAX Process in and move ahead immediately.

**Complexity of situation.** This process will obviously be effective in a highly complex selling situation. But the process is also a powerful tool in less complex scenarios, where the emphasis is on using the process efficiently and closing quickly. Even companies that transact sales activities primarily over the phone can use and benefit from the process.

**Public sector accounts.** Even with customers in the public sector, who often rely on systematized rules for the buying process, this process can help you stand out as a value-added business partner.

One of our clients, a telecommunications company, was faced with losing a big customer, the city of Hartford, Connecticut. The company had experienced performance problems, and the city had opted to send the job out to bid. Our client decided to apply the process and swung into full research mode. They involved a disgruntled evaluator in the process and really turned him around. Elevating the level of contact, they moved beyond the IS department to deliver a presentation to the city manager. By using the process, they prevented the unraveling of the entire relationship and in fact solidified a long-term partnership with the city. The evaluator who had started out foursquare against them wound up feeling so strongly in their favor that he eagerly agreed to participate in a video extolling the company's solutions.

## REAL-WORLD EXAMPLE

As we conclude this overview of the IMPAX Process, we'd like to close with an anecdote from a client situation that really demonstrates the power of the process and how research, communication, and presentation work in the field. This case study is from Superior Corporation, one of the leading check printers in the world. We worked very closely with Superior to exploit an opportunity they had identified in the Canadian market.

At the time, they had no customers in Canada. In the midst of the selling effort to one of Canada's leading banking and financial institutions, they began to feel they were being dragged down, particularly on the issue of price. To elevate their access and get to senior-level decision makers who could appreciate Superior's value story, our client felt they had to rethink their sales approach. Because they were new to the market and because they faced competition from some top companies, Superior knew they weren't going to win this business based solely on price. They decided they could only win by selling value—specifically selling value to people who could buy value.

They conducted a planning session, beginning with the end in mind. It was very simple: they identified the steps to take and the time frame to make it happen. They began by leveraging the Internet to gather data, then continued with research meetings. Gathering information by following the 95-5 rule, they talked only 5 percent of the time to ask questions and let the customer talk the other 95 percent of the time. The research delivered two key results. First, in just three calls, they learned more about the bank than they had ever known, multiplying their knowledge of the business. Second, they developed a network of coaches. These coaches came to support Superior and helped them gain access to senior-level people, particularly the executive vice president of the corporation. They had one shot at this executive.

Beyond Selling Value means consistently applying the 95-5 rule—listening 95 percent of the time and only talking 5 percent—during your research efforts.

Superior knew their challenge was to make a good first impression. They delivered a high-impact business presentation. The Superior salesperson stood in front of the executive vice president and talked about something a little unusual—the bank's business. The executive had never seen anything like this before: "A vendor talking about us?" The approach may not be rocket science, but it was still a first. The agenda went as follows. The rep began by sharing what Superior had learned about the financial institution. Next, the rep talked about Superior and why, based on their understanding of the bank's business, Superior could become a strategic resource. Given this start, the presentation was much more powerful. They put it in context. They wrapped up with the business fit. In the end, they said to that executive, "Working together, we can help you accomplish some of your critical objectives."

By this time, the executive no longer saw Superior as a mere check printer. He looked at them as a business resource. And that's probably the essence of selling value, something we can all appreciate. If you're a value provider, you want to be seen as a business resource, and that's what happened here. The presentation delivered such a high impact that in the middle, the executive turned to the group and said, "I can't believe how much they know about our business." This is a common response.

> Beyond Selling Value means that you are responsible for the customer's perception of your value. You must first believe in your heart that what you do is more than just selling products—that you bring value to your customer's business.

As a result, the executive vice president became deeply involved in the sale. He wanted to work with Superior because of the business resource that Superior could provide. By the way, if we stopped thinking about business resource, we could easily start thinking, "Wait a minute! Superior is a check printer. It's ink on paper! That's a commodity." But what company can't be commoditized, if they let themselves? Microsoft? Software's a commodity. ExxonMobil? It's just gas, right? Northwest Airlines? Airline travel is just a commodity. IBM? Hardware. DuPont? Chemicals. Xerox? What, no one else can make a photocopy? You get the point. None of these products are commodities unless the client perceives them that way. Ink on paper, high-quality checks, great business relationship—not a commodity. Superior won the business, established a beachhead in Canada, and became one of the leading suppliers in Canada with the goal to be the primary check supplier in the entire country.

## CONCLUSION

By now, we hope you've got some enthusiasm for what you can accomplish using the IMPAX Process and you're ready to learn more about it. But before diving into research, we would like to close by sharing with you a thought from Abraham Lincoln. It's a play on the time-worn cliché that good things come to those who wait. We all probably heard that one at least a few times when we were growing up. Lincoln had a slightly different take. He said, "Good things may come to those who wait, but only the things left by the people who hustle." Lincoln was right. To win you have to hustle. If you want to win, and break out of the Vendor Trap that the gatekeepers and product evaluators keep setting for you, you need to rethink the way you sell value.

And that's just what the chapters that follow offer—the best strategies and tactics for sales professionals who want to win by selling to the executives who can buy value, not by gouging margins on the altar of price-based competition. With that in mind, let's get started with the process and dive into the research stage.

# The Power of
# RESEARCH

Research forms the foundation of the entire process. Whatever your goal with a target account—new business development, expanding your relationship with an existing customer, closing on a specific solution, etc.—all the steps that follow depend on doing the right kind of research. Research allows you to gain access and to present the power of a business relationship to those top-level executives who make long-term, value-based buying decisions.

Depending on your personal preferences, you may not consider doing research the most exciting part of the sales process; on the other hand, you may love the opportunity to turn over every rock and search every crevice to get at the elusive inside scoop on a target account. Regardless of your aptitudes, doing effective research remains absolutely critical to success with this process.

As any great athlete knows, your level of performance in the championship game depends greatly on how well you've prepared for that moment—and even helps determine whether you get there in the first place. As you'll see, research is the hard work that lets you shine when your moment in the spotlight arrives.

> *"Success is where preparation and opportunity meet."*—Bobby Unser

## A MASTER'S EXPERIENCE

Legendary golfer Sam Snead knew the value of research, as he proved during a practice round before the 1967 Masters, when he challenged South African golfer Bobby Cole to a friendly wager.

Reaching the tee at Augusta National's 13th hole, a par 5 with a slight dogleg to the left guarded by pine trees, Snead, then 55, said to the 23-year-old

Cole, "You know, Bobby, when I was your age, I could knock the ball over those pine trees."

Cole, who was much bigger than Snead, accepted the elder statesman's challenge. He lined up and uncorked a monster tee shot, but the ball failed to clear the trees and disappeared amidst the pines. Incredulous, he turned to Snead and said, "I couldn't get the ball over those trees. How on earth did you do it?"

Snead smiled and said, "Bobby, when I was your age, those trees were only 20 feet tall."

That day Bobby Cole learned an important lesson about doing his homework.

## WHY DO RESEARCH?

Let's take a look at the three key benefits research offers sales professionals using this process:

1. *Credibility.* Time and again, sales professionals using the process have leveraged the quality and depth of their research to blow away upper-level decision makers. You know your research has paid off when the target of your presentation, a senior-level executive, responds by saying, "You know more about our business than most of the people who work here." Good research also gives you a level of credibility in the decision maker's eyes that will prove crucial when you propose a strong business relationship with that customer's organization.
2. *Professionalism.* Effective, applied research is also key to elevating your own level of professionalism. High-achieving salespeople know more about their customers than mere product issues. They do research to improve their understanding of a customer's entire business *from the customer's perspective.* They become empowered to make recommendations that extend beyond the limited range of a product solution. In the decision maker's eyes, these salespeople become true business resources, the kind who stand out from the throngs of vendors trying to cram more products into an already crowded marketplace.
3. *Distinction from the competition.* Today, the differences among competing products have shrunk to the point where they are almost indistinguishable to many buyers. This is particularly true with senior-level executives, who tend to focus more on long-term strategic issues than side-by-side product comparisons. By doing research, you set yourself apart from the competition, not by what you sell but by the way you sell and how well you understand the customer's business.

## RESEARCH IN THE REAL WORLD

So what happens to a business relationship when you do your research and elevate your understanding of the customer's business? Take the example of one client who leveraged his research to deliver a well-developed presentation to a targeted senior-level executive. The executive was enthusiastic about the business fit between the two companies and committed to a mutually beneficial path forward.

Several weeks later, after the successful implementation of the action steps, the executive was promoted to president. One of his first calls was to tell the sales rep about the promotion. He then invited the rep to participate in an off-site strategic planning meeting. Only a select few of the president's respected associates were asked to assist him in planning the organization's future.

> Beyond Selling Value means doing the "right" kind of research.

This invitation was a tremendous compliment to the sales rep and the impact he'd made as a true business professional. By using a research-driven, customer-focused selling process, he won more than the sale—he won the long-term relationship as well.

One of our clients, Martha Richardson, Director of Strategic Development with VeriFone, shared this perspective on the research process:

> I thought that my team and I were selling value, but I realized that we weren't. We weren't doing the right kind of research. We were focused on our solutions and requirements, but that's not selling value. Truly selling value means doing research around the customer's business so we can position the business value associated with our relationship. The type of research we do now helps differentiate us from our competition.

## WHAT IT ISN'T

Now that we've talked about the benefits of effective research, let's take a moment to reaffirm just what research isn't. When you're doing research, you're not conducting some boring academic exercise in a sterile environment with people in white lab coats. So you can leave the chemistry sets and protective goggles at home. For us, research is a dynamic, exciting process. It means speaking with prospects and customers face-to-face or on the phone and asking insightful, challenging questions that help develop a powerful understanding of their business.

When conducting research, you're more like a detective, gathering clues and building a case—the case you will later make to the decision maker to enter into or expand a business relationship.

# CHAPTER THREE

# Digging for Clues
## HOW TO GATHER AND UTILIZE DATA

The first step in researching a target account is gathering data. But what is data? For our purposes, we define data as the publicly available facts and figures about a company. We distinguish data from information, which is the unique insider perspective you get from conducting research meetings with people with insight on the target account. We'll talk more about information in the next chapter. For now we'll focus on data.

> Keep in mind one of Steven Covey's seven habits of successful people: seek first to understand, then to be understood.

Just what data is publicly available depends on what kind of account you're chasing, specifically whether the company is publicly or privately held. So let's start by taking a look at some data source options with publicly held companies.

## COMPANY DATA SOURCES

Three primary reports published by publicly held companies can aid your search for key data about a target organization: annual reports, quarterly reports, and 10K reports.

### Annual Report

Companies use the annual report to inform shareholders and other stakeholders about the business's past performance and the company's future direction and objectives. You should investigate specific sections of the annual report:

**The president's letter.** The first, and for our purposes most important, section of the annual report is the president's letter. Here, the president or CEO discusses both the past year and the year to come and shares some of the strategies the company plans to implement to achieve the next year's goals. This section should give you a pretty good understanding of this company's business objectives and some key strategies. After reading the president's letter, you should have a basic grip on the big picture direction of this business.

**The year in review.** Many annual reports include an interesting section called "The Year in Review" or something similar. The company lists the highlights of the past year, including such items as new product introductions, new company acquisitions, key personnel promotions, or the divestiture of subsidiaries or divisions. The reports generally strike a positive note, speaking glowingly of the company's recent history.

Although we typically associate annual reports with publicly traded companies, many privately held companies produce internal annual reports. These are often sent to employees and sometimes also to key outsiders, such as suppliers and customers.

One more note about the annual report: Woody Allen once said, "Eighty percent of life is just showing up." Think about it—how often do people read their own company's annual report, much less take a highlighter and really pore over it? Not very often. Simply by reading the target company's annual report, you're already ahead of that 80 percent mark. This is the kind of activity that later will inspire the senior-level decision maker to utter those famous words: "You know more about our business than the people who work here." Just by showing up, you're ahead of the pack, and by doing a little preparation, you can put some real distance between you and your typical vendor-trapped competitors.

Most people don't read their own company's annual report. Imagine what an advantage you gain by reading your customers'.

Caution: Remember, the annual report is essentially a communications and sales tool for a publicly traded company's stock sale and performance. The reality behind all the enthusiastic analysis may not be as rosy as it appears in the annual report.

Companies will often bend over backwards to put a positive spin on their performance in the annual report. We recall an oil company that was desperate to show charts with a positive growth pattern, despite negative sales growth from the previous year. Their solution: graphs depicting five-year windows instead of the typical one-year windows.

## Quarterly Reports

Annual reports offer a wealth of great data about a company, but because they only come out once a year, the information can get a little stale. If you're nine or ten months past the annual report publication date and you want fresher data, quarterly reports offer a great solution. Quarterly reports should provide you with a more current perspective on how the company is measuring up to objectives laid out at the beginning of the year. Bear in mind, however, that you'll likely only be able to get quarterly reports from publicly traded companies.

## 10K Report

Any company that trades stock on a U.S. exchange is required to produce a 10K report for the Securities & Exchange Commission. Because it's not directed at shareholders, the 10K isn't as glossy as the annual report, but for that reason many consider it a more realistic assessment of the company. In addition to overviewing the company's business, marketplace, and competition, the 10K report also provides additional background information on the board of directors and company officers.

# OTHER DATA SOURCES

## D&B Business Information Report

Whether you're pursuing a publicly or privately held company, you'll probably want to look at the company's D&B Business Information Report. This report contains a great deal of credit information which, depending on what you're looking for, may or may not be valuable to you. But beyond credit information, the D&B also includes helpful data such as estimated annual sales, a description of current events and highlights, and a listing of the officers of the company including background profiles. This report also lists related companies, whether subsidiary or parent companies. Whatever you're after, it's a great place to start, especially when you're looking for data on privately held companies.

Data gathering can even help you build rapport. We had one client who was struggling to make a connection with an important decision maker. He read the executive's bio in a D&B report and discovered that they had both attended the University of Notre Dame. Armed with this information, he used the shared background to get the decision maker to open up and from that starting point built a strong business relationship.

## Articles

Recent articles are also a great place to look for current data. You can search the Internet or electronic databases for articles specifically about the target company, or you can look to general business publications and industry trade journals for data on recent events, product introductions, marketplace positioning, and so forth.

## Internal Publications

Company brochures, media kits, product literature, and internal newsletters are often overlooked but nonetheless important sources of data.

## Brochures and Media Kits

Company brochures and media kits tell us how the customer wants to be perceived in the marketplace. We can see whether they consider themselves "the quality company," "the service company," "the one-stop shop," or a niche player with one specific solution.

## Newsletters

Internal newsletters should help you understand recent events, promotions, company buzzwords, and new product introductions as well as the culture of the organization. You can see where they place emphasis, for example, on recent safety programs or on environmental initiatives. Social events like softball games, outings, or company functions are frequently covered as well. Newsletters may even feature interviews with upper-level executives talking about the state of the business. As a supplier, you may be able to get on the company newsletter mailing list.

## Others

But there's more. How about brokerage reports, which provide extremely up-to-date data? Management bios can help you gather background about the decision maker to whom you'll be presenting. Many companies today also air Web casts of analysts' calls that you can tune in to for great current source materials. "Who's Who" listings can also prove helpful, particularly when you're targeting specific key executives. News releases highlight events that can provide pinpoint information that applies directly to your efforts. Finally, you may also be able to get hold of speeches by company executives to industry associations and stockholder meetings.

While gathering data, one client pursuing a banking account thought to ask for copies of any speeches made by company executives. He obtained six different speech transcripts, two of which happened to have been given by the bank's vice chairman—the very decision maker he planned to present to. During the presentation, this rep made sure to include references to the vice chairman's speeches and some of the key related points. The executive was impressed with the rep's thoroughness and felt like the rep really "got it," as he put it. Can you imagine what that seemingly small step—asking for the speech transcripts—wound up doing for the sales rep's credibility in the decision maker's eyes? The lesson: it never hurts to ask for additional data sources.

## GETTING YOUR HANDS ON THE DATA

Now you know what you're looking for, but how do you get hold of these diverse data sources? You've got a few options.

*"Knowledge is knowing . . . or knowing where to find out."—Alvin Toffler*

## The Internet

Of course the Internet is a limitless source of all kinds of data, even about small and medium-sized companies. But because the Net is so vast, while it provides a means of quickly accessing data, it can also prolong your efforts. Following are a few tips on using the Internet to get data on your accounts.

**Company Web site.**  Your target account probably has a Web site, and this is the best place to begin looking for publicly available data. Here you will most likely find the company's public face—how they present themselves to

> The best place to gather data on a specific company is the company's Web site.

potential customers and investors. Usually, the site can be found simply by typing the company's name into your Web browser's URL window (as in <www.unitedteacozies.com>).

However, sometimes the site address is not so obvious, or it links to some organization other than the one you are trying to find. (An example of this is IMPAX Corporation's Web site, which is found at <www.impaxcorp .com>, not <www.impax.com>.) In this case, you may need to use a search engine to find the correct Web site.

Search engines.  Search engines can help narrow your search from among the millions of Web pages on the Internet. They enable you to enter key words related to your search, then provide links to related pages. There are a variety of search engine options, including the following:

- *General search engines.* These do not specialize in any particular category of Web sites, so they work best with general and easy-to-find words and phrases. Most work very well, despite vastly different technical approaches. Some general search engines include:
  - Google <www.google.com>
  - Yahoo! <www.yahoo.com>
  - Excite <www.excite.com>
  - Lycos <www.lycos.com>
- *Metasearch engines.* General search engines sometimes provide you with thousands of "hits" or links, only a few of which are useful. Metasearch engines are designed to search through several general search engines simultaneously and provide you with only the most relevant hits. Examples include:
  - Dog Pile <www.dogpile.com>
  - Metacrawler <www.metacrawler.com>
  - Ask Jeeves <www.askjeeves.com>
- *Specialized search engines.* Some companies have specialized the data they provide around a specific subject matter. These search engines can be especially useful when you are looking for information about an industry, a company, an application or function, or even a person. Here are some excellent research sites:
  - For profiles on U.S. public (and some private) companies: <www .hoovers.com>

- For trade journal articles from hundreds of industries: <www
  .northernlight.com>
- For in-depth information about companies: <www.company
  sleuth.com>
- For Canadian companies: <www.sedar.com>
- For international market reports: <www.tradeport.org/ts/countries>

## Beyond Search Engines

In addition to the search engines and industry-specific sites, you may consider some of the business press sites, such as *The Wall Street Journal* <www.wsj.com>, *Fortune* <www.fortune.com>, *Forbes* <www.forbes.com>, and even the sites of general newspapers. These may be worth a look, and most contain internal search engines that allow you to search their archives for company names, people's names, or other words and phrases.

Finally, services such as Yahoo! and many others allow you, the user, to personalize the information they present by letting you specify the companies, industries, and issues in which you are most interested. These are ideally suited to help you stay abreast of developments related to your target accounts.

If you're already Web savvy, we're not telling you anything you don't already know. But if you're not currently using the Web to gather data on your target accounts, it's probably time to start, and these sites are a few great places to begin your investigations.

But as even casual Web users know, the Internet is a fluid, growing, rapidly changing entity, with Web sites emerging and evaporating so abruptly that keeping up can be difficult. Your best bet is to find a strategy for gathering account data quickly on the Web that works for you, then constantly hone your techniques to take advantage of new technologies to further streamline the process.

## A Phone Call Away

Contrary to popular belief, you don't have to be a stockholder to obtain corporate reports. When you're chasing after data on a publicly held company, you should have little trouble getting everything you want simply by asking. Call the company's main number, then ask for "annual reports." Some companies call the department "shareholder information," others call it "stockholder relations." Don't try to figure it out; simply ask for "annual reports," and the receptionist will direct you to the right department.

When you're connected, ask the person to send you the annual report, 10K report, and the two or three most recent quarterly reports. Most likely you won't be asked why you want them, but if you are, simply say that you're preparing for an upcoming meeting and you want to make sure you've done your homework. Follow up by asking if they happen to have a media kit, any company brochures, product literature, or company newsletters that they could include with your mailing. In positioning your request, you could ask them this question: "If I were a recent college graduate interviewing with your organization, what kind of data could I get to do my homework?" Typically, people will be glad to help out and will actually overdeliver and send even more than you ask for.

Also, if you plan to be dealing with this account for some time in the future, ask to have your name put on their mailing list. All you have to do is ask, and you'll be added to the list of people who automatically receive these reports as they come out. Half the challenge with data is getting it in the first place; the other half is keeping it current.

When calling a privately held company, your request may vary depending on the size of the company. If it's a large company, the process is very similar to that described above, except that they may not have an annual report or quarterly report, and they won't have a 10K report. You can still ask for any data they may have to help you better understand their company. With a smaller company, you may want to ask to speak to public relations or marketing. When you're talking to them, if you sense they don't have much data, ask them for a press kit. A press kit is a collection of company brochures, articles, and other materials that are frequently available for publications interested in writing about the company.

## Library

In addition to public libraries, many companies have an internal library or other source of data, often unbeknownst to the salespeople who work there (shocking!). We're not suggesting that you should don Coke-bottle glasses and turn into a bookworm, but if your company does offer this resource, which can help you track down the data quickly, it makes sense to take advantage of it and capitalize on the opportunity.

## On the Road

Many customers make the data sources you're interested in available right in their lobbies or other common areas. While you're visiting an account, take a look around for newsletters and product literature. Investigate what's posted on bulletin boards. Ask whether the office has a public information or public relations contact. If so, share with this person that you're trying to learn as much as possible about the company and that you'd be interested in obtaining any company publications like newsletters, brochures, company highlights, fact sheets, and executive bios.

## Coaches

Another way to gather data is by working with your coach or coaches—the people with inside information and access who truly want to help you win. Explain your objective—to obtain as much as possible of the publicly available facts and figures on the target account. Give them the right kind of direction and specifics, asking for annual reports—external and internal—brochures, fact sheets, highlights, and news releases, and your coaches will typically overdeliver.

At one point, one of our clients was trying to sell into Cargill, one of North America's largest privately held companies. He was sure that there was simply no data to be had. A contact agreed to a 20-minute meeting, so they shifted into full 95-5 research meeting mode. The call lasted more than two hours, and the reps walked out with so many data sources they could hardly carry it all—internal newsletters, org charts, and even videos about Cargill. Even with private companies, data is like truth on the X-Files: it's out there.

## One Last Thought . . .

Clearly, a great deal of data is available. The key is to get the data and get it efficiently. You want to obtain as much data as possible, but you want to spend less time getting it than you've already spent reading about it.

> Remember, getting the data is administrative; using it is strategic.

## USING DATA

Once you've got all these data sources in hand, you'll need to know how to use them. One client, Jim Harvin, an Executive Vice President at Burnham Insurance, looks at the topic this way, "Every sales rep knows that they should get data, but how many of them do it on a regular basis? We get the data, and we leverage it to help us position our value as we do our research and get in front of decision makers."

Typically, we look to data with two goals in mind: to understand the business and to build credibility.

## Understand the Business

Clearly, these materials will give you a better understanding of the customer's business. You're looking to understand the big-picture issues being addressed by the corporation—the vision, mission, market, objectives, strategies, business issues, and the organization. These are the issues you uncap the highlighter for. There's a great deal to be learned, and it's all geared toward helping you gain access and eventually make a powerful business presentation to the decision maker.

A good way to think about what you need while reviewing data sources is an acronym we call *POSTI*. This stands for Profile, Objectives, Strategies, Trends, and Issues. Perusing annual reports, 10Ks, brochures, news releases, and speeches, you're likely to find statements like:

- "This year, we celebrate our 50th year in business." (Profile)
- "This year, we will grow our business at least two points faster than our industry's average." (Objectives)
- "Critical to our success this year is the rollout of our new technology platform." (Strategies)
- "As our industry experiences major consolidations. . . ." (Trends)
- "Looming legislative action causes us uncertainty." (Issues)

These are just a few examples, but POSTI is a good memory tool to keep in mind as you look at your sources. It really helps to bring the data to life.

## Build Credibility

The other way you use data is to build your initial credibility. With the data in hand, you can formulate intelligent, well-researched questions. Are you looking to undermine your efforts as soon as you walk in the customer's office? Then go into that account and ask, "What do you do?" or "So how's the economy doing around here?" It's like slapping the customer in the face. Essentially you're saying, "You aren't important enough for me to even bother with the most basic precall homework."

> During a research meeting, we pulled out a customer's annual report we had highlighted and written on and used it to ask questions. The contact reached over, grabbed the report, and said, "Let me take a look at that. I haven't seen it yet." Then, as he looked over all our highlights and marks, he commented, "Wow, you've really done your homework."

By contrast, when you've gotten the data and done your homework, you can come in with much more intelligent questions. You can say to the customer, "It's our understanding that the economy in your region has been mired in a lengthy recession, yet your organization has prospered in spite of this. How have you been able to accomplish this?" This question communicates very powerfully to the contact or coach that you've invested some significant time, even before the first meeting.

Simply gathering data doesn't mean you're going beyond selling value, but how you use the data does. Most salespeople, if they gather data at all, look for opportunities to sell their product—new plant openings, system upgrades, etc. Moving beyond traditional value selling means using data to understand the customer's critical business issues that reveal the business fit between your two companies, not simply the openings where you might be able to shove more product in.

So how can you put your data to use during the selling cycle? Here are just a few possibilities:

- *Use it in account planning.* The data will help you in developing your current understanding of the customer's business.
- *Prepare for a research meeting.* Review the data prior to a research meeting to build a baseline understanding of the company, which will allow you to generate a list of questions to ask during the meeting.
- *Assist in a research meeting.* It's a good idea to bring your data sources along to a research meeting and at some point during the call actually refer to them as you ask a question. Pulling out your data shows that you cared enough to prepare.
- *Identify research meeting contacts.* If you don't have any leads, looking through the data may produce names of potential research meeting contacts.
- *Develop your business presentation.* Data can help tremendously as you gather key points for the presentation—specifically for the profile, objectives, strategies, and business issues pages.

Gathering and using data can have a significant impact on your credibility with customers and prospects. Take Felicia Wilson's experience. She's an account manager with Hyperion, a leader in business performance management. Here's how she describes her research process selling into a major consumer packaged goods company:

In preparing for a research meeting with a senior manager, I did my homework on the company—gathering data from their annual report, 10K, recent press releases, and even watching a Web-cast about the company's latest financial results hosted by their CEO. Because of the insight I had gained about the company through research, I was able to ask the senior executive some real thought-provoking questions. The impact was even more significant than I expected: right in the middle of our meeting, the senior executive stopped me and said, "I wish all of our suppliers would take the time to understand our business as well as Hyperion does." It was music to my ears. Getting the right data and knowing what to do with it has given me another way to differentiate myself.

We've seen it over and over again, and it bears repeating: a little research goes a long way.

As we've mentioned, data helps in another way when you're writing a business presentation. One of our clients found herself in a quick turnaround situation as she prepared to present to a senior-level decision maker at Eli Lilly. She had very little time to do research and ended up having to rely on data for 90 percent of her customer knowledge. Although she was concerned about the short time frame, she felt she didn't have any alternative but to rely on what she could get quickly. As she was presenting to the senior executive, he stopped her and said, "It's unbelievable how much you know about us. None of this is public information, how did you learn so much about us?" She didn't have the heart to tell him that almost all of her presentation came from data.

## KILLER APPLICATIONS

At first glance, gathering and investigating these data sources may seem to be most valuable for salespeople calling on new prospects. In fact, research can prove just as powerful for reps calling on longstanding customers. We use the saying, "The longer you're doing business with a customer, the greater the odds that you don't understand their business." By staying up-to-date with your customers and their business, you impress them with your efforts, and they recognize that you take their needs and your relationship very seriously.

## CONCLUSION

As you move forward gathering data, however, it's important to ask yourself one question: how much is enough? Remember, you want to spend less time gathering data than it takes to read this chapter. Data helps you understand the target company, particularly big-picture direction and objective issues. But you also need to be careful to avoid "analysis paralysis." You don't want to get so bogged down in compiling and interpreting data that you never make it out to the customer.

As you gather and use data, bear in mind Voltaire's words of caution: "The best is the enemy of the good." Get the data, get it quickly, and keep the process moving forward.

The amount of data available varies from one account to another. Fortune 500 companies will have reams and reams of data, while smaller, privately held companies may offer much slimmer pickings. But one aspect you can control is how much time you spend gathering the data. If you're in a general business territory with hundreds of prospects and you're trying to sell value in a one-call or two-call close, you'll tend to spend less time doing data gathering than someone with just a few strategic accounts. In either case, however, just a little research can do wonders to help you break out of a customer's impression of you as a vendor.

Whatever kind of customers you're calling on, the key is to keep your file current with recent, regularly updated data. So make it a habit in every account situation you face to collect the data quickly and then commit to keeping a steady supply of fresh materials coming in.

# CHAPTER FOUR

# Keys to the Customer Kingdom
## THE FIVE RESEARCH ELEMENTS

Two pirates, Angus and Jean Paul, who hadn't seen each other in years, suddenly crossed paths one day. Here's how their conversation went:

**Jean Paul:** Angus, it's great to see you, but I've got to be honest. You look terrible. What happened?

**Angus:** Oh, you must mean the peg leg. Well, I fell from the rigging one day, and before they could pull me out a shark got to me.

**Jean Paul:** That's a real shame. But I've got to be honest, it's not just the peg leg.

**Angus:** Oh, you're talking about the hook. Well, I went up against a young swashbuckler. I guess I'm not as quick as I used to be, and, well, he got my hand, sad to say.

**Jean Paul:** That's terrible! But, you know, that's not all of it either.

**Angus:** Oh, you're talking about the eye patch. Well, I was up in the crow's nest one day, a seagull flew overhead, and the droppings went right in there and cost me the eye.

**Jean Paul:** Now wait a second. I understand about the shark and the leg, and the swashbuckler and the hand, but I don't understand how some bird droppings can cost you an eye.

**Angus:** Well you would, if it was your first day with the hook.

Most jokes carry an element of truth in them, and this one is no exception. The lesson is that in almost any situation there is more to the story than simply what appears on the surface. That's what this chapter is all about—building a deeper understanding of the customer organization you've targeted.

> *"Beyond Selling Value is about earning the business by learning the business."*—Dunc Hawkins, SSA Ontario

## GOING IN—INFORMATION GATHERING

In the last chapter, we talked about one element of research—gathering data. Next, we're going to cover information—what we call the *insider's perspective*. This is the information you learn from working with and talking to people who have an insider's perspective about the target account. Either they work there, or they're otherwise familiar with the company.

But what kind of information are you looking for? An almost limitless amount of knowledge about your customers is available. If you're going to use your research to develop a high-impact business presentation to a key decision maker, you need to classify the information you gather. For that purpose, we divide information into five distinct categories, called the Research Elements, which we'll cover one by one (see Figure 4.1).

### Research Element #1: Corporate Profile/Direction

Corporate Profile/Direction is the big picture. Where is the company now? How did they get there? Where do they want to be in the future? How are they going to achieve that? What's impeding them? What are their opportunities?

It is here, in the understanding of the customer's business, that most reps fall short. Typically, they understand the customer's need or application, but they lack a grasp of such critical business issues as the names of the customer's top ten customers, the company's heritage, and the concerns that keep the CEO awake at night. This is why, when sales managers ask their reps the question, "What does the customer do?", they tend to get answers like, "Oh, about $50,000 a year" or "80 units per quarter," instead of, "They are a leading _____ company with a mission of . . ."

Creating a corporate profile can be compared to building a house, and each individual piece of information is like one building block. Let's take a look at some of the issues to consider and the questions you'll have to answer to construct your corporate profile.

FIGURE 4.1    The Research Elements

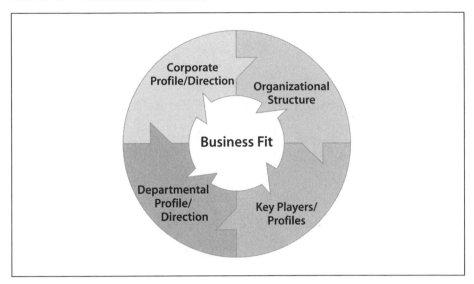

**Profile.** To understand the customer's organization, you begin by getting a firm grasp on the facts and figures that make this company unique. Some of the questions you may want to consider include:

- What are the company's products or services?
- What's their market share position?
- Who are their top five or ten customers?
- Are they trending up, trending down, or holding steady?
- What are their major divisions and locations?
- How many employees do they have?
- What's the company history—what path led the company to its current position?
- Are there any other characteristics that make this company stand out?

Beyond Selling Value means knowing a great deal more about your customers than an address and phone number. As Karen Kracher of John Harland Company puts it, "In order to be a consultant to your customers, you have to understand their customers."

**Issues.** You'll also want to investigate the activities going on within as well as outside the company that are influencing the corporate direction. Consider:

- What's happening in this company's industry?
- What are the key external impacts on their business? Government regulation? Environmental pressures? Competition? The economy?
- What are the trends in the company organization—in terms of growth, hiring, new products, and in the industry?
- What major events have affected the business? Examples include new product introductions, new divisions, acquisitions, etc.
- What are the key challenges facing the business?
- What are the CEO's top three to five issues or concerns?

**Financial condition.** By understanding the target company's financial condition, you can begin to identify the pressures that senior-level executives are under. Ask:

- What are their key performance indicators, financial and otherwise?
- How does the company measure its success?
- What is the company's financial condition? How are they performing, both against their own objectives and compared to the rest of the industry?
- What are their revenues and their profitability?

**Culture.** It's important to understand how this company views itself and its place in the market. Think about these questions:

- What's the corporate culture?
- What are some of the organization's basic philosophies?
- How does the company view itself? Are they conservative? Trendsetters?
- What's the company's personality? Is it a fun, invigorating, exciting place to work, or does a more traditional, staid atmosphere prevail?

**Competitive environment.** Naturally, any thorough understanding of a company's business will include a sober assessment of competitive issues. Questions to ask about the company include:

- Who are the their closest competitors?
- How do they differentiate themselves?
- What is their single greatest competitive advantage?
- How are they viewed by their competition and by their customers?

> *"In this industry, we're only as smart as our dumbest competitor."*
> —*Robert Crandall, CEO, American Airlines.*
>
> Who are your customers' competitors?

**Future direction.** If you hope to join forces with the target company, it makes sense to determine just what they have planned for the future—their objectives and strategies. First, you must understand the difference between vision, mission, objectives, strategies, and tactics:

- *Vision* is typically a statement of future condition.
- *Mission* is traditionally what the company does and how they do it.
- *Objectives* are measurable and tend to be financially oriented (revenue, profit, market share, etc.).
- *Strategies* are how the company is going to implement and attain these objectives (invest in R&D, acquire companies, raise capital, introduce new products, etc.).
- *Tactics* are the specific, day-to-day action steps to implement these strategies.

With these definitions in mind, think about your target account. Consider:

- What are the company's mission and vision?
- What are their major opportunities for future growth?
- What are the company's objectives (what they're trying to accomplish and by when) and their strategies (how they'll do it)?
- What are the CEO's top three priorities?
- How will the business be different two years from today?
- What are the customer's critical business objectives?
- How will the company achieve these objectives?
- What strategies are in place or are being put in place to accomplish the objectives?
- What are some of the company's key projects or initiatives?
- What are the company's critical success factors?

The questions concerning the customer's critical business objectives may make up the single most important aspect of the corporate profile and direction. When we talk about the customer's business objectives, it's not enough to know that the customer wants to increase sales and profitability while reducing costs. That's too basic—who doesn't want to increase sales and profitability and reduce costs? Instead, we need to delve deeper to understand their quantified business objectives and any related strategies.

For example, if the company has a 15-percent compound growth rate as a stated objective, what strategies are in place to help them achieve these results? Are they growing their sales force? Investing in new technology? Opening additional manufacturing facilities and increasing manufacturing capacity? Or are they improving training or offering new value-added services to their customers? What are the specific strategies behind each objective?

Let's say one of their objectives is to reduce expenses. If so, what strategies are in place to make that happen? Are they reducing head count, cutting back on programs, or selling subsidiaries or facilities? What expenses are being cut and how?

Then again, maybe the company has stated that they want to grow. Okay, let's understand how much and by when. Do they want to improve the quality of their products? If so, what are their metrics and benchmarks? If quality is important, how do they measure quality improvement, and what strategies are in place? What quality programs are they embarking on? What quality programs already exist? Who manages these quality efforts?

Remember when we said that an almost limitless amount of information is available about customer organizations? We weren't kidding. In fact, the above questions address just some of what we want to understand about the company's big picture. Bear in mind that if you understand just a tenth of these issues, you'll already know more about this company than 99 percent of the other sales professionals calling on the account.

## Research Element #2: Organizational Structure

Organizational structure refers to the traditional boxes and lines that lay out a company's organizational hierarchy. When it comes to selling, this area of research seems to have faded into obscurity. But we have an excuse for not creating org charts on our customers, right? Today's corporate hierarchies are too unstable. They're like computers: as soon as a new org chart comes out, it's already obsolete. But that's really just a cop-out. While it's true that most customer organizations are dynamic and constantly changing, nonetheless, no matter the size or complexity of the account, a variety of buying influences and different people will fill different roles.

The question becomes, if you're going to sell value, can you afford not to put together an organizational chart? Realistically, you still need to have something down on paper identifying your coaches as well as the contacts, evaluators, gatekeepers, and the true decision maker.

With that in mind, let's take a look at the three different ways to think about organizational structure.

There are three different views of an organization: how things are supposed to work; how things really work; and how things work when people are done working.

**1. The formal chart.** Here we're talking about the boxes and lines, names and titles, the reporting structure—the road map of the account. You'll want to know:

- How is the company formally structured to achieve the company objectives?
- What's the chain of command that the company makes public, if any?
- How many major business segments are there?
- How do the different departments interact?

Another way to think about the formal structure is *how are things supposed to work?*

A typical organizational chart might look like the one in Figure 4.2.

**2. The informal chart.** If the formal chart is how things are supposed to work, the informal chart reflects how things actually get done. This is what insider perspective is all about.

---

FIGURE 4.2   Organizational Chart

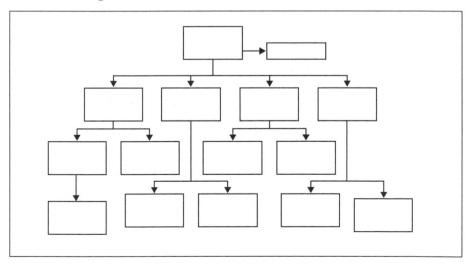

FIGURE 4.3    Influence Box

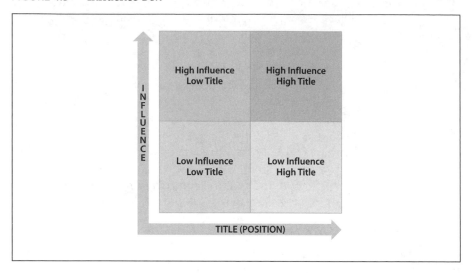

Often we hear salespeople say, "We didn't get the business—it was a political decision." The words *political* and *politics* take on a negative connotation for many people. Politics, however, is a major factor in any organization. To succeed, you need to know how to recognize, work with, and leverage a company's informal or political structure.

People also frequently associate power with job title. This correlation does not always hold. Also, accessibility is frequently inversely related to influence. That's why many sales efforts are conducted at low influence/ high accessibility levels.

One key note to remember: Don't be fooled by job titles. As anyone knows who's ever had to do business with a manager who also happens to be the CEO's brother-in-law, the title on a person's business card does not always equate to his or her influence within an organization.

The model in Figure 4.3 illustrates how to analyze players of power and influence within an organization.

Your knowledge of your prospect or customer and coach network are your best means of learning the customer's political structure and influence level.

Ask yourself these questions when trying to identify the influential players within the organization:

- What do you need to know from your coaches about the influence of key players at your target account?
- What level of influence does your coach or your coaches have? Gatekeeper? Evaluator? User? Contact?
- What are the dotted line responsibilities and key relationships that make things happen?
- Who are the people with significant influence in the organization?
- To whom does the decision maker turn for guidance?
- Who hired whom within the organization?
- Who has been behind recent internal changes such as personnel, philosophy, policy, etc.?
- Who has the responsibility for the highest visibility projects in the company?

The best business reasons alone are not always enough. You also need to understand the political influences on the decision maker.

**3. The social chart.**   What are the key social relationships at work? At any company, interpersonal relationships affect every aspect of the company. Another way you might think about the social chart is *how do things work when people aren't working?*

Beyond the three types of org charts, you're also going to want to find out the following:

- Where in the organization does the current supplier have the strongest relationships?
- Who makes the final recommendations?
- Is a committee typically involved in buying decisions?
- What is the decision making process?
- Who is the decision maker?
- Who are the players involved in achieving the primary corporate objectives?

Why is it so critical to understand the company's organizational structure? By mapping out where the decision maker, coaches, potential coaches, contacts, evaluators, and gatekeepers all reside, you gain perspective not only on what you know, but also on what you don't know. Where do you lack coaches? Where are the gatekeeper booby traps you need to avoid? Do you know who has influence? Who are the senior-level decision makers? If you don't know, how can you find out?

## Obtaining the Org Chart

So how do you get your hands on the target company's organizational chart? After all, they're not just going to hand it over, are they? Actually, they might. Often, simply by asking, you will find that some customers are glad to share their org charts with you, particularly if you have strong coaches. If this is the case, and a recently updated organizational structure is yours for the asking, take advantage of the opportunity.

It's easier today to get org charts than it used to be. During the 1970s and 1980s, companies tended to guard their org charts and mark them *confidential use only* or *internal use only*. Today, the veil of secrecy has been lifted, and the org charts are much more accessible.

But sometimes customers hesitate, often responding with something like, "Well, we don't have a formal chart laid out" or "The one we have is so outdated it won't do you any good." If you get this kind of response, that's your cue to break out the notebook and start drawing boxes and dotted lines.

Walk the person through, asking probing questions about the organizational structure. Take comprehensive notes, and pause frequently to confirm your understanding. Say, "Am I getting this right? Is this the correct reporting structure? How do you spell her name again? What was his title?"

Really work with the customer. The more enthusiasm and interest you show in developing a complete organizational structure, the greater investment your contact will make in helping you get it right.

Another way to build an org chart is to ask the customer for help with fixing a very rudimentary one you already have. If you've done some homework on the account, whether through data gathering or research meetings, simply put together a very preliminary chart, but do get it down on paper. Pull in any resources you have, whether research meeting notes, names and titles from data sources like newsletters and annual reports, and anyplace else you can.

Then, at some point during the research meeting, ease into the org chart conversation with the contact by saying something like, "You know, Jay, you've mentioned Deanna's name a couple of times during our discussion. I have to admit, I'm not sure where she fits into the organization." Then hand Jay your written org chart and ask, "Could you help me understand where she fits on this chart?" Frequently the customer will take the initiative to pick up a pencil (to use the eraser, more often than not) to start making revisions and do the work for you.

## Buying Roles

In this chapter, we've been tossing around a few terms to describe the different individuals and the varying roles they play in the customer organization. While these terms are, by and large, self-explanatory, it's important to make clear what we mean by the labels we use.

**Contact.** Almost anyone can be a contact—a name in a file, a person we met at a trade show, a friend of a friend, and so on. For our purposes we define a contact as someone who is:

- Knowledgeable about the company
- Credible within the organization
- Willing to meet with us
- Able to provide useful information

> Remember: A contact is not necessarily in your corner. A contact can easily share all the same information with a competitor.

**Coach.** A coach is a special kind of contact. We'll go into more detail about the coach in Chapter 5, but for now we'll define a coach as someone who has all the characteristics of the contact listed above, but who also:

- Shares information completely
- Is willing to provide insight and direction
- Helps you develop your strategy
- Provides reliable, subjective analysis about the buying organization
- Wants you to win
- Wins if you win

The two most important coach characteristics are these last two, that she wants you to win and that she wins if you win. We'll explore all these characteristics more fully in the next chapter.

Another characteristic of an exceptional coach is that he is proactive. Many times, a great coach will come to you before you even know there's a problem or an opportunity. Admittedly, not all good coaches are proactive, but it's a terrific asset when they are.

**Decision maker.** There's no doubt about the decision maker's role in the sale. The decision maker is the person who:

- Establishes the priority of projects
- Is concerned about the economic health of the business
- Focuses on the future
- Asks "Why?"
- Can buy value, not just price
- Can say "yes" even if everyone else says "no"
- Can also say "no" when everyone else says "yes"

Remember: For any given sale, there is only one true decision maker.

When asked why he robbed banks, gangster Willie Sutton famously replied, "Because that's where the money is." If Sutton had been a sales professional selling in today's marketplace, he'd have skipped the purchasing agents and product evaluators to focus on decision makers for the same reason. You should too.

When we say that the decision maker is someone who can say "yes" when everyone else says "no," it's important to clarify: say "yes" to what? A decision maker may or may not be the person who says "yes" to a $100 order for more toner for the office copier. That's often a little mundane for most higher-level decision makers. But a decision maker is definitely the person who can bless a strategic, long-term relationship between your two companies.

*"Committees are groups that keep minutes and lose hours."*
*—Milton Berle*

One question we hear frequently is, "What do you do when a committee is making the decision?" We believe that, despite the push for employee empowerment and the decentralization of power, even supposedly "decision making" committees have to report to true decision makers or have individual decision makers sitting on the committee. As a result, we are hesitant to say that committees make decisions. Consider the following experience shared with us by a client, Bob Karel:

> I was selling to a coveted prospect in the backyard of our biggest competitor. I had just learned this process and had a presentation opportunity the following week to a buying committee. I made a great business presentation, and they voted on the spot to give my company the business for the first time ever. The next day, however, the table turned as the president, for the first time, overrode a committee's decision. The committee only made the decision if it supported what the decision maker wanted.

**Evaluator.** Evaluators often come disguised as decision makers but in fact are not empowered to make substantive decisions. Evaluators go by many names, but one of the most common is *purchasing agent*. An evaluator typically may:

- Be most closely tied to your company's products
- Be a gatekeeper
- Be able to say no to you but needs to get approval from upstairs before saying yes
- Be able to recommend
- Be a key influencer to the decision maker
- Be concerned about product specs and financials
- Be focused on the present
- Ask "What?" and not "Why?"

> One good way to start to understand who the decision maker is: during the course of your sales process, if someone tells you, "I'm the decision maker," that's a good sign that this person is an evaluator. Decision makers will more typically say something like, "My people make those kinds of decisions."

Evaluators are made, not born. They even take classes. They learn how to evaluate better while salespeople are learning to sell better. One of our clients, a regional vice president of sales for a multinational company, found this out when he was invited to attend a company meeting. He wasn't sure what the meeting was about but was told that a consultant was going to talk about a topic related to sales.

It turned out that the consultant was pitching a training course. His entire premise was that salespeople needed to be stopped. "Salespeople are immoral," he explained, "and their unethical practice of trying to get to decision makers needs to be squashed. We need to keep them down. This whole notion of trying to sell value is a crock. We need to pin them down and trap them with our purchasing people." This was his entire premise.

Meanwhile the RVP, who was our best coach and a key influencer on the decision maker and was responsible for spending hundreds of thousands of dollars on training to help his people sell value, was getting more and more livid as the man spoke. At the end of the presentation, he addressed the consultant.

"Let me make sure I understand your premise," he said. "Salespeople are immoral and unethical? And I'm unethical for leading them toward a vision of selling value? So you're saying we should relegate ourselves to selling to purchasing people so we can get garbage for margins and have the crap beat out of us in the marketplace?"

Of course the consultant was unprepared for this. He had nothing to say. He hadn't done his research. He didn't know who was going to be in the meeting. Instead of asking any questions, he just came in with his premise. And for that he got killed and escorted out personally by the RVP.

**Gatekeeper.**  For most salespeople, gatekeepers are all too familiar. Like evaluators, they can say "no" (in fact, they're quite good at it), but they can't say "yes." Gatekeepers also:

- Restrict access to other key players
- Block your strategy
- Limit your effectiveness
- Can be either subtle or overt
- Can be either antagonistic or friendly

Gatekeepers come in all stripes. Some are overtly hostile, while others are a little more subtle—smiling the whole time while ushering you out the door. In many cases, the subtle, friendly gatekeepers provide a more difficult challenge than their more antagonistic counterparts.

Some salespeople believe they can convert gatekeepers, that if they do a great job of selling value, then the gatekeeper will throw away the grid and realize the advantages of buying based on value instead of mere product feature and price issues. This reminds us of the following age-old parable about the scorpion and the frog:

> One day a scorpion was walking along the riverbank trying to find a way to get across the river, when he came upon a frog. The scorpion asked the frog to take him across the river on his back. The frog quickly replied, "No I will not give you a ride." The scorpion asked why not. The frog said, "Because, Mr. Scorpion, if I were to give you a ride on my back, we would only get halfway across and you would sting me, and then I would drown."
>
> Quickly, the scorpion replied, "But Mr. Frog, if I were on your back and stung you and you drowned, then I would drown also." The frog considered this for a minute and then said, "I guess you're right. Okay, I will give you a ride." The scorpion jumped on the frog's back, and they started to cross the river.
>
> Half way across the river, the frog felt a sharp pain in his back as the scorpion pierced him with his stinger. The frog immediately started to panic as he felt the venom race through his veins, paralyzing him. Just as he took his last breath and they were both about to go down, the frog looked at the scorpion and asked, "But why did you sting me? Now we will both drown." The scorpion replied, "Because that is my nature."

It is the gatekeeper's nature to put you on the grid. If you choose to expend energy trying to convert gatekeepers and bring them around to the concept of buying value, chances are you're going to wind up like the frog, getting stung.

**User.** User is probably the most self-explanatory label of all. These are the people who will actually use your product or service. Users typically:

- Are personnel whose daily work will be affected by your product or service
- Are implementation oriented
- Take a tactical view versus a strategic one
- Focus on the past and present rather than the future, except to ask, "How will this affect me?"

> Users want to know how your solution will affect them, but they likely will not be concerned about how the solution affects their company.

FIGURE 4.4    Sample Org Chart

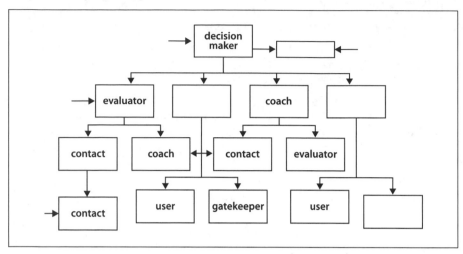

As you put your preliminary organizational chart together, think about buying roles. As each name is placed in a box, ask yourself, "Is this person a decision maker? A coach? An evaluator? A gatekeeper? A user? A contact?" Then jot down those notations right on the organization structure.

Let's take a look at a sample org chart with buying roles listed on the chart (Figure 4.4).

## Research Element #3: Key Players/Profiles

As we develop our understanding of the target account, of course we want to identify who the key players are. But beyond simple identification, we also want to build profiles on these key players. For our coaches and decision makers, we want to make those profiles as detailed as we can. If you've read Harvey Mackay's bestseller, *How to Swim with the Sharks without Being Eaten Alive,* then you may be familiar with the Mackay 66. This is a very detailed list of 66 questions that Mackay Envelope sales reps have to answer about a prospect—things like education, family, marital status, business background, and lifestyle.

Whether you're able to answer all 66 questions is one thing, but Harvey's point remains valid: a great deal of information can be gathered about these key players, and a great deal of value can be gained when we do so.

Now let's consider some of the details we want to find out about these key players.

## Professional background.

- How did she get to this point? Was she brought in by a headhunter, or did she rise up through the ranks, beginning in the mailroom?
- Where was he before he got to this position?
- What does she consider her crowning success to date?
- What professional challenges is he facing?

## Personal.

- What is her personal background (schooling, family situation, hobbies)?
- Is he married?
- Is she active in a church or local community?
- Does he enjoy the arts or athletics?
- How does she spend her time when she's not working?

## Issues/concerns.

- What issues is he facing?
- What keeps her awake at night?
- What is the biggest issue he's facing now?
- What major issues is her department facing now?

## Objectives/priorities.

- What are his top priorities?
- Where would she like to take her organization?
- Where does he spend most of his time now?
- What are her personal objectives?

## Characteristics/style.

- How would you describe his personality?
- What is her dominant operating or management style?
- How does he typically make decisions?
- What is her social style (amiable, analytical, expressive, driver)?

Asking what a decision maker considers to be his or her greatest success to date can be very powerful. One of our clients, a software company, was building a profile on a senior executive in a major transportation company. In conversation with a coach, they asked what the executive would consider his greatest achievement. The coach got a quizzical look on his face, then said, incredulously, "You mean you don't know about the dream?" Our client had no idea what he was talking about, and asked what "the dream" was.

The coach explained that one night this executive woke up in the middle of the night, raced down to his kitchen, and started feverishly scribbling down notes, trying to remember the dream he'd just had. But that wasn't good enough, so he threw on some clothes and raced over to the office.

The next morning, the others in the office arrived to find him looking all disheveled, in jeans and a sweatshirt, unshaven, in a room full of flip charts with writing all over them. To top it off, he's babbling some gibberish about a dream, "I had this dream, it was unbelievable," and so forth.

Naturally, they assumed he'd gone nuts. But he wasn't nuts. In fact, he had dreamed of a way to use a satellite to track every unit of transportation 24 hours a day, 365 days a year, and that's what he was working out on the flip charts.

By the time our client arrived on the scene, "the dream" had become an integral part of company lore. Imagine the better position our client was in when he presented to the decision maker, just because he thought to ask the coach that one simple question about the president's greatest accomplishment.

> Caution: There's a great deal here to learn, but let's be careful about one thing. Don't go looking for confidential information. Digging up dirt is not an effective strategy for today's successful sales rep.

## Research Element #4: Departmental Profile/Direction

We've already talked about the corporate profile/direction. Now we're going to narrow our focus to concentrate on the specific department we're selling into. Whether that's manufacturing, distribution, quality, engineering, sales, marketing, human resources, information systems, or one of any number of other possibilities, this is the department where your product, service, or solution is going to make an impact.

As you investigate the departmental profile/direction, you want to concentrate on six key issues—this department's:

**1. Profile.** This is the internal workings of the department, how it functions and what makes it unique. Some of the questions you may want to consider include:

- What are the department's responsibilities?
- What is its mission?

- Who are the most effective people in the department?
- Who are their customers?
- What are the department's frequently used acronyms and buzzwords?

2. Relationship to corporate direction. This is the relationship between this department and the corporate direction. Before you invest a great deal of time and effort into a specific department, you have to ask yourself, "Who cares?" Too often, sales reps slog through long selling cycles only to discover that the targeted department has no leverage or clout within the company and will not get any budget for a sizeable new project. To make sure this doesn't happen to you, ask:

- What is the department doing to support the company's vision?
- How does the department interface with other departments?
- How is the department perceived in the organization?
- How will the attainment of key departmental objectives affect the corporate goals?

3. Objectives/strategies. What does the future hold for this department? Find out by determining:

- What is the department's vision?
- Is there a strategic plan for the department? If so, what is it?
- What are the short-term departmental goals?
- What are the department's critical strategies?

4. Projects. It's one thing to know where the department wants to go, but you'll also want to find out how they plan to get there. Ask:

- What are the department's major projects?
- What is the priority of these projects?
- Who is driving these projects?
- What factors will influence the success of the projects?

5. Issues/concerns. What obstacles may stand in the way of the department achieving its objectives? Find out:

- What are the department's major issues, concerns, and challenges?
- What is the most critical issue facing the department?
- What changes need to occur in the department to meet the objectives?
- If money/time were no object, what would the department fix, change, or invest in today? Why?

**6. Product fit/account qualification.** You should find out how this department traditionally makes buying decisions. Not that you plan to operate within those confines, but understanding how things typically function will certainly help you. Ask:

- Who is your current supplier? How would you describe the strengths and weaknesses of their company and solution?
- What is the department's decision making process?
- What are you looking for in your supplier?
- Can you give me an example of an outstanding supplier? What makes them outstanding?
- If you had the perfect situation, what would it include?
- What are the implications should the department's priorities not be met?
- What is the payback if the department's primary objective is achieved?

**Unique terminology.** Finally, let's make sure we find out if this department uses any unique buzzwords, acronyms, or mottos. Many companies use different words or terms to describe essentially the same thing. It's critical, however, that when we're dealing with a specific customer, we get those terms right.

Here's an example. For most finance departments, Return on Investment (ROI) is a critical concept, right? Actually, it depends. Some companies focus on CROI, or Cash Return on Investment. Others talk about ROE, or Return on Equity. Admittedly, the idea is essentially the same—they're all financial measurements against which to chart progress. But imagine how much credibility you'll generate when you walk into the customer's office already using their unique terms and phrases—and how much you'll lose if you don't.

Take the case of one IMPAX client, an accounting and consulting company. During a planning session, two of the firm's partners began arguing about how their targeted account measured financial success. One partner felt that ROI was the most critical measuring stick. The other partner believed that ROE was more important. To resolve the discrepancy, they decided that as part of a research meeting, they would ask the customer what financial metric their company used to measure success.

When they asked the question, the customer seemed surprised that they would have to ask and responded, "Well, of course we measure ROWPA." Bear in mind that this account was a chicken processing company. They considered ROWPA a universal term understood by nearly everyone. The partners in the consulting firm didn't have a clue what ROWPA meant. So they asked, "And what does ROWPA stand for, exactly?" The customer answered, with a hint of surprise in his voice, "It stands for Return On Working Poultry Assets."

You can laugh about that, and it is funny, but you can also bank on the fact that the partners used ROWPA in the presentation to the executive, because it demonstrated a true insider perspective.

Let's take another example. Many companies today have a quality department. It's great to know that quality is important to a customer, but it's even better to know which approach they take to improving quality. Is it Malcolm Baldrige? Is it a Deming approach? Maybe it's something else entirely, or a program they've developed internally. Either way, when you present to the decision maker, you're going to want to talk about quality the same way they talk about quality.

> Remember: Assumptions can really trip you up. Don't assume that the target company uses any of the same specialized terms, lingo, or acronyms you use. As you develop your research into the customer organization, repeatedly check to make sure you're always phrasing your understanding in the customer's terms.

## Research Element #5: Business Fit

Now we come to the business fit. Everything else we've discussed so far in this chapter—corporate profile/direction, organizational structure, key players/direction, and departmental profile/direction—all contribute to the business fit.

So what is it? While the business fit will be different for every account, each will always have certain elements in common. Broadly speaking, the business fit:

- Identifies the basis for a long-term, strategic relationship
- Is account-specific and strategic
- States the value of the relationship in the customer's terms

> Beyond Selling Value means focusing not on your product and product fit, but on the customer's business and the associated business fit.

Specifically, business fit is how two companies, working together, can help the customer achieve critical objectives, implement important strategies, and address important issues. For this reason, it typically focuses on senior-level management's business priorities.

To salespeople drilled in traditional selling methods, focusing on business fit may seem just short of revolutionary. "What about product?" they ask in disbelief. "When do you talk about features and benefits? What about the low price, only good until the end of the month?"

No, we're not talking about any of those things—not yet, anyway. These are product fit issues. Remember, we're presenting to senior-level decision makers, people who can buy based on value and long-term relationships. So let's draw a distinction between business fit and product fit.

| Product Fit | Business Fit |
| --- | --- |
| Looks for a specific departmental need | Addresses the customer's objectives, strategies, or major issues |
| Focuses on middle-management concerns (User) | Focuses on senior-level management concerns (decision maker) |
| Solves a short-term problem; aims to move product | Aims for a long-term strategic relationship; aims to move the customer's product |
| Dwells on your company's competitors | Focuses on supporting/creating the customer's competitive advantage |
| Measured in own terms (e.g., sales, dollars, volume quota) | Measured in customer's terms (ROE, cost savings) |
| Focuses on price | Focuses on value |

**Product fit examples.** Most salespeople are already well versed in product fit. But just in case, following is a brief list of some common product fit statements that salespeople stuck in the Vendor Trap typically highlight when selling to product evaluators and other gatekeepers. You may even recognize a few from your own selling efforts. Examples include:

- Leverages faster processing.
- Has 10+ years of experience.
- Utilizes smaller packaging.
- Provides quick turnaround.
- Enables increased throughput.
- Allows for a higher number of users.
- Comes in multiple colors.
- Supports enhanced capacity.

- Uses highest quality parts.
- Leverages experienced team of resources.
- Provides for smooth implementation.
- Has locations around the world.
- Focuses on quality and innovation.
- Has grown to be the market share leader.

**Business fit examples.**  But business fit is different, right? Business fit moves beyond the mere product fit to consider more strategic issues. One way to take that step is to look at your product fit and ask, "So what?" How does this product fit impact the customer's business—objectives, issues, strategies, direction, etc.?

So let's say you're selling to a big account, Fuzzy Dice Manufacturers International (FDMI), the company recognized worldwide as the "IBM of rearview mirror accessories." Some business fit statement examples you and your company might stress include:

- Builds on strong existing relationship with FDMI.
- Supports FDMI's corporate philosophy.
- Builds on a set of common values.
- Directly supports key initiatives.
- Enhances attainment of critical business objectives.
- Supports FDMI's position as a leader in rearview mirror accessories.
- Supports FDMI's competitive advantage/strengths.
- Complements FDMI's business direction.
- Leverages resources and skills.
- Complements FDMI's global expansion.
- Helps to address key department issues.
- Develops a win-win partnership.
- Helps accelerate FDMI's attainment of business objectives.
- Provides critical growth tools.
- Provides additional resources in support of FDMI's innovative direction.
- Helps to address critical business issues.

**Flow.**  When you present the business fit to the customer, you will have distilled it down to its essentials, typically in the form of a series of simple, concise, bulleted statements.

The flow begins with a general statement sharing how the relationship between your two companies can help the customer achieve stated business objectives and address key strategic and business issues. One such statement might be: "The relationship supports and enhances your profitability objective."

Here you've concisely communicated that a relationship between your two companies will align with the customer's focus on improving profitability.

Next you might support that general statement with additional bullets that identify specific products or services your company offers. Because you'll be delivering this presentation to a senior-level decision maker, someone who appreciates the value of a long-term business relationship, you'll want to provide just enough background to make your point, then move on. Try not to get bogged down in too much product or technical information.

Depending on your proposed solution, your follow-up bullet points might share how you can assist the customer in developing a competitive advantage. Perhaps your relationship is consistent with their culture and the way they do business. The possibilities are nearly limitless and will vary depending on the customer and the solution. The point is to understand the customer's business objectives and then tie yourself to that vision. Help your customers understand how, by working with you, they can achieve and realize their vision and mission.

> In developing your business fit, look beyond just your products, services, and solutions. Think more broadly. Consider your competencies, skill sets, areas of expertise, and the expertise of other divisions and functions.

**Business fit in the real world.**    To illustrate business fit in an actual customer situation, let's take a look at a powerful business fit uncovered by a client of ours—DuPont—while selling agricultural chemicals to a Canadian grain company using this process.

The grain company was the DuPont sales rep's largest account, but the chemical product he sold was perceived as little more than a commodity by the customer, and competition for the business was severe. Recognizing that changing market conditions in the grain industry would compel the customer to focus on cutting expenses, the rep chose to apply the process to differentiate himself proactively from the competition.

As the highest-priced supplier in the industry, DuPont was also vulnerable to price-based threats from competitors or potential pressure from the customer to offer substantial discounts. And, even though the grain company was the rep's largest account, he still felt he had few coaches within the account and was not dealing with the true decision maker.

He conducted an account planning session to identify gaps in his customer knowledge, and out of that session, three research meetings were scheduled and conducted. As a result of the research meetings, the rep learned a great deal about the grain company's business and developed an appropriate access strategy.

FIGURE 4.5    DuPont Business Fit Page

### The [Grain Company/DuPont] Business Fit

- Capitalizes on current relationship
- Builds on a set of common values
  —Safety
  —Environment
  —People
  —Customers
- Complements [Grain Company's] business direction
  —Improved profitability
  —Improved inventory management
  —Modified distribution network

Three weeks later, the DuPont sales rep had the opportunity to make a business presentation to the grain company president. He made a typical presentation, beginning by sharing some of what he had learned about the customer's business. The president was visibly enthusiastic about DuPont's understanding of his business and expressed surprise at how well DuPont understood his business.

The highlight of the presentation was the business fit, which looked like a typical IMPAX presentation business fit. The presentation page of bulleted business fit points looked like the one in Figure 4.5.

To the uninitiated, the first bullet point—"Capitalizes on current relationship"—may not seem particularly impressive. To the grain company president, however, there was significant impact because, as DuPont recognized, he had recently sponsored a rightsizing project aimed at cutting the company's supplier base by 40 percent. DuPont wanted to make sure he was aware that a relationship between the two companies already existed before he started trimming the fat.

Essentially, with this point DuPont hoped to establish that they were aware of the rightsizing program but felt there were compelling reasons DuPont shouldn't be subject to it. In an effort to show the president how successful the relationship had been, they mentioned the new Web-based distribution system that had just been implemented between the two companies as well as the blue ribbon earned for their cooperative marketing campaign in an industry association contest. DuPont wanted to ensure that the president understood the nature of the current relationship, knowing that, at a management level, he would appreciate the relationship's benefits.

Again, to those unfamiliar with the account the second bullet—"Builds on a set of common values"—might seem like straightforward, boilerplate stuff. Yet, for this opportunity, the bullet powerfully communicated DuPont's message to the president: "These are DuPont's values; they're also your values." In fact, the rep's research indicated that the grain company originally modeled their corporate values in part after DuPont's. The rep definitely wanted the decision maker to understand that important connection.

Regarding the theme of shared values, the DuPont representative talked about the first sub-bullet, saying, "Both of our companies value safety, and we would love to learn more about your Safety First Program." The executive responded strongly, saying, "No problem, but I want to learn more about what you're doing with safety initiatives—you're the best at safety."

Continuing with this theme, the rep reflected on another high-priority value for both companies: becoming stronger environmental stewards. The grain company president took an immediate interest and responded by saying, "You know, I have to give a speech on environmental issues at a major industry association meeting, and I was wondering if someone from DuPont could come out and talk to me about environmental issues facing the industry today." While no one on the company payroll had that exact job description, DuPont could certainly find any number of people to work with this executive for a daily fee for his industry meeting. By this point in the presentation, the president was beginning to look upon DuPont not as just one of many agricultural chemical vendors, but as a business resource to help him as he considered the environmental issues facing his company and his industry.

The next bullet point—"Complements [grain company's] business direction"—emphasized a high impact element of the DuPont business fit. They wanted to communicate that an expanded relationship between the two organizations would complement the grain company's business direction and objectives and help move the company forward in ways that were important to the president. DuPont proposed, for example, to help improve the grain company's profitability. How? Because although DuPont's products were expensive compared to most competitors, they were also highly profitable to the customer. In fact, Dupont chemicals delivered the highest gross margin among products the grain company offered for sale to its customers.

As a result, counter to the appearance of a high dollar cost associated with DuPont products, it was actually highly profitable for the company to offer DuPont chemicals. Farmers were willing to pay more for DuPont solutions. At the executive level, however, the president typically would never have known this. But with this information, he began to look upon DuPont as a profit generator for his company, not as an overpriced vendor.

The other two sub-bullets about "improved inventory management" and "modified distribution network" related to a very important issue on the president's mind. The grain company's customers were clamoring for just-in-time solutions. As things stood, they were forced to stock excess levels of agricultural chemical solutions in their grain elevator locations to satisfy the changing needs of their customer, the farmer. This arrangement was expensive and taxing. It required separate building facilities that had to meet certain regulations. It also required specific training for the elevator managers in chemical handling and special shipping arrangements, and the elevator managers were becoming frustrated. Customers were saying to the grain company, "We want to get to a position where we don't have to store your chemicals. We want them just in time."

Clearly, this major issue was weighing on the president's mind. How could he get agricultural chemicals to the farmers on a just-in-time basis? In his presentation, the DuPont rep explained that DuPont's distribution network experts could help the president design a network that would build efficiencies into the company's distribution. He also shared with the president one strategic attribute of DuPont's chemical solutions—that they came in a granular, not liquid, form, and as such could be shipped via common carrier on any commercial handler on an overnight basis. What this meant was that the grain company could ship its agricultural chemical solutions to its customers from a central location in Winnipeg, delivering the just-in-time solutions the customers wanted so badly.

This point is critical, because it illustrates the essential difference between product fit and business fit. From a product fit standpoint, the rep might have simply said, "We have granular solutions." But that doesn't mean anything to the president. By contrast, the business fit carried much more weight with the president. The granular nature of the product allows him to assist his customers in achieving their desire for just-in-time delivery of his services. He doesn't concern himself with granularity vs. liquid; he only cares about what granularity means—customer satisfaction and customer retention.

What percentage of sales reps would have focused on granularity vs. profitability or customer satisfaction?

In the end, DuPont was able to position not the product fit but the business fit with the grain company president, relating to him on his terms—profitability, client satisfaction, and company values—instead of on a product fit basis of granularity or product performance. He could never have appreciated the product benefits, but he truly valued the prospect of attaining his business objectives.

The outcome of this effort was that the president became much more enthusiastic about his company's relationship with DuPont. He began to look at DuPont not as a product vendor but as a business resource, and he wanted to learn more about DuPont's safety programs and environmental perspectives. Bottom line: the DuPont rep defended his position and expanded his relationship with this important customer.

This example should give you a much firmer understanding of business fit and how business fit differs from product fit. Product fit drives business fit. You typically start with your understanding of the product fit and say, "So what?" How can this product fit and our relationship help this decision maker and the company attain objectives, implement strategies, and/or address issues?

This concept of business fit is a powerful tool for moving beyond traditional value selling. Consider the perspective of Errol Schoenfish, a client of ours with Microsoft Great Plains Business Solutions:

> Business fit really is different. For years, salespeople have been trying to get to senior-level decision makers, but when we got there, we were underwhelming. Business fit has given us a tool to show decision makers how we can help them resolve critical issues and attain objectives. They can now see us as a business resource, not just a product vendor.

We'll provide a more detailed guide for delivering your business fit in Chapter 10 when we talk about putting together and delivering your presentation to the decision maker.

## CONCLUSION

Looking back over the five Research Elements—corporate profile/direction, organizational structure, key players/profiles, departmental profile/direction, and business fit—it may seem awfully time-consuming to gather all that information. In fact, the information can be collected quite quickly. Depending on the opportunity, you may have to make just one or two calls. The important point is not that you spend a lot of time gathering information; it's that you spend the little time you have to gather the right information.

But we also hope that as you read through this chapter, you're already getting excited thinking about potential target companies, imagining the power of walking in to present to a senior-level decision maker with all this information under your belt. Invigorating, isn't it? This enthusiasm will also help you develop an effective coach network, the topic covered in the next chapter.

# CHAPTER FIVE

# The Advice Squad

## HOW TO BUILD AN EFFECTIVE COACH NETWORK

Have you ever experienced the power of having a great coach?

Anyone who's achieved success in sales can probably look back and identify who their coaches were and what role those coaches played. You may not have known you were being coached at the time, but in retrospect a coach's influence is almost always clear. Here's a story that highlights the role of a good coach.

Remember the stormy relationship between New York Yankees owner George Steinbrenner and his manager Billy Martin? Steinbrenner hired Martin five separate times to manage the Yankees—and fired him five times, too. After one such firing, Steinbrenner replaced Martin with Yogi Berra. The story later came out that the newly hired Berra, while rummaging around in his desk, found two envelopes that Martin had left behind. They were labeled *Number 1* and *Number 2*. Both were sealed and addressed "To my successor," and below that was written, "Open only in case of emergency."

Berra started out the season well, but eventually the Yankees hit a slump and lost a few in a row. Steinbrenner lit into Berra, and the manager rushed to his office to open envelope one. Inside was a single sheet of paper. On it was written, "Blame it all on me."

"Terrific," Berra thought, and he did exactly that. The team soon turned things around and got back in the winning column, temporarily soothing Steinbrenner's temper. Four weeks later, however, the Yankees ran into another losing streak. Again Steinbrenner went ballistic. Berra raced back to the office and opened up envelope number two. This time the piece of paper said, "Prepare two envelopes."

Talk about great coaching. It may not have done Yogi any good with the Yankees's boss, but there's no question that developing strong coach relationships is critical to sales success and avoiding the Vendor Trap. A good coach network can be your most important asset as you move forward in the sales process. Your coaches will help you gather the information you need to develop a strategy for success.

As you build your network of coaches, remember that you want to understand the target business from a broad and varied perspective. If you operate in a general business territory with a hundred or more accounts, one coach for an individual account may be terrific. But, if you're operating in more of a strategic account mode, one coach will typically not be sufficient to build that broad perspective. Also, having a great coach is wonderful, but what do you do when that person transfers to the company's Kuala Lumpur office? That's another reason why developing a *coach network,* or a series of coaches, is so important. The larger the account and more significant the opportunity, the more important a coach network becomes.

## WHAT IS A COACH?

In school, identifying our coaches was easy. They were the ones in gym shorts who spent most of the time blowing whistles and yelling about obscure concepts like "playing defense." Sometimes they even had "Coach" emblazoned across their T-shirts.

In the sales sphere, coaches are not as easy to identify. So let's highlight some of the characteristics we look for in a good coach.

First, coaches are typically *knowledgeable.* They can help us learn more about the business and the key players than we already know. Coaches offer an inside perspective that's critical to complete our understanding of the customer's business.

Second, if the coach works for the customer organization—they don't always, but if they do—they should be *credible* and respected within the organization. Without credibility, a coach's value is limited.

Third, coaches are *willing to help;* they'll spend time with you, they'll guide you, and they'll refer you to other coaches.

Fourth, a coach *wants you to win.* This point is important: your coach wants you to win—not your competition, not somebody else, but you. That's why, in a competitive situation, you don't share coaches with a competitor. A contact who may want you to win or may want your competition to win is just that—a contact. Your coach wants you to win.

Fifth, the coach *wins if you win.* This point gets to the heart of what having a good coach means. The coach has to feel a win when you win.

Sixth, in an ideal situation, a coach will be *proactive* on your behalf. These coaches are of hall-of-fame caliber. They're people who will call you out of the blue to fill you in on some new development or to let you know about a competitive threat. When you have a coach who will take the initiative to warn you about what the competition's doing, then you know you've got a great coach.

We like to say that a great coach is someone who's smart enough to answer questions you're not smart enough to ask. The relationship can be like playing chess with a master who's always three or four moves ahead of you. When you find one of these coaches, you know it—and you gladly give them the steering wheel to take you where you want to go.

> A great coach is someone who's smart enough to answer questions you're not smart enough to ask.

How critical is a proactive coach? Consider the case of a new client IMPAX was working with. The first time we met with this client to go over their strategy, they brought to the table 30 accounts they wanted to sell to using the process. But they also mentioned one account they didn't want to use the process with. We were curious, and asked why. It turned out that this was their biggest client, and they had planned a big joint golf outing that was coming up.

Now we believe in golf and in building social relationships with customers. Whether that means you should base your strategy for managing your number one account on golf is another matter. We inquired a little further and found out that of the 25 people from the customer organization they'd invited, 23 were coming. Great, nearly everyone's coming, right? So which two sent their regrets? Naturally, they were the two most senior players—historically the decision makers. But still, 23 out of 25 isn't bad.

The outing came off without a hitch. There were coolers in the back of the golf carts, rest stops along the way, and a break for lunch after the front nine with a beautiful spread laid out. Then they had more good times on the back nine, more coolers, more rest stops, and plenty of cocktails and good-natured ribbing afterwards at the 19th hole. Unquestionably, everyone had a great time.

So what happened three weeks later? You've probably already guessed—the sales organization received a "Dear John" letter. Not even a phone call from their biggest customer, just a letter to say, "We're no longer doing business together." Staring at that letter, they couldn't help but think back to the golf outing and the fact that probably half the people joking around on the links and enjoying the expensive buffet knew what was coming. Yet no one said a thing. No one gave them a head's up. If just one person had taken them aside and said, "Hey, you've got to look out for this," the result might have been different. That's why a proactive coach can be so critical. But hey, at least they got in a good day of golf, right?

## HOW DO COACHES WIN?

A good coach will win when you win. But what does that mean, exactly? In fact, your coach can win in many ways, some of which are obvious, but others are not. Let's take a look at some sample wins for the coach.

> *"Always think in terms of what the other person wants."*
> *—James Van Fleet*

**Personal win.** This win is the least complicated. Some coaches want you to win because they know you, they like you, and they'd like to see you be successful. A personal win is a perfectly valid win.

**Professional win.** One of the most common ways coaches win is by doing their jobs better, achieving their goals, and helping their companies meet objectives. You and your solution may represent a way for a coach to make these things happen.

Personal development is another aspect of the professional win. A coach may want you to win so that she will grow as a professional. Maybe she feels she can gain new experience or strengthen her resumé by working with your product or solution or going through your training.

**Recognition win.** This is an extremely powerful win. Some coaches win simply by receiving recognition from their own organization, and that recognition can take a variety of forms. Maybe they'll be applauded for identifying a need and solving a specific problem. Or perhaps they'll develop a reputation among peers for effectively handling suppliers and vendors. Whatever form it takes, internal recognition offers one of the most attractive and common coach wins to keep an eye out for.

**Negative win.** A coach may want you to win because he really wants someone else to lose. Politics are a reality in nearly any business environment, and we'd be naïve to pretend otherwise. It's a perfectly legitimate win that you can accept and leverage, but it's a bit tenuous. Political breezes change rapidly, and you don't want to get caught in a shifting wind. If possible, follow up by trying to find a more positive win to leverage in the future.

**Interest win.** This is a very basic win. Some coaches will want to see you win simply because you went to the trouble to ask their opinion. Have you ever had someone approach you for help—maybe a recent college graduate asking you to look at a resumé and provide some guidance? Didn't you want to help that person, even if you had no vested interest in whether they landed a job or not? Sometimes people just appreciate being asked, and that feeling becomes a win for them.

> *"We all admire the wisdom of people who come to us for advice."*
> —Jack Herbert

**Information flow win.** As you do more homework, chances are you'll be gaining insights even your coaches may not have. Another win can come from your ability to share what you're hearing with your coach—confidentially, of course.

These are some of the most common wins your coaches may experience, but they're by no means the only ones. Other possible coach wins include:

- Resolution of a business issue
- Control of others
- More leisure time
- More freedom
- Lifestyle change
- Company politics

The point is not to look for any specific win—let's not quibble too much over what our coach gets out of helping us. If a coach wants to help because you're both Civil War buffs, or another likes you because you remind her of a favorite character from the Harry Potter books, terrific. Be glad they get something out of being your coach, and take full advantage of the opportunity.

> Zig Ziglar says, "You can get everything in life you want, if you will just help enough other people get what they want." Find their win, and you help your coaches get what they want.

## WHAT CAN A COACH DO?

Now that we've discussed what you can do for a coach, let's talk about what a coach can do for you. How does a coach help you win?

Of course the most obvious way is that a coach can help *broaden your research* to strengthen your understanding of the target account. Your coaches will frequently have specific areas of expertise where their insights will be particularly valuable.

A coach can also *recommend strategies.* These strategies may focus on different elements of the selling process. For instance, one coach recently emphasized to an IMPAX client that the company's CFO was the likely decision maker. Our client asked, "So how do you recommend we gain access to the CFO?" The coach picked up the phone and said, "When would you like to see him?" That phone call clearly indicated the strength and credibility of this coach. Not only did he know how the rep could reach the CFO, he could also make it happen.

Along the same lines, a coach can help you *identify subtleties* within the account—items like their unique terms, their key issues, and the priority areas of interest for each of the key players. A good coach will help you understand whether to talk to the decision maker about Return on Investment, Return on Equity, or, if appropriate, Return on Working Poultry Assets.

A coach can also help you *build a groundswell of interest.* You want people to be excited about your effort, to the point where they're actually talking about it among themselves. A coach can help generate that excitement.

Another important service a coach can provide is to *refer you to other coaches* who can strengthen and broaden your understanding of the business. As you're conducting your research, you might say to a coach, "You can relate to what we're going through as we try to improve our understanding of your business. Is there anyone in related departments that could help us strengthen our perspective? For instance, whom should we talk to in marketing or in engineering?"

A coach can also help you by *reviewing your presentation.* As you produce the business presentation you plan to deliver to the decision maker, you want to make sure you're using the right terms, picking up the subtleties, and prioritizing the right areas. Having a strong, capable coach to walk you through and review the presentation is invaluable.

Finally, working with a coach to *gain access to the decision maker* can make for a very efficient and powerful strategy. A credible, well-positioned coach who can assist you in gaining access is a very valuable asset indeed. If not, you may want to write an Access Letter. A good coach will review that letter for content and make sure your request is on target. (We'll talk more about writing the Access Letter in Chapter 8.)

Gaining access to senior-level decision makers may not be a problem you face. If you have name recognition and a good reputation, then you may be able to get to the people you want to see. For many sales professionals, however, that is not the case, and the biggest benefit a coach can offer is that precious access to the decision maker.

### Easel Does It

Sometimes a great coach will step up and help in ways you could never predict. One sales rep using the process arrived at the customer's office ready to present to a senior-level decision maker, only to realize that he didn't have an easel for his flip chart, nor did the company. Thankfully, the rep had a terrific coach who offered to stand in as the easel. The coach got up and held the flip chart while the rep went through his presentation, flipping each successive page over the coach's head. Now that was one supportive coach, both literally and figuratively.

## WHERE COACHES RESIDE

Your coaches are out there waiting to help you close great, profitable, long-term sales, but they're not going to waltz in your office door. You've got to go out and find them. In fact, sometimes in the process, you can get pretty creative in locating and developing coaches. So where should you begin your search? Here are a few ideas.

**User department.** Whether it's engineering, information systems, manufacturing, or some other division, the user department is a fairly typical place to seek out coaches. Whether the target account is a prospect or an existing customer, with your credibility and expertise in the field, the user department can prove to be a fertile breeding ground for coaches. Contacts from the user department whom you develop into coaches will frequently become strong advocates to help you win. They understand your solution, and the win is typically very clear to them.

> Be careful—gatekeepers also tend to congregate at the user level. Bear in mind also that, while people in the user department are often good at helping you understand their needs and applications, they may not be able to help you understand the big-picture issues facing the company. If you conduct research exclusively at the user level, you might not get the broad business research you're looking for.

**Related departments.** A number of IMPAX clients have found that departments just one step up or back in the value chain, or perhaps a step to the side, can contribute excellent coaches as well.

**Ex-employees.** Ex-employees can provide an interesting perspective that may not be available from current employees. Of course, you should take into consideration the circumstances that led to the person's departure, as those circumstances may affect their value as a coach. But as a rule, ex-employees tend to be very open to talking about their old employer and industry. One potentially fertile ground to check for ex-employee coaches is among recent retirees.

**Your company.** Depending of course on the type of company you work for and your industry, you may have potential coaches under your own roof. In fact, many sales organizations have multiple people who have interfaced with an individual customer. They include people who have previously sold to or managed the account, technical personnel, or others who have performed work at the customer's site. So next time you run into a coworker in the office kitchenette, instead of making the usual comment about the lackluster quality of company coffee, try, "Hey, let me ask you something. Have you ever worked with International Ball Bearings?" You may well discover someone who can help build your knowledge about the customer.

**Other companies.** Companies up and down the value chain from your target customer may contain coaches as well. Your target company's suppliers and customers can provide terrific insights, and you may well have contacts or know others in these organizations who can provide unique perspectives. Also, think about approaching your existing customers in other companies. If they compete with the target company, they may have yet another unique perspective you'll want to explore.

> Within the companies you search for coaches, a good level to begin your search is in entry-level management. These folks make ideal coaches, because they're typically in tune with the front-line issues that their companies face, but they also understand these concerns from a broader corporate perspective.

Finding coaches provides you with the opportunity to get creative and think outside the box. Don't restrict yourself just to speaking with people in the decision making process. That's a recipe for gaining only a limited perspective on the account. Instead, cast a wide net for someone who can help you understand this account. When you attend sales association or industry meetings, ask the people you meet if they know anyone who can help you. You might also consider talking to the target company's salespeople and sales managers. After all, sales professionals love to talk about their companies and what they do—why not take advantage?

Also, if you're desperate enough, you may want to put together an e-mail list of contacts—friends, relatives, neighbors, former coworkers, fellow college alumni, people you know from church or civic groups, other youth soccer parents, old army buddies, former cellmates—anyone who might know something about the account or put you in contact with someone else who can coach you. In your message, ask, "Who knows someone who knows someone at Amalgamated Urinal Mints?" Then follow up with any positive responses you get.

Chasing down coaches gives you the chance to exercise all that networking brainpower you never even knew you had.

## Going Farther Afield for Coaches

As you think about your target accounts, you may have already identified enough existing coaches to field a full volleyball team—with a couple of substitutions no less. That's great. But then again, you may not have any likely candidates on the radar screen.

If you're faced with the unfortunate situation of no coaching prospects and no contacts who might be developed into coaches, then you will probably have to ratchet up the creativity another notch. Your task is to dig up names of people you can call and ask to meet with. Perhaps you can get a customer's annual report or newsletter and find some possibilities there. Another option is to search through the customer's Web page. Go ahead and call anyone you think might make good coach candidates and work to schedule brief research meetings. Yes, you have to be aggressive, but this strategy can absolutely be effective as well.

# DEVELOPING YOUR COACHES

Coaches are like muscles—they perform best when fully developed. In the last chapter, we defined what a contact is—someone who will meet with you and become a research source. Now let's share some thoughts about turning a contact into a coach, a person who wants you to win and wins if you win.

As we mentioned, if you're starting out of the gates with strong coaches, that's great. But you can probably never have enough coaches, so developing new ones is always beneficial.

Naturally, every situation is unique, so there is no single formula for developing a coach relationship. That said, a number of common elements contribute to the process. Let's take a look at some of these elements.

FIGURE 5.1    Coach Development

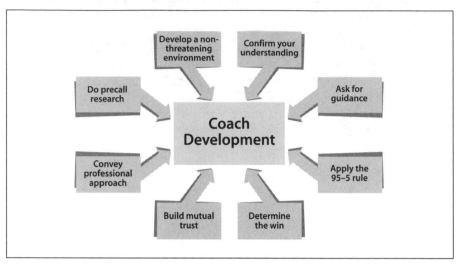

## Do Your Homework

When you first meet someone face-to-face, you want to establish your credibility and show that you've invested some effort ahead of time. As we've mentioned before, you don't want to walk into a contact's office in an unfamiliar city, start picking up knickknacks off the desk, and open with, "So, how's the economy around here?" Instead, you should do your precall research to develop a baseline knowledge of the company. This way, you can open with a much more detailed, powerful question.

Typically, you'll want that question to have a positive spin, but it doesn't have to. You might say, "I understand that the regional economy has been suffering through a recession for quite some time, yet throughout this period you've sustained an impressive growth pattern. How have you managed to accomplish so much while your competitors have struggled?" It may seem paradoxical, but by asking an informed question, you actually answer a number of potential questions the contact may have about you. You're no longer a completely unknown commodity. Right away, you show that you've done your homework and you're not going to waste his or her time. This instant credibility really helps get contacts to open up.

## Be Nonthreatening

Contacts who don't know you or only know you a little won't know what to expect. But they're probably used to being sold to. That's why we recommend proactively stating to the person at the very outset that you're not there to sell. You can also add that, while you think that a good fit may exist between your two companies, you're not prepared to sell their organization anything—yet. Say that to be effective in the selling process and make the best use of everyone's time—including theirs—you have to do your homework, and talking to them is one way to do it. Persuaded that you're not going to try to sell them anything, they'll relax, which should make it easier for you to gain momentum in the research process.

> *"A promise must never be broken."—Alexander Hamilton*

By the way, when you promise you're not going to sell during a research call, making good on your promise is critical. It doesn't matter if the call is going like gangbusters and you're building so much rapport that you think you may have a new best friend on your hands—don't try to sell. That's the vendor side of you trying to escape. Suppress it. Stick to your plan, and use that positive energy to build groundswell and move the process forward.

> Beyond Selling Value means sticking to your promise to focus on the customer and not slam product.

## Be Subtle

There's one subtlety we stress about developing coaches. Remember to emphasize that you are there to confirm what you've already learned about the organization and to expand that understanding. Don't say that you want to come in and learn their business. It just sounds too imposing. Imagine if someone said to you, "I'd like to come in and talk to you so that I can learn your business." Better clear your calendar, right? You'd probably want to respond by saying, "Why don't you go to the library?"

Because you don't want to frighten off a good potential coach, instead say you want to confirm your understanding of their business. This approach implies that you already have some background. It also sounds more manageable and puts less of a burden on the other person. The distinction is subtle but can make a big difference in helping to convert a contact into a coach.

> "I'd like to confirm my understanding," is preferable to, "Teach me about your company."

## Ask and Ye Shall Receive

Typically, when we're learning something new—whether how to play golf, build a Web page, drive a stick shift, or almost anything—we get coaching. There's no reason why that shouldn't apply when you're earning your livelihood too.

Thankfully, asking for guidance—and specifically for coaching—is generally well received. But coaches won't just come to you. You have to ask for the coaching and the guidance. Typically, the people you ask will be more than willing to help. In fact, they'll probably wind up giving you more than you ask for. So don't hesitate to ask for the help.

## The Score Is 95-5

Remember when we said to emphasize to the potential coach that you're not there to sell anything? There's no better way to prove it than by following the 95-5 rule. When you meet with a contact to confirm your understanding of the business, you should talk 5 percent of the time and let the customer do the other 95 percent of the talking. During that 95 percent that the customer is talking, you should be listening. By spending the vast majority of the meeting just listening, you build momentum and establish that you are primarily interested in the insights the customer has to share. Typically, you will note that the customer becomes personally involved in the meeting and begins to take ownership of helping you accomplish your objectives.

> *"You can make more friends in two months by becoming interested in other people than you can in two years by trying to get people interested in you."—Dale Carnegie*

## Find the Win

The next element of this formula is to determine the contact's win. To turn a contact into a coach, you have to figure out the contact's WIFM (What's in It For Me?). It doesn't matter whether the win is personal, professional, or political, as long as it's there, but you've got to find out what it is.

This is not always easy. Sometimes getting to the heart of a coach's win takes months. But you have to keep at it, to find the win and leverage it. Coaches need to understand that you can help them attain their business objectives and that by helping you, they're also helping themselves.

You already take great pains to listen carefully to find your coaches' wins, right? Of course you do. But many salespeople—other than you, that is—have been taught to talk, not to listen. Yes, it's true! So for them, we want to make this point clear: listen to your coaches, and they will reveal what they hope to achieve by helping you win.

## Trust a Must

It should already be apparent from the nature of the relationship you're trying to establish that you develop coaches on a basis of mutual trust. For a coach relationship to work, it must operate on mutual trust. Why? Because so much is at stake. You're moving forward with your selling process, trusting that the insights coaches share with you are accurate, and they're trusting you as well—trusting that the thoughts they share will be used in a professional manner and that you will maintain an appropriate level of confidentiality. Building mutual trust is never easy, but it is critical.

How do you build trust? One great way is to be a good listener. In fact, effective listening is a critical element in nearly everything you'll do to build relationships. Your contacts need to understand that you're actively listening to the insights and subtleties (even the ones that aren't so subtle) they share and that you'll be professional enough to use them properly.

The French playwright Jean Giraudoux once said, "The secret of success is sincerity. Once you can fake that, you've got it made." But when you're dealing with coaches, asking them to open up and share personal assessments and inside information, faking sincerity won't cut it. To build that necessary trust, you've got to show coaches that you're sincere and will not betray the trust they place in you.

## ONWARD AND UPWARD

Ideally, with these elements to guide you, you'll take your list of contacts and turn it into a list of strong, powerful coaches. You'll have created relationships based on mutual trust and professionalism that help you learn enough about the target account to move forward, while delivering valid wins for the coaches who've helped you along the way.

Let's make one last point about coach relationships. Have you ever been in a situation where your coach in one instance was not your coach later on? If so, you know how frustrating this can be. Sometimes you can look back on a situation and, with the benefit of hindsight, come to realize why a coach wasn't a coach after all. Often, that coach's win disappeared, faded, or changed over time. The point is, don't take a coach's win for granted. You have to work to make sure the win is strong, clear, and current, even as circumstances change.

## EXTRAORDINARY COACHING

As we close our thoughts on coaches, we'd like to share a phenomenal coach story from a client of ours, Gary Jarosz, a former IBM sales manager. Calling on a company where IBM had some business but wanted to expand the relationship, Gary and a colleague conducted a research meeting with the CFO. Here's how Gary describes that meeting:

With this opportunity, we really wanted to get to the president and CEO, but we didn't have an avenue, so we needed to do some research to find out what their hooks were. We got together to meet with the CFO.

About 15 minutes into what was, until then, a relatively straightforward research meeting, the CFO mentioned that he'd been with the company for 40-some years. We stopped for a moment and said, "Wow, what's so great about any company—and this one in particular—that you'd stay for that long?"

With that prompt, he began to open up. He launched into a story about how as a teenager, he had suffered from a debilitating disease and doctors didn't think he would live very long. He even heard the doctor tell his parents just to try to make him comfortable, because he didn't have much longer.

But he had set a goal for himself, he told us, which was to get a job. Despite the illness, he was determined to earn a check before he died.

An agency helped him land an interview, and during the interview he was hired on the spot. He really appreciated the opportunity, because he considered himself grotesque to look at. The disease had given him a sickly appearance, so he was surprised the company would hire him. Yet through the sickness the company stood by him. In fact, during his first week, people stopped by hourly to introduce themselves and offer help. They really made a point to make him feel welcome. And of course, contrary to the doctors' predictions, he did recover and survive.

At the end of the story he said, with tears rolling down his cheeks, "How could I ever leave?" He wasn't the only one with tears in his eyes. His was a very moving story. He added, "By the way, people around here don't really know this about me. I'd prefer if we could keep this just between us." We'd known him for 30 minutes, and he'd already shared this very personal story that only a select few of his coworkers knew.

From this point forward, we had little trouble scheduling a meeting with the president. The CFO had trusted us enough to share this story—it was no surprise that he supported the rest of our effort. We got to present to the president and achieved our goal to expand the relationship.

This is an extraordinary story. Most of your research meetings will not be so emotionally charged. But your coaches do need to trust you before they will open up. What made that happen for Gary and IBM was five things:

1. They asked good questions.
2. They actively listened.
3. They were sincere.
4. They made the coach feel comfortable to the point where he'd open up and share.
5. The coach trusted the sales reps.

When these things come together for you with good coaches, the obstacles begin to fall pretty quickly, and you really jump-start the sales process.

## CONCLUSION

Building a coach network is a bit like cultivating a garden. No, coaches are not going to pop up overnight, in full bloom and ready to walk you into the decision maker's office. Instead, you have to plant the seeds by doing your homework and then nurture the relationship by demonstrating your professionalism, building trust, and showing potential coaches that by helping you, they'll also be helping themselves. The larger and more lucrative the opportunity, the more cultivation and nurturing you have to do to grow that coach network. But you'll soon realize that the effort was worth it, when the competition starts being weeded out entirely. So grab your watering can and go get yourself some coaches.

# CHAPTER SIX

# The Inside Stuff

## FUNDAMENTALS OF THE
## RESEARCH MEETING

At this point we've talked about the benefits of building a coach network, and by now you should have a pretty good idea how and where to locate the best coaching candidates. Of course, it's one thing to get a hold of potential coaches, but it's another entirely knowing what to do with them when you've got them. In this chapter, we're going to talk about the research meeting and how to meet with your contacts and coaches to gain critical insights about your target accounts.

But first, we'd like to share a story about a friend of ours traveling on business in London, England.

Not very familiar with the city and finding he had a free evening, he stopped in at a club where he had a guest membership. Hoping to strike up a conversation with a distinguished looking Englishman sitting nearby, he said, "May I buy you a drink?" "No," said the Britisher coolly. "Don't drink. Tried it once and didn't like it." So our friend ordered a drink for himself, then tried another tack with the gentleman. "Can I interest you in a cigar?" "No. Don't smoke. Tried tobacco once and didn't like it." Our friend thought for a minute and then, noticing a deck of cards on a nearby table, said, "Maybe you would like to join me in a game of gin rummy?" "No," replied the Brit. "Don't like playing card games. Tried it once and didn't like it. However, my son will be dropping in after a bit. Perhaps he will join you." Our friend settled back in his chair and said, "Your only child, I presume?"

Okay, maybe this scenario doesn't qualify as a true research meeting, but as our friend discovered, you can gain a great deal of insight just by asking a few pointed questions. And that *is* the goal of the research meeting—to elicit insights from your contacts and coaches, the kind of information that's only accessible by talking to people who know the inside scoop on the account.

*"Wisdom is the reward you get for a lifetime of listening when you'd have preferred to talk."—Doug Larson*

## WHAT IS A RESEARCH MEETING?

The research meeting is a distinct type of meeting where the focus is on improving your understanding of the target customer's or prospect's business. It is not a product-focused sales call. This is where you put the 95-5 rule to work as you move beyond data to gain the real insider's perspective. As Cathy Barthel, a regional sales executive for National Car Rental Systems, says, "Some people might think this isn't a sales call. It's a sales call all right—a great one. The question is: 'What are you selling—a product or yourself?'"

> Beyond Selling Value means conducting more customer research meetings and fewer product-focused sales calls.

Research meetings can be done in person or over the phone, and how long they last is up to you and your contact. How many research meetings you'll make on a specific account will also depend on the nature of the opportunity. In an account with a great deal of potential, you may conduct many research meetings. At other times, two or three meetings may be sufficient, or maybe even just one. Then again, if you're pressed for time and have to move quickly, you may make fewer than you'd like just to take advantage of the chance to present to an important decision maker. How many research meetings you'll conduct for a specific opportunity will depend on how many you believe will adequately prepare you for presenting to the decision maker.

Each research meeting should help you move forward in the cycle. If, after two or three meetings, you still don't understand who the decision maker is, how you can gain access to this person, and some of his or her primary concerns, then you need to reexamine how you're conducting research meetings. Your focus should remain on the five research elements we talked about in Chapter 4:

1. Corporate profile/direction
2. Organization structure
3. Key players/profiles
4. Departmental profile/direction
5. Business fit

Research meetings also help you create a groundswell of interest. In fact, for many sales reps, that's half the battle. As you conduct meetings, schedule that presentation to the decision maker and do a little additional research before delivering the presentation—the momentum should be building the entire time.

There's another important point to be made here about the research meeting stage. Unlike traditional vendor-based sales methods that allow product evaluators and gatekeepers to control your destiny, research meetings help you maintain control to avoid gatekeepers and the Vendor Trap as you progress through the selling cycle.

## RESEARCH MEETING OBJECTIVES

We list four primary objectives for the research meeting:

1. *Insider perspective.* As we explored in Chapter 3, we can get plenty of information on companies through publicly available data sources. The purpose of the research meeting is to move beyond this level to gain an insider's perspective and broaden our understanding of what really goes on within the account.
2. *Business fit.* During your research meetings, you'll learn a great deal about a range of issues at the target account. Of course, you won't be able to address all the challenges facing the company, but some you will. That's where you can make an impact and where you hone the business fit between your two companies.
3. *Coach development.* Besides learning more about the target account, during research meetings you'll also learn more about your contacts and coaches. You can take this opportunity to turn contacts into coaches and strengthen your existing coach relationships.
4. *Groundswell.* As we mentioned before, more than simply an opportunity to exchange information, the research meeting helps you build a groundswell or an aura of excitement and momentum about your selling cycle and the process. Contacts who walk out of a research meeting with you should feel good about the process and curious about where you'll go next. They're not used to being asked these questions. Frequently, they'll talk to colleagues and say, "Hey, did you talk to these folks? What was your meeting like? I wonder how they're going to present their findings." That's what building groundswell is all about, and it can be very rewarding.

The research meeting process generally consists of five distinct steps, as presented in Figure 6.1.

FIGURE 6.1   Process Chart

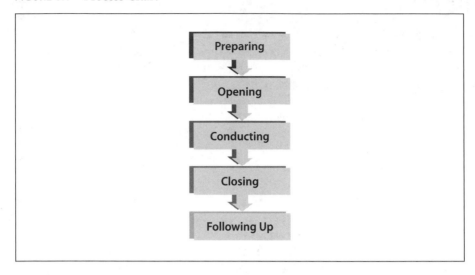

## PREPARING FOR THE RESEARCH MEETING

### Making Your Selection

In selecting the initial research contact, a coach or strong contact is a good place to start. It's easier to build momentum with these people. But if you don't have a coach or a strong contact, then start wherever you can.

### Scheduling

Bear in mind, however, that the research meeting is different from a traditional, product-oriented sales call. That becomes apparent as soon as you pick up the phone to schedule the meeting. What you say during that scheduling phone call will probably depend on the existing relationship between you and the person on the other end of the line.

With your existing coaches, the call is straightforward. If, on the other hand, the person will be receiving this call out of the blue, the request should be a little more formal. The way you phrase your request will largely determine whether you get the meeting at all. For that reason, we generally recommend you highlight these key points while making the request:

- *Vary your positioning* of the request according to your relationship with the contact/coach.
- Let the person know that you sense there is a *strong fit* between your two companies.

- Make a *specific request* for a meeting to better understand their business. State that your goal is "to confirm my understanding" vs. "to learn about your business."
- Recognize the *contact's role.*
- Request a *one-on-one* meeting.

In asking for the research meeting, you only need to be as aggressive in hitting all these points as the relationship warrants. New contacts may require that you mention each of these key points and then close on getting that meeting. But with existing coaches, you shouldn't have to do as much of a selling job.

## Scheduling Scripts

Let's say, for example, that you don't know anyone at the target account. However, you've gotten hold of an annual report and a newsletter, and from those sources you identified a middle manager whose position and power are unclear to you. This person could be a potential gatekeeper, a potential coach, or someone of no use to you at all. At this point you don't know. Your script for the call might go like this:

Hi, Tom. This is Ann Reed with Refrigerator Magnets International. I sense a strong fit between our companies, and so for the past few weeks I've been doing some homework on your organization. I recognize the role you play in the novelties department, and your insights would be very valuable to me. I wonder if you could spend 20 to 30 minutes to meet with me one-on-one so that I can confirm and expand my understanding of your business. What time next week would be convenient?

Note that the tone of the request is nonthreatening. You're not asking this complete stranger to explain the company's entire 120-year history and then go over a detailed floor plan of the headquarters building. All you're asking for is to confirm your understanding of the business, which sounds pretty innocuous.

Let's take another case where you have a contact you've been calling on for a while but the conversations have been primarily product-focused, not aimed at any broad, strategic business issues. During your scheduling call, you might say:

You know, we've been meeting for the past several months, and we've talked about a number of issues. It occurred to me after our last meeting that I've neglected to step back from these product discussions and spend a little time trying to understand the bigger picture. How would it be if we met briefly next week, one-on-one, so that I could confirm some of the things I've learned and gain some of your insights into broader business issues and the roles of some of the other key players?

Again, when you make this request, be sure to hit the key points—that you think there's a fit, you want to confirm what you've learned, you recognize the role they play, you want the meeting to be just the two of you, and then you close. You want to get that meeting.

> Be careful not to become an example of the best intentions gone awry. Consider the case of the sales rep who did everything right, until he called the customer to ask for the meeting and said, "Can I come in and learn about your company?" only to have the contact respond, "Hell no, that's too much work," and hang up the phone.

## Logistics

Proper logistics play an important role in making sure your research meeting goes smoothly and effectively. As we mentioned, good research meetings can be done face-to-face or over the phone. Here we're going to focus on the logistics of research meetings you conduct in person.

**Your place or mine?**  First, if at all possible, the research meeting should be held at the customer's location. Why? There are a few reasons. One, at their own home base, customers have ready access to helpful data sources like newsletters, annual reports, or organizational charts. Also, being in a place where your contact can introduce you to others who may be helpful is convenient. Finally, by going to the customer's location, you communicate that you appreciate that this person is spending time to meet you and that you want to make it as easy as possible on them.

We've noticed that some people struggle with the idea of going to the customer location to conduct the research meeting. They typically say they'd prefer to meet over a meal at a restaurant. The meal meeting poses a number of problems. First, you're likely to be plagued by frequent interruptions, which will hamper your efforts to build momentum through the call. Second, taking notes while you're eating can be difficult, and you'll often wind up with as much tomato sauce as ink on your notepad. Unless you've got a photographic memory, a research meeting is only as good as the notes that come out of it, so if possible, avoid the meal meeting.

A research meeting is only as good as the notes you take.

Even within the customer's location, some places are better than others to conduct your research meeting. Open areas, like the cafeteria or a bank of cubicles, pose concerns about privacy and interruptions. Even meeting in the person's office, where interruptions are still likely to take place, can be challenging.

We believe the best place to meet is in a conference room, where interruptions are much less likely to occur and privacy is enhanced.

Keep in mind that privacy is critical to the research meeting; not so much because you're going to be gathering confidential information, but because you're trying to build momentum. You want that person to feel free to answer your questions without any concerns about others overhearing.

But you don't always get what you want. Sometimes contacts or coaches insist that they can only meet you over a meal. This circumstance isn't optimal, but it's better than nothing, so you'll want to take advantage of the opportunity and just make the best of it. In these cases, try to leverage the opportunity into a follow-up research meeting in the person's office. When you finish the meal, recap some of the highlights of the issues you talked about, then ask if you can continue the meeting for just a few minutes in his or her office to make sure you're getting the most out of this important conversation.

If you plan to conduct a research meeting over the phone, don't take it for granted that when you call, the contact will be in and ready to spend a half hour with you. Work with the contact or an administrator to get on the person's calendar.

**Who's on the guest list?** Who should attend a research meeting? One important element is that you only want to call on one person at a time. Why just one person? First of all, you're looking for true insights from an individual perspective. By calling on only one person, you enhance your ability to do that. When you call into a situation with both a manager and a subordinate present, you'll find you're much more likely to get the manager's perspective, even when the subordinate is talking. Also, if two people are peers, they may look back and forth at one another, each waiting for the other to take the lead, and that's no way to get candid insights or to build momentum.

**Meeting duration.** Another question is how long the meeting should last. As with many other aspects of the process, each situation is different. Typically, if you're calling on someone you've never met before, just ask for a brief meeting—20 to 30 minutes is a good length. On the other hand, if you're calling on a coach with whom you've worked before, go ahead and ask for an hour. It all depends on your relationship with the other person.

**Plan of attack.** Okay, you've called and scheduled the research meeting, and you're eager for the opportunity to hear the interesting insights your contact has to share. Terrific! Now, let's take care of the last few details you'll want to address before your meeting. To ensure a successful research meeting, follow these guidelines in your planning:

- Gather and analyze your data in advance.
- Develop the opening for the research meeting.
- Define a questioning strategy based on what you already know versus what you need to know and whom you're calling.
- Develop a flow of the meeting based on the research elements.
- Determine your desired action.
- Bring an account folder with the customer's name written on it to reinforce the impression that you have been collecting data and information on the account.

By compiling your data and going over your materials beforehand, you'll seem more credible during the research meeting. Also, this will help you develop an opening to the research meeting that demonstrates insight. Your questioning strategy should include questions that force the other person to sit back and think about the answers. To formulate your list of questions, consider your primary objectives for the meeting. Translate these objectives into five to ten questions that, when answered, will dramatically improve your understanding of the account.

Finally, in the folder you bring along with the account's name prominently displayed, include the annual report, your additional notes, and any of the newsletters, brochures, magazine articles, or other data sources you've acquired. Your contact or coach can't help but notice that you're really doing your homework.

## OPENING THE RESEARCH MEETING

For a typical research meeting, you will want to use the five research elements to guide you through the call. But first you need to open the conversation in a way that sets the tone for the entire meeting.

> In a research meeting, what you say in the first 60 seconds can determine what will happen during the next 60 minutes.

A quotation we like to cite that describes the opening of a research meeting is, "Expectations minus reality equals stress." So, when you open the meeting, restate the reason you're there. Whatever you said to get the meeting in the first place, say it again as your opening.

With this in mind, here is how Ann Reed from Refrigerator Magnets International might open her research meeting:

Tom, thanks for your time today. I really appreciate it. As I mentioned on the phone, I believe there might be a good fit between our companies, and with that in mind I've been doing some homework. As I came to understand the role you play in the organization, I thought that I could really learn a lot from this conversation with you. You were kind enough to give me 30 minutes on your calendar. Do you still have until 9:30 today? Great.

But again, depending on how you positioned yourself to gain the meeting, adjust your opening script to restate that point.

In some situations, depending on whom you're calling on and your relationship with them, you may want to mention that anything said during the meeting will remain confidential and that any notes you take will be exclusively for your own use.

## CONDUCTING THE RESEARCH MEETING

The research meeting typically represents the first time during the process when you will be face-to-face with a coach or contact. As they say in action movies, this time it's personal. It's also your first opportunity to use the 95-5 rule and show the customer (if your contact is part of the customer's organization) that you sell differently than the vendors you're competing with. As Tom Mezera, Senior Vice President of Sales & Marketing Operations for Metavante (a subsidiary of Marshall & Ilsley), says, "We want our sales process to be part of our competitive advantage. It's hard to do that if the questions we're asking are focused only on where our solution fits. We needed to take an approach to questioning that took us to the next level—one that truly demonstrated our interest in our customer's business."

You'll need two critical skills to conduct an effective research meeting. They are *questioning* and *listening.* Let's take an in-depth look at each of these two elements.

## Question Everything

> *"Quality questions create a quality life. Successful people ask better questions and, as a result, they get better answers."* —Anthony Robbins

As we've mentioned, effective questioning is critical for the research meeting to serve its purpose. Issues to think about include the types of questions, characteristics of good questions, and questioning techniques.

**Types.**   You can ask several types of questions during the research meeting.

First are *open-ended questions.* An open-ended question requires a detailed answer from the other person and usually begins with words like *What, When, How,* and *Why.* "What are the top three priorities for your department this year?" is a typical open-ended question.

Second are *closed-ended questions.* A closed-ended question requires only a one-word answer, typically either yes or no. These questions can be harmful, but they can also be helpful. They can be harmful in that they can limit interaction and the contact's involvement. But they can be helpful in redirecting a line of questioning or transitioning to another topic. "Is quality a priority for your organization?", "Who is responsible for that initiative?", "What year did you join the company?", and "Is there anything else I need to know about this initiative?" are examples of closed-ended questions.

Next are *assumptive questions,* which presuppose an answer. A typical assumptive question might be, "The economy is tough but your company always succeeds, doesn't it?" An assumptive question can do a couple of things for you. First, it provides a smooth launch into a new topic. This example might be effective for transitioning into talking about the company's strategy for success. Typically, people respond well to assumptive questions.

You can also use assumptive questions to size up the person you're talking to. If the contact jumps on an assumptive question and answers with enthusiasm, that person may be a strong coach candidate. But if you ask an assumptive question early in the call and receive little more than a shrug of the shoulders in response, you know you're going to have to work hard on this person to get any substantive answers.

Then there are the truly *high-impact questions*. These questions get the other person to sit back and reflect for a moment before answering. Examples of high-impact questions include:

- How do you feel about the trend toward developing more corporate partnerships?
- If budget weren't an issue, how would you resolve this situation?
- What two or three initiatives will make the most impact on the growth of this company in the next year?
- How do you think market consolidation in the industry will affect your department?

> Beyond Selling Value means asking questions that cause your contact to sit back and say, "Let me think about that. No one's ever asked me that before."

Questions that begin "How do you think . . ." and "How do you feel about . . ." generally invite involvement and elicit thoughtful responses. Another terrific high-impact question is, "When your boss is lying awake at night because something about the business is bothering him, what's on his mind?" You'll know you've asked a powerful question when the customer responds, "Hmm, nobody's ever asked me that before."

> *"Good questions outrank easy answers."* —*Paul A. Samuelson*

**Characteristics.**  Effective questions have some primary characteristics:

- They're brief, clear, and relevant.
- They provide a logical flow to the meeting so that you aren't just skipping around randomly.
- They require thought before a response.
- They get the contact involved through sharing feelings, thinking, or speculating.

**Techniques.**  One of the best questioning techniques, of course, is to follow the 95-5 rule. Bear in mind that you need to keep your questions succinct and listen attentively to the answer. Another great questioning technique is to make sure you're asking thought-provoking questions. The more creative the question, the more thought provoking it is. Here are some of the most effective techniques for getting thoughtful answers out of your contacts during the research meeting:

- *The Domino Effect.* Ask add-on questions in a progressive manner, getting deeper into the topic and avoiding hopping around from topic to topic.
- *Close But No Cigar.* Use closed-ended questions judiciously. Closed-ended questions can help direct the research meeting, but an effective interviewer uses them sparingly.
- *The Turnaround.* Don't say it—turn it into a question. As tempting as making a statement may be, instead find a way to ask a question. For example, rather than saying, "That's why you moved to the Malcolm Baldrige criteria," ask, "Is that what led you to the Malcolm Baldrige criteria?" Now, whether the answer is yes or no, you have another series of questions to ask.
- *The Straw Man.* Using a so-called straw man, imply the presence of another person and invite interviewees to put themselves in that person's shoes. An example might be, "If a new president were to take over this organization tomorrow, what's the first thing he or she would change?"
- *Follow the Leader.* Provide a lead example. If you sense that your interviewee is stumped, an effective technique is to throw out a line and provide an example of what you mean. For instance, if you ask, "What are the two or three biggest market issues you're facing today?" and all you receive is a blank stare, you might say, "Is the proliferation of competition on your mind? Or is one of your issues market consolidation?"

> *"No man really becomes a fool, until he stops asking questions."*
> —*Charles Steinmetz*

**Say What?**  Of course the most important questioning technique is to listen effectively. As we mentioned before, during the meeting you should be following the 95-5 rule, getting the other person to talk 95 percent of the time while you talk only 5 percent.

So what should you be doing during the 95 percent of the meeting when you're not talking? Fiddling with your watch? Thinking about whether to order chili fries for lunch? Building a ship in a bottle? No, of course you should be actively listening to what your contact is saying.

When business guru Mark McCormack was preparing to write the best-selling *What They Don't Teach You at Harvard Business School*, he asked a number of successful friends, several of them corporate chairmen, what business

> *"When people talk, listen completely. Most people never listen."*
> —*Ernest Hemingway*

advice they would give if they were writing the book. Almost without exception and often at the top of their list, they told him, "Learn to be a good listener."

While the average person can speak at about 175 words per minute, the average listener can hear and register about 400 words per minute or more. This substantial difference poses a significant challenge for business professionals, particularly salespeople, who typically are inclined more towards talking than listening. But attentive, effective listening is critical to making the research meeting productive. Here are a few techniques to help you listen effectively:

- Pause before you ask your next question.
- Listen to the person's answer, then make sure you understand what he or she is saying by asking a clarifying question.
- Don't interrupt, except to get clarification of a point.
- Feed enough information back so that the contact knows you're paying attention.
- Take notes. Taking notes is precisely the type of activity that separates professional salespeople from the pack. It also demonstrates an interest and commitment to the contact or coach and shows that you value their insights.
- Listen actively by leveraging body language—use strong eye contact, face the person directly, and assume an attentive posture.

When contacts meet with you for the first time, they aren't sure what to expect. When you ask good questions, listen effectively, and take notes, you send a powerful message that you value them and their time. That, in turn, helps you gain their trust. In fact, one of the interesting outcomes of effective questions is that the customer truly views the meeting as a terrific sales call. They genuinely appreciate the opportunity to share their insights and feelings. Contacts will often say after a research meeting, "That was the best sales call I've ever been a part of." And why not? They just talked about nothing but themselves for an hour. You'll even find that people begin to look forward to meeting with you, just to find out what additional insights you're gathering from other research meetings.

One of the side benefits to conducting great research meetings is that you begin to generate a buzz and groundswell around what you're doing. When one rep was using the process to sell business solutions to a nationwide food

Bob was beginning to sense some negative body language from his interviewer.

Remember, the contact needs to see—and hear—you listening.

distributor, he conducted four interviews in one afternoon. By the time he was leaving, a number of other people from the target company approached him to ask, "When are you going to interview me?" The first interviews had been so powerful and effective that word had raced around the building, to the point where only a few hours later, potential contacts and coaches were signing up to participate.

One Tonight Show guest Jay Leno looked forward to interviewing was 60 Minutes correspondent Mike Wallace. When asked why, Leno said, "I find that people who listen for a living always have something interesting to say."

The point is that when you do it right, the research meeting can create a sense of mystique around who you are and what you're doing. Again, this is when the barriers start to fall and your path to the decision maker opens up.

# WRAPPING UP THE RESEARCH MEETING

## Going into Overtime

Research meetings are notorious for running over their allotted time. This is because the contacts are engaged, appreciate your professional approach, and enjoy the opportunity to talk about themselves and their business. So don't let your schedule be a slave to the length of time you asked for. During a research meeting, you want to build momentum, and when that happens, the meetings tend to run long. Prepare for this by scheduling plenty of available time around the research meetings.

Handling a meeting that goes over the appointed closing point requires some delicacy, however. If you originally scheduled a half-hour meeting, but the momentum is going strong as you near the 30-minute mark, try saying to the person, "You initially agreed to a 30-minute meeting. I really appreciate the insights you're sharing. Can we continue a little longer?" In most cases, the customer will be glad to keep talking. But remember to plan for this. You never want to be forced to cut off a contact as he or she builds up a head of steam just so that you can run out to another appointment.

## Closing the Research Meeting

Even the best research meetings do come to an end, however. At that point, how you conclude the research meeting is very important. You want to maintain the level of professionalism and integrity you established before and during the meeting, while also opening up the possibility of further research meetings and contacts within the client organization. For this reason, begin wrapping up the conversation a few minutes before your agreed-upon time is up.

The closing strategies you'll use will depend on the person you called on, your perception of that person's role, what you still need in the process, and the type of relationship you want to develop with this contact. These strategies are:

- *Show appreciation.* Express gratitude for your contact's time and knowledge. "Debbie, I appreciate your insights, and I learned a lot. For instance, I didn't know how aggressive the company's growth plan is. . . ."
- *Summarize.* Restate a few of the key points of the meeting, emphasizing whatever the contact stressed. Then make a statement reiterating that you feel a business fit exists between your companies. "I understand that the next few months are critical to achieving the department's objectives and that you have a lot at stake here. I see a strong fit between Foghorns, Inc. and Associated Earplugs."

> *"Listening, not imitation, may be the sincerest form of flattery."*
> —Dr. Joyce Brothers

- *Request referrals.* Ask for other contacts. "Now that you know the kind of information that I'm looking for—and why—whom would you recommend I talk to in other parts of the organization to give me another perspective or refine my understanding?"

If appropriate, ask if the contact is willing to call the other contact(s) to prepare for your call. "Would you be willing to call Tom Willis to let him know that I'll be calling?"

Remember, willingness to help you meet others is one of the qualifications of a good coach.

- *Request an open door.* Ask if you can call in the future to clarify issues. "As I continue to do my homework, I would like to be able to call you to review what I learn and determine the relevance to our business fit."

Often, your ability to share information about what's going on in other parts of the company delivers a great win for your contact or coach.

- *Position the next step.* If you believe that this contact is comfortable enough, begin to elevate the level of your relationship.
    - *Describe your objective.* "Louise, I'm excited about the outstanding business fit between our companies. I'm putting together a business presentation to George Jefferson, and I would really appreciate your input."
    - *Ask for the names of other key players.* "Who else do you think should be at that meeting, Louise?"
    - *Tell your contact what your next steps will be.* "I'll be making a few more calls like this one to make sure I understand your company and the business fit."
    - *Ask advice on setting up the meeting.* "If you were me, Louise, how would you go about scheduling this presentation meeting?"

Essentially, a research meeting has two likely conclusions. Following are two complete closing scripts to conclude each kind of meeting.

**1. Coach potential.** If things go well and the contact has opened up and shared thoughtful insights while demonstrating a genuine interest in helping you develop your research, then you'll want to conclude by hitting all these key points. Here's a full script of a possible conclusion:

> Louise, thank you so much for the time you spent with me today. I really appreciate it. And I've learned a great deal as well. I was particularly surprised to learn about your growth through acquisition strategy. Thanks for sharing it.
>
> As you know, Louise, I'm trying to gain a broad understanding of the business, but I really don't know anyone in engineering or sales. Is there someone you might suggest I talk to who could help me strengthen my overall perspective on the business?
>
> And by the way, Louise, as I'm doing that, if I run into something that doesn't necessarily jibe with what we've talked about today or that throws me for a loop, would you mind if I just picked your brain a little bit more? That would be great, thank you.
>
> As our conversation unfolded, I feel even stronger about the business fit between our companies. But after doing that work, it's clear to me that I need to reach George Jefferson and present to him the business fit between our companies. Do you have any suggestions or recommendations as to how I might reach him and schedule that meeting? Who else do you think would be appropriate to have at that meeting?
>
> And Louise, as I draft that presentation, would you be open to reviewing it before I give it? Thank you so much.

**2. No coach potential.** At other times, however, although you appreciate the person's time and efforts, you may not see the relationship going any further. Here's what you might say in that circumstance:

> Florence, thank you so much for the time you spent with me today. I really appreciate it. And I've learned a great deal as well. I was particularly surprised to learn about your growth through acquisition strategy. Thanks for sharing it.
>
> Florence, as I'm doing some additional homework, if I hear something that I don't understand or doesn't necessarily jibe with what we've talked about today, would you mind if I gave you a call and picked your brain a little bit more? That would be great, thank you.

With this contact, the difference is that you don't go into the follow-up issues. In the meeting, you have to make some judgment calls, and one of them is: do I think this person is going to be credible with the decision maker? If the answer is no, then clearly you're not going to want to ask them to help you schedule your meeting with the decision maker.

You don't have to ask for the moon every time you close a meeting. Sometimes you just need to get out. By using this type of language, you move on—without sacrificing any of your professionalism.

## FLOW OF THE RESEARCH MEETING

The first four research elements should provide you with a logical framework to guide your research meeting. As you recall, they are:

1. Corporate profile/direction
2. Organizational structure
3. Key players/profiles
4. Departmental profile/direction

The fifth research element, business fit, is something you will work on after you've conducted your research.

With these elements in mind, let's take a look at a couple of sample research meeting flows.

Let's say you already have a solid relationship with the contact. In that case, your meeting might flow this way:

Hard-hitting opening question ⟶
Corporate profile/direction ⟶
Departmental profile/direction ⟶
Organization structure ⟶
Key players/profiles ⟶
Close on desired action

But if you don't have much prior contact with the person, you may prefer to ease into the conversation by asking questions the contact will feel comfortable answering, before moving on to more sensitive, high-impact questions. Here's how the flow might go for this meeting:

1. Personal introduction/contact's background
2. Departmental profile/direction

3. Organizational structure
4. Key players/profiles
5. Corporate profile/direction
6. Close on desired action

## Opening

Here is a typical research meeting opening:

Thank you for taking the time to meet today. As I mentioned, I'd like to take a step back to better understand the big picture, confirm my understanding of your business direction, and gain your insights. This understanding will enable us to serve your interests better and bring ideas and solutions to the table on a timely, proactive basis.

## Body

Here's an outline of the key questions and transitions you might use during the body of the research meeting. See Appendix A for additional research meeting questions. This particular outline is for a meeting where you do not know the contact very well.

> *"Judge a man by his questions, rather than by his answers."—Voltaire*
>
> This is your chance to ask great questions.

Personal introduction/contact's background questions:

- How long have you been with the company?
- Can you tell me a little about your role and responsibilities?
- What projects or initiatives do you spend most of your time on?
- What are your key measures of success?
- What are the most pressing issues you're facing?
- If money or time were no object, what would you fix, change, or invest in today? Why?

Transition from personal to departmental profile/direction by asking:

- How do your initiatives relate to the objectives of the department?

Departmental profile/direction questions:

- How does your department support the CEO's objectives?
- What challenges do you face in attaining these objectives?
- What are the top projects for the department?
- How would you prioritize these projects?
- What strategies are in place to help reach these objectives?
- What would occur if these objectives were not achieved?
- Who would be the most affected and why?
- What would the payback be if you accomplish the objectives?

Transition to organizational structure by asking:

- How is your department structured to achieve its objectives?

Organizational structure questions:

- If we look beyond your department, can you help me understand how the department fits into the broader organization?
- In the time you've been here, I'm sure this structure has changed a lot. How has it changed?
- Do you foresee more changes? What will drive that change?

Transition to key players/profiles question:

- It would appear you work closely with Kristin [the decision maker]. Can you help me understand her background and current responsibilities?

Key players/profiles questions:

- What are the major issues facing her department right now?
- What are her top priorities?
- What would her legacy be if she were to move on today?

Transition to corporate profile/direction:

- How do her priorities support the overall objectives of the company?

Corporate profile/direction questions:

- What are the corporation's critical objectives?
- What are the CEO's top three priorities?

- Where do you see the business in the future, both in the short-term and the long-term?
- What strategies are in place, or being put in place, to achieve these objectives?
- What are some of the major projects or initiatives within the company?
- What are the company's critical success factors?
- What are the key challenges facing your business?
- What is the biggest issue facing your company today?
- What are the CEO's top three to five issues or concerns?

*"It is better to know some of the questions than all of the answers."*
*—James Thurber*

## Close

Here's what a typical close might sound like as you wrap up a meeting with someone who has developed into a coach or strong contact:

"Thank you. I really appreciate your time. I've learned so much in the past half hour. In fact, I was surprised to learn that. . . .

As you know, I'm trying to gain a broad understanding of the business. Who else would you suggest I talk to?

As I continue to do my homework, do you mind if I call you as questions come up?

Our conversation has reinforced my belief in a strong business fit between our companies. After doing additional homework, I would like to convey this business fit by delivering a business relationship presentation.

Whom do you think should attend this meeting? What would be the best way to schedule this meeting?

Would you be open to reviewing the presentation prior to this meeting?

Thank you again. I look forward to talking to you soon."

## FOLLOWING UP THE RESEARCH MEETING

Your involvement doesn't end with the research meeting. Remember, you're trying to develop a network of coaches to help you make an impact with the decision maker. That's why it's important to nurture your budding contacts by following up professionally after the research meeting.

Your follow-up strategy may depend on whom you're calling and what you'd like to see happen with your relationship in the future. One option is to send a written thank-you note to the person. You can also simply leave a thank-you message via voice mail or e-mail. Then, as you progress toward the presentation, keep in contact for clarification and updates.

## COMMON CHALLENGES

By carefully preparing for a research meeting, you reduce the chances of encountering situations beyond your control. Unfortunately, there's no way to completely eliminate unexpected problems that may arise. Here are a couple of the more common unanticipated challenges you might face and some suggestions for how to handle them.

### Additional Attendees

| *If . . .* | *Then . . .* |
|---|---|
| You walk into the contact's office and he picks up the phone and says he's calling others to attend. | Ask if you might schedule separate appointments to see others. Example: *"Today, I'd like to meet with you individually—to get your point of view on things."* |
| You walk into the contact's office and there is an additional person there. | Keep the meeting brief and position yourself for return one-on-one meetings. You may also be able to reposition the meeting immediately to meet with one of the people and make an appointment to return to meet with the other. |

| *If . . .* | *Then . . .* |
| --- | --- |
| You walk into the contact's office and there are three or more people there. | Clarify the reason for your visit and your interest in speaking one-on-one.<br>Example:<br>*"I seem to have been unclear about my intentions for this meeting. Frankly, I'm not here to do a presentation, but I'll be happy to schedule one."*<br>*"In the meantime, I'd like to meet with each of you individually—to get your insight into the issues—before I meet with you again as a group."* |

## Changes to the Plan

| *If . . .* | *Then . . .* |
| --- | --- |
| Your contact turns out to be a gatekeeper. | Close the meeting as soon as you can. The longer you stay, the greater your chances of being blocked further.<br>Do not mention your intention to do a presentation to senior-level management. It's easier to apologize for going over the gatekeeper's head if you were not told not to do so. |
| Your contact gives you less time than agreed on. | If less than 20 minutes, stress the importance of what you hoped to accomplish and say that you'd like to reschedule. See if the contact can suggest some others that you can meet with.<br>Ask the appropriate questions to ensure that the contact is not sending you to a gatekeeper. |

## Common Temptations

Being alert to challenges the contact may throw in your path can help you focus on the goals of your meeting. But sometimes the problems originate with you. Some of the ways salespeople undermine their own efforts during research meetings include:

> One rule of silence is that someone's going to fill it.

**Talking too much.** It's nearly impossible to listen too much during a research meeting. But it is possible to talk too much. The 95-5 rule will help you gain the most out of this meeting. If you're the type who likes to talk, suppress that urge. Every time you speak, you discourage the contact from providing you with additional information. The same goes for the urge to fill empty spaces. When you ask a challenging question that forces the contact to think, resist the temptation to break the silence. One rule of silence is that somebody's going to fill it. The question is Who? You want the contact to fill the silence. Often the best answer you get is the second answer, so let it flow. Be patient, and the contact will reward you.

> When you ask a question, often the best answer you get is the second one, so let it flow.

**Digging for dirt.** It's best to avoid confidential topics. You are looking for that critical insider perspective, but you don't want to hear personal gossip. Although you are likely asking questions most salespeople calling on the account wouldn't think to ask, you're still a professional conducting a sales call, and by delving into confidential areas you reduce your level of professionalism.

**Handling objections.** Salespeople have a nearly instinctive urge to handle objections. Resist this compulsion as well. Instead, focus on understanding the concern. Ask questions, encourage the contact to talk about the objection, and listen to the answers. Don't look to find solutions during the research meeting. Remember:

- This meeting is an information-gathering session, not a sales call.
- Objections provide you with insights into challenges the company currently faces. You can use these insights later when you formulate your solution fit and business fit with the client company.

- Responding to an objection with further questions shows the contact that you're not avoiding the issue. Ask: Where? When? What? Why? How?

**Unleashing the product hammer.** The purpose of the research meeting is to help you understand more about the contact's organization; it's not an opportunity for you to begin selling the customer on the wonders of your company's latest model of widget. You will have plenty of time to talk product and service later on. If you gain a meeting under the pretense that you're only interested in gathering information and then proceed to sell during that meeting, your credibility is immediately at risk. Admittedly, you are selling something, but it's not a product or service. You're selling the customer on your approach to building relationships and the way you work with customers. If you are compelled to discuss product issues, make sure to conclude the research portion of the meeting first.

This is how Fred Caprio, Regional Vice President of Sales with Securian Financial Network, describes it.

> This is a big challenge. Our people have been taught to find the opportunity to close, and take advantage of it. And yet, that's not the right thing to do in this situation. This is our chance to ask great questions and listen to the answers. There's more power in waiting, presenting to the decision maker, and closing the person who can actually say yes.

## AN UNCOMMON CHALLENGE

Remember when you found the bike your parents were planning to give you for your birthday a week ahead of time, hidden in the garage? Well, you couldn't exactly take it out and start riding it, could you? No, you had to wait until the time was right before hopping on and cruising the neighborhood. The same principle applies when you realize that your contact is actually the decision maker. Despite the fact that a gift has fallen into your lap, now is not the time to start tearing at the wrapping paper.

Why? Let's revisit a couple of the premises we talked about in Chapter 2. Remember these?

- Senior-level management is more likely to buy from us based on what we know about them than on what they know about us.
- You don't get a second chance to make a good first impression.

You typically don't want to conduct a research meeting with the decision maker. You want to come back and make a strong business presentation to this person. Even though research meetings are effective and can be differentiating on their own, you're better positioned to make that impressive and compelling first impression during the presentation than in a research meeting.

Admittedly, your contact won't turn out to be the decision maker very often, but if they are, you'll want to be prepared. So how will you know if the contact is the decision maker? A few clues are:

- The contact is in the corner office and has a certain "decision-maker presence."
- As you peruse the org chart, you notice that the contact's name is in a key spot.
- When you ask, "Besides you, who else is involved in making the decision?" the contact responds, "The people who work for me make the decision." If the contact says, "I make the decision," that does not necessarily mean he or she is or is not the decision maker—it just means you need to investigate further.

Once you recognize that you're meeting with a decision maker, take steps to position yourself to come back, but only after you've done some more research. Try to hit the following points:

- *You need to gather more information.* Say that you do not want to take his or her time until you've had the chance to talk to others in the organization and learn more about their business issues.
- *Get names.* Ask for the names of some of the decision maker's managers who might meet with you to discuss their business priorities and issues. One question you could use is, "Whom do I need to talk to in order to be ready for our meeting?"
- *Make a brief inquiry.* Ask a few questions about his or her top priorities and issues before you go.
- *Make yourself scarce.* Even if the person seems receptive to speaking with you at greater length now, resist the urge to stay too long.
- *Get a date.* Confirm a date for a business presentation, and allow enough time to prepare.

Your goal for handling the "contact turns out to be decision maker" situation is twofold. First, you want to leverage the meeting to help you gain access to good research contacts (and prospective coaches), and you want to walk out with a scheduled presentation to the decision maker. These are two of the greatest challenges you'll face during the process, and if you can accomplish them both in a matter of minutes, you're operating well ahead of the curve.

## CONCLUSION

How powerful can a research meeting be? Consider the case of one of our clients, a sales professional in the long distance communications industry.

During a relatively typical research meeting with the vice president of marketing for a prospective client, this rep was doing a nice job of following the 95-5 rule, asking great questions and really engaging the VP. About 20 minutes in, the VP suddenly interrupted the conversation, asked the rep to "hold on," and picked up the phone to call someone else into the meeting. The other person came in, and the VP asks him to "just sit and watch for a while."

The rep began again, and after the meeting concluded was formally introduced to the third person, who turned out to be the VP of sales. The marketing VP was so impressed with the research meeting, that he wanted the sales VP to see it. As the two of them agreed afterwards, this was exactly the kind of call their reps needed to make. That's an impressive outcome, and not a bad "sales call."

> "A good listener is not only popular everywhere, but after a while he gets to know something." —Wilson Mizner

In this chapter, we've covered a lot of details about the research meeting. It may seem a bit overwhelming, but it's not. Once you have a little practice under your belt, preparing for and conducting great research meetings can become second nature to you. The other thing is, they're fun. It's invigorating to sit across from your contacts and coaches as they become more animated talking about what they do and how they hope to accomplish their professional goals. You can't help but get caught up in the excitement. Once you start doing research calls, you'll begin to marvel at how little you used to know about the companies you were selling into.

# The Power of
# COMMUNICATION

"Information is power."

We've all heard this quote a thousand times. And almost everyone believes it's true. But is it? We have a slightly different take on it. We say information is not power; applying information is. After all, how many times have you lost deals despite having all the right information? You had what you needed, but you didn't use it correctly. The rest of this book focuses on applying research. We answer one critical question: how do you use research to gain access to decision makers and deal effectively with gatekeepers so you can present the business fit between your two companies?

> Information is not power; applying information is.

## LEVERAGING RESEARCH

At this point, you've probably gained a great deal of insight about the account. And terrific as all that information is, you'll eventually confront one of the realities of operating in today's business environment—you can do enough research to open your own historical archive on a target company, and it won't guarantee you an appointment in front of a busy, hard-to-reach, top-level executive. For that, you need an effective access strategy.

And that's what the communication stage of the process is all about—leveraging your research to gain access to the decision-making level, while dealing effectively with any gatekeepers who crop up to try to block you, control you, or ensnare you in the vendor trap.

For this reason, the communication section is divided into two parts. In the first chapter, we'll discuss how to evaluate your target account and develop an appropriate strategy for gaining access to the senior-level decision maker. We'll also dedicate a chapter to one specific strategy—the

Access Letter, a powerful tool for getting in to see those particularly hard-to-reach executives.

> Beyond Selling Value is all about not trying to sell value to people who can't buy value and not being blocked by people who can say "no" but can't say "yes."

The second section is all about gatekeepers—who they are and why they want to block or control you. You'll also learn a range of strategies for going over or around them—or even converting them into coaches.

But communication does not exist in a vacuum. The research you've gathered so far will be critical in helping you develop the strategies you'll use to deal with those gatekeepers and to schedule that presentation to the decision maker.

As Greg McCamus, President, Enterprise Communications Solutions for Sprint Canada, points out, access is critical:

It's never more evident than in this aspect of the process that good intentions aren't enough. We can do the best research, but if we can't get to the person who can buy our value and instead get stuck with the person who can't, so what? All the good intentions won't buy us anything—we have to execute.

# CHAPTER SEVEN

# Two Feet in the Door

## HOW TO GAIN ACCESS TO SENIOR-LEVEL DECISION MAKERS

A true decision maker is like that ripe, delicious piece of fruit hanging off the upper branch of a tree. You can see it, but how are you going to reach it? Sometimes the answer is simple, like getting yourself a ladder. But other times, you have to be creative and think of a solution that might elude your competitors, like renting a helicopter or hiring a trained monkey to climb up there for you.

Admittedly, this is not the case for everyone. Some salespeople, on the strength of their name recognition, corporate reputation, and personal credibility, can merely pick up the phone and get a meeting scheduled with senior-level executives. If that's the case for you, great. You should take full advantage of those leverage points.

## ACCESS STRATEGIES

One of the goals of the process is to schedule the presentation to the decision maker as soon as possible. If you have the kind of relationship with the decision maker that allows you to book the meeting first, do it. You can do your research after the presentation is scheduled, and the research will no doubt be easier, as you'll be able to leverage the upcoming meeting. If, however, you need to do some research before you can figure out how to gain access to the decision maker, welcome to the club.

Difficult as getting that foot in the door can sometimes be, you have a number of strategies available to you, as indicated by the pyramid in Figure 7.1.

Let's review those strategies, from top to bottom.

### Decision Maker Initiates

Sometimes decision makers call you, right out of the blue. It probably doesn't happen as often as we'd like, but it does happen.

FIGURE 7.1   Access Strategies Pyramid

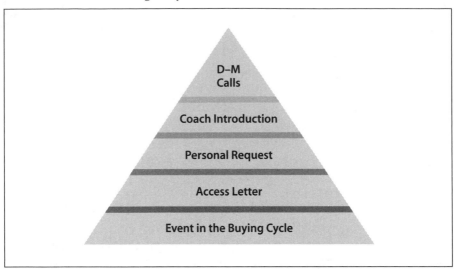

A sales rep we work with was sitting at his desk just before lunch, when he received an unusual phone call. Over the phone line came a man's booming voice. This man said that he was on the board of directors of a Fortune 500 company and that he used to be president of another Fortune 500 company. "My former company used to do a great deal of business with you," he bellowed. "Now I get here only to discover that we're not doing any. I want someone who can come in and tell me how we can do business together."

The rep reacted the same way a lot of us might. He said, "Oh, shut up, Drew," thinking this was a prank being perpetrated by the friend he was about to go to lunch with. But it wasn't Drew. The man was who he said he was, on the board of directors for this huge potential customer. The rep quickly recovered from his embarrassment and was able to position a business presentation. He laughs about it now, but imagine his horror at that moment of recognition that the caller wasn't Drew and wasn't playing a practical joke.

*"A wise man turns chance into good fortune."*—Thomas Fuller

We love this story because it shows that yes, indeed, sometimes decision makers do call you. But you can't simply sit by the phone, expecting decision makers to call you and ask when the two of you can get together. Not unless your short-term goals include collecting unemployment benefits. It's much better to be prepared to take advantage of these rare opportunities by effectively using the process.

> Sometimes when a decision maker calls you, it's because there's a problem. Don't despair—this is a great chance to use the process. What better way to communicate with the decision maker than to present around issues as well as opportunities?

So let's take a look at a couple more strategies you have at your disposal for gaining that critical presentation to the decision maker.

## Leverage a Coach

Your coach network can be your most valuable asset in getting to the decision maker, provided you have a coach who is credible enough to make the call for you. But just because a coach is on your side and wants you to get the meeting, you can't take for granted that he or she will position the request correctly.

Take the example of a sales rep we worked with and introduced to the process. With one account, he had been doing everything wrong in a very traditional, vendor-oriented way—calling on product people, positioning product, and doing demos. Six months' worth of product sales later, he still didn't have a sale or a commitment. Then one day the "decision maker" (really a gatekeeper) woke up and kicked him out, effectively ending the sales cycle. This is when we got involved, and as a result he decided to try the process.

He scheduled a number of research calls with people at the company he had never met—they were just names in a file—and he picked up the phone and called them cold. One of the people he met with was clearly a coach. The rep could tell because this person would answer questions the rep hadn't even thought to ask yet (a clear sign of a coach).

> A credible coach can be your most valuable asset in getting to the decision maker.

What also became clear was that the rep had to get to the coach's boss's boss—the CFO of the company. He asked, "Ed, how do you suggest I get to John?" Ed picked up the phone and said, "When would you like to see him?"

Even though the rep hadn't asked Ed to schedule the presentation, Ed was willing to do it, which was terrific. So why did the rep ask Ed to hang up the phone? Because he didn't want to jeopardize the opportunity.

By this point, the rep had already invested significant effort into demonstrating that he wasn't a typical vendor and that he didn't sell just like everyone else. But what happens to all that effort when Ed picks up the phone, calls the decision maker, and says, "John, I've got a vendor here in my office. He seems pretty sharp, and I think you should set aside an hour to talk to him."? The decision maker is bound to say, "Vendor? I don't deal with vendors. Why don't you take care of it?"

Instead, the rep asked Ed to hang up the phone, then talked him through the positioning to make sure he knew precisely what to ask for: a one-hour meeting to lay out the value of a business relationship in addressing certain concerns facing the CFO and his company. Armed with that coaching, Ed was ready to pick up the phone again.

> Beyond Selling Value means more than simply leveraging a coach to get to the decision maker; it means picking the right coach and preparing him or her to get you a yes.

**Coaching the coach.**  Faced with this situation, can you be sure your coach is going to say the wrong thing? No. And if he or she does misspeak, is the decision maker guaranteed to react so negatively? Again, no. Maybe you would get the meeting after all. But why take the chance? Instead, before anyone picks up the phone, try to provide your coaches with a little preliminary coaching of their own.

Clearly, phrasing is extremely important. Tell your coaches to position the meeting as a business presentation that will focus on "business issues and priorities," not as a product presentation. Also, your coach's job is to get you a meeting, not to sell your product or service, so make sure he or she doesn't make the mistake of telling the decision maker how much faster, stronger, or less expensive your widget is than any others on the market.

**Coach cultivation.**  Because getting this presentation scheduled should be your goal, even during the research stage, the research meeting is a good place to begin educating your coaches on how to make this call for you. During a research meeting, you might broach the topic by saying this to your coach:

> Bosley, before our companies commit too many resources, we need to confirm the business fit. To do that, we'd like to request a meeting

with Charlie. We'd like to have a couple of weeks to finish doing our homework and preparing. How would you suggest we go about scheduling that meeting?

This approach gives the coach the opportunity to decide whether he or she is the right person to set up the meeting or, alternatively, to give you advice on what the right strategy might be.

**Separate but not equal.** One key concept we like to stress is that *not all coaches are created equal.* None of the people in this comic is the right coach. To leverage a coach to get to the decision maker, you need to find someone who is in the loop. This is important to remember as you strategize your progress through an account or opportunity.

Some people make things happen, some watch what happens, and others say, "What happened?" Find the right coach who can make things happen.

For instance, take the example of a client of ours, Jay Zack, a managing director with RSM McGladrey, a large accounting and consulting firm. He describes a situation he faced selling into an industrial food products company.

> We were working to get to the president. We had developed two coaches within the account, the VP of manufacturing and the VP of finance. We then had to figure out which would be a better coach to help us get to the president.
>
> In doing our homework, we found out that the president had only been with the company for six or seven months. We knew we had to better understand who had his ear. Probing further, we discovered that the VP of manufacturing was also newly hired and had come along with the president, whereas the VP of finance had been with the company for years. In our research, one of the key questions we asked was, "When the president makes a decision, whom does he turn to?" Not surprisingly, we learned that the president generally looked for counsel to the VP of manufacturing, who had come with him to the company.
>
> Without thinking to ask this question, we might have leveraged either coach to try to get the meeting. But this one piece of information helped make it clear that we should leverage the coach with greater influence to increase the odds of getting the meeting.

This story underscores a few key points, including the importance of asking the right questions as well as the value of cultivating multiple coaches within an opportunity. But just as critical a lesson to understand is that not all coaches are created equal.

> Don't use coaches who aren't credible with the decision maker or who for any reason are reluctant to request the meeting.

## Personal Request

Another effective strategy for scheduling a presentation meeting with a decision maker is to have someone outside the client's organization (possibly you) make the request. Let's look at the best way to go about this approach.

**Do it yourself.** If you decide to make the request yourself, bear in mind that going it alone carries certain risks.

For example, have you ever found it impossible to reach a prospect over the phone during typical business hours, so you began calling before 9 AM and after 6 PM, just to avoid the secretary? You might have even put in your calendar to call this person every day, once at 7:30 AM and once at 6:30 PM. So day in and day out, you make these calls, sometimes getting the secretary, sometimes voice mail, but you're persistent. The calls become just another part of your routine.

Then, two months into this program, something unexpected happens. The decision maker actually answers the phone! And what do you say? This moment you've been working so hard towards and anticipating for so long finally arrives, and all you can think to say is, "Wow, you're really hard to get a hold of!" Perfect. Nice and smooth. With a hook like that, who wouldn't want to talk to you?

The point is the same as the one in the dandruff shampoo ads: you only get one chance to make a first impression. Foul it up, and the entire opportunity may evaporate.

> If you have a close enough relationship with the decision maker to schedule this meeting yourself, terrific—do it. But don't take anything for granted. Prepare yourself thoroughly before you make the call.

So when you do call, make sure you're professional and that you've thought through the request ahead of time. Phrasing is just as important here as when your coach makes the call. Be ready to state that your presentation will address some specific objectives, strategies, and/or issues, and then close on the meeting. Remember to position the meeting as a business presentation, not a product presentation or a sales call. This is a one-shot opportunity, so you'd better be prepared to make your case and then to close well.

Finally, don't paint yourself into a corner. If the decision maker responds to your request with something like, "Sounds great. Let's do it in six months," be prepared to address this stall by highlighting aspects of the business fit that give the decision maker a compelling reason to schedule the meeting sooner.

## Let Someone Else Do It

The opposite of doing it yourself is to have someone else do it for you. Anyone with the credibility to schedule this meeting on your behalf is a candidate, whether it's your manager, another executive from your company, or a coach from another company entirely.

Finding that person may give you another opportunity to flex your creative muscles. You may be familiar with the "small world" concept of Six Degrees of Separation (or its pop cultural cousin, Six Degrees of Kevin Bacon). The theory posits that any given person—a Mongolian goatherder, a Russian cosmonaut, or your TGIFriday's server—can reach any other individual through a network of six personal contacts. Regardless of whether the theory is true, seemingly unrelated people are often interconnected, frequently in ways even they are unaware of. You should use this to your advantage.

For example, consider the case of a client of ours—a rep with a multinational telecommunications firm—who was calling into a large cable systems provider. The rep had been dealing predominantly with the engineering and purchasing departments, where he was viewed as little more than a typical vendor. His goal was to get higher in the organization, specifically to the executive vice president.

Without a viable access strategy, he decided to get creative and think outside the box in search of a connection. One option: He sent an exploratory e-mail mentioning the target company and executive to his own VP of sales, who forwarded it to his peers throughout the company. Soon, a senior executive in a different part of the company responded, saying that he sat on an industry board with the targeted decision maker.

The rep sat down with his internal coach (the senior executive) and coached him on how to help the rep gain access. By educating the executive on the proper way to approach the decision maker and how to phrase the request, the rep won the meeting with the targeted EVP. And what was that EVP's name? Kevin Bacon. No, that's not true. But what is true is that a good access strategy may well be out there, if you're diligent and creative enough to go find it.

> Don't be too proud and think you have to schedule the presentation yourself or not at all. Leverage anyone who can help you get the meeting set.

## Other Approaches

These are just a few strategies—there are plenty more. Some customers have an established buying process in place, which culminates in a presentation to the decision maker or a committee. Many sales organizations opt to defer to this buying cycle. It may not be your first choice, but it is a viable strategy. You just have to make sure the decision maker is involved in the process.

If you're forced to use this strategy, don't despair. Using the business presentation in this setting can provide a tremendous competitive advantage.

Then there are other, more unorthodox approaches. We once had a client who was a former New York City police officer with just such a unique strategy. Burly, imposing, aggressive—he was clearly not the type of guy you'd want to mess with. He told us his strategy was to "wait customers out." He'd show up at their offices early in the morning and wouldn't let them kick him out until he saw the boss. Now this approach probably isn't the best for everyone—especially if you're under 250 pounds—but it worked for him. If you have a strategy that works, go with it. Get that meeting.

## CONCLUSION

As you prepare to schedule this meeting, keep in mind Theodore Roosevelt's thoughts on decisiveness. He said, "In any moment of decision, the best thing you can do is the right thing. The next best thing you can do is the wrong thing, and the worst thing you can do is nothing."

There's no one right or wrong way to gain access. Know your situation and take a shot. And if that doesn't work, try something else. As a matter of fact, one thing you might try is an Access Letter, outlined in Chapter 8. This letter is a tool that has proven remarkably powerful in winning presentations to senior-level executives when you're not in a position to ask for the meeting directly and you have no coaches with the credibility to call the decision maker.

# CHAPTER EIGHT

# The Write Stuff

## COMPOSING THE ACCESS LETTER

Legendary baseball manager Casey Stengel used to say that a baseball team consists of three types of players—the ones who hate you, the ones who love you, and the ones who are undecided. The key to management, he added, was keeping the ones who hate you away from the ones who are undecided.

A similar principle applies to senior-level decision makers. No, none of them hate you—we hope not, at least. But of those upper-level executives, a small percentage will probably see you with very little coaxing. At the other end of the spectrum are those few who will never meet with you, no matter what you do. Where you prove your mettle, however, is with the large group in the middle, the ones Stengel called the undecideds. They may or may not meet with you, depending on whether you can reach them in the first place and then how you position the meeting.

Despite all the research and coach cultivation you do, sometimes the access strategies described in Chapter 7—leveraging a coach, scheduling the presentation yourself, or having someone else schedule the presentation for you—remain unavailable to you. If that's the case, don't worry. You still have a very powerful tool at your disposal in the Access Letter.

The Access Letter is a research-driven, reader-oriented letter designed to win that presentation. It demonstrates your understanding of the decision maker's organization, strategies, issues, and objectives while emphasizing a possible relationship between your two companies. Unlike typical sales letters, the focus of this letter is not on you and your company but on the customer's company and the pressing business issues it faces.

> Beyond Selling Value means sending sales letters that don't sell solutions; they sell you as a business resource.

FIGURE 8.1    Access Letter Process

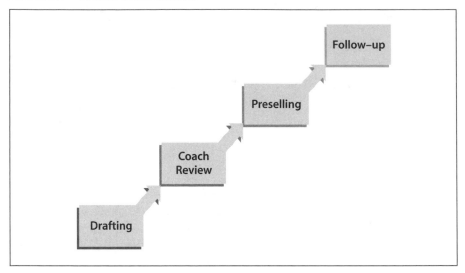

The Access Letter process consists of four parts. Let's take a look at each part and how they all work to help you get that presentation scheduled.

## DRAFTING THE ACCESS LETTER

Before you can begin writing your letter, you should organize your research notes and other materials and categorize that information as *objectives, strategies,* and *issues.* Do this at both the *corporate* and *department* levels. Focus on research that applies specifically to this company and leverage critical industry trends and marketplace concerns. You also need to consider the profile you've constructed on the decision maker you're targeting with this letter. Ask yourself questions like: "If she were to leave today, what contributions would she be most remembered for?" and "When he is driving to work, what are the top two or three business priorities on his mind?"

Here's how we typically structure an effective Access Letter:

- *Opening.* In the opening paragraph, refer to the decision maker's past accomplishments or successes.
- *Concerns.* Next, mention some of the decision maker's critical objectives and concerns that you've identified during your research.
- *Future.* Refer to the future possibility that your company may be able to address those issues or concerns or help the decision maker's company achieve its critical objectives.

- *Request.* Next, make a request for a business presentation. That's a business presentation, not a product demo or product presentation.
- *Close.* Conclude the letter by closing on what specifically you will do to schedule the presentation meeting.

> *"To be a bore is to tell everything."—Voltaire*
>
> To compel instead of bore, focus on the reader.

## WRITING STYLE

How you write the letter is almost as important as what you write, so keep a few guidelines in mind as you're putting together your draft:

- *Be clear.* Use concise, unequivocal language. If you have concerns about spelling, grammar, or formatting, simply find a qualified colleague to look the letter over.
- *Lingo.* Use the customer's unique terminology and acronyms wherever appropriate. This subtly conveys that you have an insider's perspective on the organization.
- *Keep it short.* You should be able to communicate everything you need to say in 1 to 1½ pages.
- *No empty praise.* When you're talking about the decision maker's accomplishments, this is no time to be vague—support the reference with specific details. You want the decision maker to know immediately that you've done your homework, and that you're not merely floating empty compliments.
- *Focus.* This is a short letter, so keep your comments focused. Sell the business presentation, not your company's products or services. Explain briefly that the presentation will key on a business relationship between your two organizations, tailored toward how you can help them achieve their goals or deal with critical issues.
- *Details.* Check and double-check to be sure you've got the decision maker's correct title and the spelling of his or her full name, including middle initial. Don't hesitate to call a coach about this. There's no better way to undermine all your exhaustive research than by blowing a small but critical detail.
- *Sign off.* As you conclude the letter, think twice about including your title. A corporate CFO, for example, might not be particularly impressed by the title *account manager*. In fact, misguided as they may be, some

people will tune out a letter as soon as they see a salesperson's title. If sharing your title puts your efforts at risk , simply include your name.

> *"Nothing in life is more important than the ability to communicate effectively."—Gerald Ford*

## SAMPLE LETTER

Now that you understand the components that go into an Access Letter, let's see how these guidelines come together where ink meets paper. The Access Letter in Figure 8.2 comes from a client of ours—a major information services company—selling to GE Capital, a financial subsidiary of General Electric.

GE Capital was the rep's largest customer, but he wasn't satisfied with the relationship. He wasn't selling the value he wanted to sell. They looked at him as a commodity, and he always faced pressure on price and margins—typical Vendor Trap stuff. He was looking to change the game.

Using the sales process, the rep did his research. One key point he learned was that the senior-level executive he wanted to reach at GE Capital had recently received a call from the CEO—Jack Welch. One of their customers had gone out of business, and Welch was calling to ask about the company's exposure. The targeted executive had no answer and had to utter those three words no one likes to say to Jack Welch: "I don't know." It took him three weeks to come up with an answer.

When our client heard this, he recognized a great business fit between the two companies. Note the third bullet item in the letter's second paragraph. Although an outside observer wouldn't recognize anything extraordinary, the decision maker understood the implied message: "The next time one of your major customers fails, you won't have to sweat for three weeks to be able to answer the CEO's questions."

As you look over this letter, note the following key points:

- The letter engages the decision maker immediately with a compliment, then substantiates the praise with some background.
- The letter flows smoothly from sentence to sentence and from one paragraph to the next, building toward the action—scheduling a presentation.
- The research is evident. Only someone who's done a fair amount of homework could write this letter.

FIGURE 8.2    GE Capital Letter

Information Services Corp.
Schroeder, NJ 12100

Mr. Smith
Senior Vice President
GE Capital

Dear Mr. Smith,

We recognize and respect the integral role that you play in guiding the sophisticated issues of risk management that impact GE Capital's 22 businesses.

Particularly in light of the current business climate of overcapacity, shrinking markets, and possibly disinflation, you may be reviewing such basic, yet pivotal, issues as:

- How to best manage the risks associated with the complexity of asset management flow and transaction businesses
- Defining the concentration of risk by assets and industry
- Evaluating the impact of specific customers across the 22 GE Capital businesses
- Protecting GE Capital's AAA rating, particularly as it relates to determining acceptable levels of delinquencies

We are prepared to address these issues and others. That is why we are contacting you directly to schedule a presentation meeting.

As a point of reference, Information Services Corp. is currently very involved in all of GE Capital's businesses. As a result, we are prepared to present recommendations, for your consideration, that can impact all GE Capital businesses.

Our presentation will be concise and the content relevant. This initial meeting can be held to under one hour.

I'll contact your office in a few days with the hope that Ms. Jones can confirm your availability for our presentation, preferably during the week of January 11.

I look forward to meeting you.

Cordially,

- The tone is respectful of the decision maker's time and position. The writer recognizes that the decision maker is busy and allows a broad time frame for the presentation to be scheduled, while suggesting that he'll handle the details with the decision maker's assistant.

> Like the ad campaign that suggested, "This is not your father's Oldsmobile," this is not your father's traditional sales letter. It's not about you, your company, and your products; it's about your customer and his or her issues and objectives.

Now put yourself in the position of this decision maker. Would you agree to the meeting, as he did? Why or why not?

Just the fact that the letter links the rep's research to issues known to be of particular interest to the decision maker might have been enough to win the meeting. With the back of his neck still warm from the CEO's hot breath, how could the executive not think, "Hey, anyone who can get me a fast answer for my boss is worth an hour of my time?"

Beyond that, the letter is also low pressure. The salesperson expresses interest in a business relationship, not in hawking 100 gross units of his company's latest product line.

Finally, the letter stresses that the meeting will only take one hour, demonstrating an awareness of the value of the decision maker's time and making it easier for him to say yes.

The national account manager who sent this letter had this to say about why the letter worked so well:

> The reason it worked is that it focused on the executive and the areas where I knew he had some pain. Once he read it, he felt it was worth it to spend an hour with me to see if we really could help him with these issues. A typical sales letter would never have worked with him.

Was this letter guaranteed to get the meeting? No, of course not. As we noted before, you can go all out and buy commercial time during the Super Bowl to ask for the opportunity to present, and some decision makers still won't see you. With that in mind, your goal is to give yourself the best possible chance to convince the decision maker that sitting down with you is worth an hour of time. The Access Letter is a powerful tool for achieving that goal.

While the Access Letter follows a relatively standard template, you will need to rework the blueprint to suit each opportunity. To assist, we've included an additional sample Access Letter in Appendix B.

## COACH REVIEW

Whenever possible, review a draft of your letter with a coach. Admittedly, if you're running and gunning and your sales cycle doesn't allow a lot of time for navel gazing, you may not have the opportunity. But if you're operating in more of a strategic account environment, take the time to sit down with a coach and go over the letter together. Make sure the letter is accurate, timely, and sensitive to the issues facing the decision maker.

Here's one note of caution with the coach review process: bear in mind that people aren't always comfortable offering criticisms or judgments of others' work. Be explicit with the coach that you're looking for honest, constructive feedback. Don't accept, "It looks fine to me," for an answer. Get specific suggestions for improvement. Make sure you've listed the right issues and concerns, highlighted the right objectives, and got the terminology down. These are the keys to an accurate, effective letter.

> If necessary, remind the coach that your goal is not to sell a product presentation but a business presentation.

Finally, after you've incorporated the coach's suggested changes, it may be a good idea to have a manager or trusted colleague give your letter a final once-over. It's often difficult to proofread objectively and find errors in our own work, and this last filter may catch any mistakes you or the coach overlooked.

> *"Many receive advice; only the wise profit from it."—Publilius Syrus*

The Access Letter is probably not the only letter you'll write as a part of the process. Others include thank you letters, presentation confirmation letters, and presentation follow-up letters. Ideally, once you've become familiar with the process, you'll develop a template for each of the letters you tend to send, so you won't have to write each one from scratch.

## PRESELLING THE ACCESS LETTER

Now that you've drafted and reviewed the letter, it's ready to be stamped and dropped in the mail to the decision maker, right? Sure, if you want your letter added to his or her heap of daily incoming mail, reminiscent of the courtroom scene from *Miracle on 34th Street.* No, you've worked too hard on this letter to see it mixed in with all the preapproved credit card offers and sweepstakes come-ons.

> The best letter in the world won't get you a meeting if it never gets read.

Instead, you need to presell the letter to help ensure that the decision maker will read it. To properly presell the letter, begin by calling the decision maker's administrator directly to introduce yourself and your company. Explain the relevance of your call and that while doing some homework on the company, you've learned about a number of key issues the company faces. Then mention that you've written a letter asking for the opportunity to make a business presentation to the decision maker describing how your two companies, working together, could address some of these issues.

At this point, it's important to be assumptive. You're not asking whether it's okay to send the letter; you're merely letting the administrator know that it's coming and asking for advice about the best way to get it in front of the decision maker. Describe the letter's appearance, and tell the administrator how and when you'll be sending it.

Next, ask if it would be okay to call back to confirm that the letter has arrived. This is not much to ask for, and the administrator will typically agree readily. Next, ask if the administrator will place your letter with the mail that the decision maker will see over the next few days. Notice that you're not asking for the administrator to make sure that the decision maker sees the letter right away—that may be too forward. Instead, you ask for minimal effort on the administrator's part—to put your letter in with a pile of other letters.

When you ask for the minimum, people typically overdeliver. In this case, you've subtly recognized the important role the administrator plays, while assumptively yet respectfully positioning your request to secure his or her support. This approach is usually enough to spur the administrator to take the initiative to make sure the decision maker sees your letter.

> Often, when you ask for the minimum, you get the maximum.

Here's an example of how you might script a typical preselling phone call:

Hello, Miss Hathaway, my name is Harry Hartel from Cement Pond Construction, Inc. I've had meetings recently with some of the people in your organization such as Jethro Bodine and Jed Clampett, and we discussed a number of critical issues that Mr. Drysdale [the decision maker] might be facing. I'm sending a letter to Mr. Drysdale today to request a brief business presentation meeting to address some of those issues and others during the weeks of either March 2nd or March 9th. This meeting will be held to under one hour, and I'm wondering if those are the right weeks to request, or is there a better week that I should suggest?

The administrator may say those dates are fine or may suggest others. You then continue:

I'll send the letter today. You'll see it in a 9×12 envelope with a green CPC logo in the upper corner. Miss Hathaway, I know that Mr. Drysdale gets a lot of mail every day. I'm wondering if it would be okay for me to call back to confirm that the letter has indeed arrived?

Chances are that the administrator will certainly agree. Then continue:

Miss Hathaway, would you mind placing this with the mail he'll see over the next few business days? Great. I'll call in a day or so to make sure the letter's arrived. Thanks so much for your help.

After hanging up, place the 9×12 envelope into a courier envelope and express it to the administrator right away. Then, when you call back, you can confirm that the letter has arrived and follow up appropriately with the decision maker.

> It's not enough to send an e-mail or a regular letter; you're better off sending your letter via overnight courier.

All this preselling may seem like a lot of hoops to jump through, but it pays great dividends in demonstrating that you are thorough, professional, and worth taking seriously. Plus, you've begun to develop a relationship with the administrator, determined which dates will work best for the decision maker, and minimized the chances that the letter will be lost or misplaced. Not bad for a single phone call.

> Don't fall back into the Vendor Trap by attaching brochures to this letter.

Even with the Access Letter, you have to be careful not to step back into the Vendor Trap, even for a moment. As a cautionary tale, recall the sales rep who wrote an excellent Access Letter but thought he'd go one step further and attach a bunch of brochures. Where do you think that letter ended up? That's right—in the wastebasket, along with his chances of getting the presentation.

## FOLLOWING UP ON THE ACCESS LETTER

Now that you've presold and sent the letter, you have only one more step—following up. On its own, the letter may get you an eager call from the decision maker, ready to schedule the presentation. But, as with every other aspect of this process, you don't want to take any chances. You want to follow up on the letter diligently to give yourself the greatest likelihood of a date to present to the decision maker.

And following up on the letter is simple. You just do what you said you were going to do. Call the administrator to confirm that the letter arrived. But when you call, be prepared to speak with the decision maker. Often, once they see a letter like this one, decision makers are eager to know who wrote it, so have your notes handy, and be ready to discuss the mutual value of a business relationship and close on scheduling the meeting. And, as we've emphasized throughout the process, remember to focus on business fit, not product fit.

Other times, you will reach the administrator and he or she will tell you that the letter has arrived but that the decision maker has not yet seen it. In this case, try to nail down a specific time to follow up again with the administrator or the decision maker. Then, when you do call back, be just as prepared to speak with the decision maker.

What can an Access Letter do for you? Take the following example of a client of ours—a partner with a professional services firm trying to get to the president of a target company for a human resources consulting opportunity. The partner had a coach but not at the right level to help him gain access. So he decided to use the Access Letter strategy. He'd gotten some good insight from the coach to build the Access Letter, so he knew it was right on and that it addressed some of the specific priorities of the president.

A couple of days after sending the letter, he followed up with the administrator and asked, "Did the president get the letter?" The administrator said, "Yes, he has received the letter, and in fact he wants to talk to you." The president came on the line and said, "I receive what seems to be 100 letters a week. I not only opened this letter, but I read it and I wanted to talk to you. That happens with maybe 1 out of those 100 letters. How did you get the insight you demonstrated in that letter?" With the obstacles removed by a well-written, hard-hitting Access Letter, the partner had a clear path to a presentation to the decision maker and a closed sale.

"I receive what seems to be 100 letters a week. I not only opened this letter, but I read it and I wanted to talk to you."

## JUST THE FAQS

We've found that many salespeople new to the process have additional questions about the Access Letter. Here's how we respond to some of the questions we hear most frequently:

**Isn't the opening patronizing?** We don't feel that it is. It is meant to start with a sincere compliment. And that's the key—the compliment has to be sincere. It should also be based on your research. By opening with a compliment that refers specifically to the decision maker's accomplishments, you separate yourself from 95 percent of the other letter writers trying to grab his or her attention.

**How long should this letter be?** Of course, it depends. However, a typical letter like this is 1 to 1½ pages. Some people get concerned that it's too short. Others will be concerned that it's too long. Generally, 1 to 1½ pages is the right amount of space to establish that you understand something about this person's issues and to position yourself as a business resource closing on a presentation meeting.

**Why should I write to them about their issues in this letter?** You're really not doing that. What you're actually doing is saying that, based on the homework you've done, you've uncovered some issues that may be important to this person (you know very well that they are). You're not trying to tell them anything about their business. You're saying, "If I understand what your business needs are, then I might be a good resource for resolving some of those issues."

**Will the decision maker read it?** Not if you don't do the work to presell the letter. The biggest potential problem with an Access Letter is going to all the trouble of writing it and then having no one read it. With the preselling strategy described in this chapter, we've found that decision makers do read the letters. And when they do, the letters get a very positive response.

As Kevin Hrusovsky, CEO of Zymark Corporation, says, "Senior executives are looking for business resources to help them address their issues and objectives. Reading a letter like this, it makes you think that the writer might be one of those resources. For me, it would be worth an hour to find out."

**Isn't the Access Letter a lot of work?**  Yes. That's why we wouldn't recommend the Access Letter as your lead strategy for gaining access to a decision maker. In our business, we only use it when we need to. If we can gain access through a personal relationship or a coach, we much prefer that. But this is a great arrow in our quiver when we need it.

**Why not use a title at the end of the letter?**  A title in a letter can send the wrong message, unless you're selling at a level on a par with your own. In many cases, the title *account manager* or *account executive* will not carry the credibility to compel a senior-level decision maker to meet with you. Instead, let the letter do the compelling, without having a title detract from what you're trying to accomplish.

## SETTING A BAD EXAMPLE

What's the worst sales letter you've ever seen? Although we've come across a lot of terrible, internally focused letters, the one in Figure 8.3 is probably the worst. It was given to us by the president of one of our clients, who kept it to show his sales team what not to do to get to senior-level executives. Of course, we've changed the names to protect the guilty.

## CONCLUSION

How do upper-level decision makers feel about receiving the Access Letter? We found out what one thought during an engagement where we were speaking to a large company meeting. As we were overviewing the process, in the middle of the section on the Access Letter, the president of the company walked in and sat down in the back row. We had a sample letter splashed up on a screen. Immediately, someone in the audience turned to the president and said, "Doug, based on this letter, would you meet with these guys?"

Suddenly we were looking at the back of 150 heads as everyone turned to hear his response. And we were nervous, because at this point he couldn't know whether we were teaching them about a good letter, a bad letter, or what. Before he could answer, one of us interrupted and said, "I'm not sure this is a fair question, because this letter wasn't written to Doug. If it were, it would be more compelling and refer to his issues. This is just an example."

People's heads slowly turned back around and the audience seemed to understand our point and think that was a fair concern. So we went back to the session. During a break soon thereafter, the president approached us and said, "You should have let me answer. I would meet anybody who wrote me

FIGURE 8.3    Bad Letter

Mr. John Winger

Dear John,

Get me past your secretary, and I can solve all your congestion problems, make your stockholders and bankers grin with idiotic delight, and as Kipling said, "Make you wonderfully sought after by five this afternoon!"

My company has a business park in Southern Oregon that enjoys very low direct labor costs (ten dollars an hour is a good wage), excellent labor availability, quality, and productivity, central access to Pacific Rim and West Coast markets, correspondingly low transportation costs, and a free trade zone status. Your manufacturing facility should be there.

I could go on about the area's ability to hold key people, it's lack of unionization, cheap facility costs and ready availability of reasonably priced housing, and abundant inexpensive water and power, but if you aren't interested by now, I've lost you. I should mention Oregon Institute of Technology, though. The number three grantor of Technology degrees (including Doctorates) in the country.

I'll phone shortly with a request to further enlighten you. Thanks for your time, and I remain

Yours,

Thomas Callahan

a letter like that. Anyone who does that kind of job understanding my business deserves an hour of my time."

Again, you can use a number of ways to gain access to senior-level decision makers, none of which is right or wrong. The key is to get the meeting scheduled with the most certainty and success with the least amount of effort. The Access Letter takes some effort, but it gets results. But whatever strategy you pick, get the meeting scheduled with the decision maker as soon as possible.

# CHAPTER NINE

# Beyond the Gatekeeper
## HOW TO BREAK
## THROUGH THE BLOCK

When gatekeepers have their way, they reduce all salespeople to vendors hawking products or services. Say, for example, you work for a computer company. Typically, a gatekeeper will expect you to sell computers. This means dealing with IT managers, reacting to opportunities or responding to bids for computers.

> *"A man is literally what he thinks."—James Allen*
>
> What do you think you are—a vendor or a business resource?

Is this where you want to be? Probably not. You would rather be dealing with line executives, learning about real business problems so that you can proactively propose *business solutions.* You want to sell value and help customers solve business problems. But gatekeepers try to prevent you from solving business problems or selling value. Their focus is on finding cost savings, not on making strategic investments.

Here's another example. If you're a sales representative for a chemical manufacturer, do you sell chemicals, or do you help customers increase and improve their own customer service? A company that buys chemicals probably wants to know about formulations, prices, availability, etc. You, on the other hand, want to provide solutions to help your customers service their customers better.

One company we worked with sold fiber to tire manufacturers. Because their fiber made up only 0.5 percent of the cost of goods sold of their customer's tires, many of the company's reps didn't feel they were worthy of getting to decision makers. Those reps were acting as their own gatekeepers. Happily, a few thought differently, and they changed the way the whole organization sold and whom they sold to.

> Beyond Selling Value means that you can't take no for an answer when it comes to getting to the decision maker.

Throughout this chapter, we'll expand on these examples, each time coming back to this crucial question: how do you sell? To sell value, you need to sell to the decision makers, who are interested in big-picture business improvements. When you sell products, however, you're selling to gatekeepers, who are only interested in buying products.

## SO WHAT IS A GATEKEEPER?

Of all the issues sales reps face, gatekeepers may be the most emotionally frustrating and professionally challenging. Gatekeepers are probably the number one cause of insomnia among sales professionals. While getting to the decision maker sounds straightforward, we know that in reality, it's a serious challenge. Beyond the right access strategy, you need to know how to go around or over gatekeepers or even work with them. This is how you get to decision makers, the people who can say "no" when everyone else says "yes" and can say "yes" when everyone else says "no."

> "I make the decisions around here" and "Let me run that up the flagpole for you," are the watchwords of today's gatekeepers.

As frustrating as they may be, gatekeepers also provide salespeople with an opportunity for creativity, because each gatekeeper you face will be different from the last. They come in all different shapes and sizes and with many personalities.

### Naughty and Nice

Sometimes, gatekeepers are antagonistic and rude, letting us know that they intend to block us. They say things like, "I make the decisions around here," "You don't need to talk to anyone else," or "I don't want you talking to anyone else." Others seem friendly, as if they truly want to help. They might say, "Hey, let me run that up the flagpole for you," "I'll take it from here," or "I'll let you know when the right time to proceed is."

Have you ever left a sales call with a smile on your face, gotten into your car, and driven away only to realize, "Hey, that guy blocked me!" He just did it in a really nice way. Regardless of whether they wear a friendly or hostile face or whether they act open or chatty, they're all gatekeepers because they want to block and control you.

## The Gatekeeper Defined

From a broad perspective, a gatekeeper is anyone who keeps you from executing your sales strategy and getting where you want to go. Gatekeepers like to block you from gaining access to other key players, especially decision makers. Typically, gatekeepers can say "no" but can rarely say "yes."

> Gatekeepers can say "no" but can rarely say "yes" to a value-oriented relationship.

While gatekeepers are not always immediately identifiable by their job titles, many are purchasing agents or product evaluators. Often, you will be told that someone is "the person you need to see." For example, if a rep who works for a components manufacturer is told, "You need to see Dan; he buys components," you can be pretty sure that Dan is a gatekeeper. His job is to evaluate and purchase components, so when you call on him, you can expect to be evaluated just like every other rep selling components—on price, product, availability, terms, discounts, your company's strengths and weaknesses, etc.

Gatekeepers exist in all areas of life, even when you least expect them. A consultant in the sales training business was dating a woman and had never met her parents. After dating for six months, the couple decided to drive a considerable distance to meet her parents for dinner. Throughout the drive, the consultant thought about what to say to make a good impression. As soon as the four of them sat down to eat, the father looked at the consultant and asked, "So, what do you do for a living?" Before the consultant could share his carefully considered and measured response, the young woman interjected, "Oh, Dad, he teaches salespeople to get around purchasing agents like you." Needless to say, the rest of the meal was less than enjoyable.

A business executive we worked with told us that when his salespeople were blocked by gatekeepers, between 90 to 95 percent of the time, the reps just accepted the block. This, he said, was the primary reason he'd brought us on board—to help his people learn effective methods for dealing with gatekeepers.

This concern is common among our clients. Yet most available sales books offer little to no coverage of this topic. As a result, even highly skilled

FIGURE 9.1    Four-Step Process Wheel

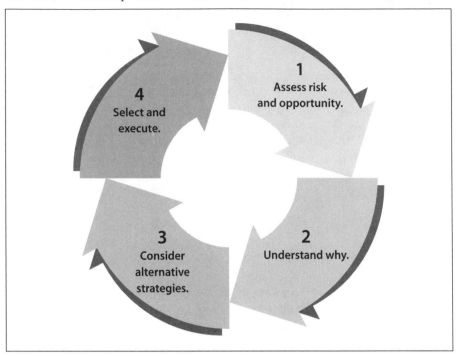

salespeople can become easily frustrated and feel powerless in the face of a gatekeeper's block.

> Guard against becoming your own gatekeeper. Often, by assuming there is a block, we limit ourselves by failing to ask the right questions.

## A FOUR-STEP PROCESS

Now that we've identified the problem, let's dive into the four-step process for dealing with gatekeepers. Like other elements of this process, this strategy is based on the methods successful salespeople practice by instinct. We've fashioned those methods into a reproducible system to help others achieve similar results. The four steps in the process are shown in Figure 9.1.

**Note of caution.** Before taking the first step toward dealing with gatekeepers, bear in mind that in today's selling environment, fewer people than ever can say "yes" to a value-oriented relationship with your company,

*"The harder you work, the harder it is to surrender."—Vince Lombardi*

You've worked hard to get to this point. You've got a good story to tell. Don't surrender lightly.

while more can say "no." The goal, therefore, is to find those senior managers who can say "yes" and to develop business relationships with them, while minimizing your vendor relationships with gatekeepers.

Also, remember that gatekeepers can be cagey. Like wooden targets on a police practice range, they can pop out of nowhere, forcing you to react. Unlike the crooks and bad guys on the range, however, gatekeepers do not wear masks or wave their guns menacingly. They're more subtle than that. But whether your contacts act hostile or friendly, if someone tries to block your path, you know you're dealing with a gatekeeper.

## Step 1. Assess the Risk and Opportunity

As we begin the four-step process for dealing with gatekeepers, remember the Woody Allen quotation: "Eighty percent of life is just showing up." At this stage, 80 percent of the opportunity is just thinking it through and continuing the effort. Remember the business executive who said that 90 to 95 percent of his reps walked away from opportunities when gatekeepers blocked them? Well, this is the point where you say, "I will not go quietly."

"I will not go quietly."

You're going to do more analysis. You're going to test yourself. You're asking, "Should I be taking this farther?" You'll compare the opportunities associated with challenging this block to the potential negative consequences. Merely by taking these steps, you are already going beyond the limits most sales reps impose on themselves.

Two questions.   The key to knowing whether to continue with an opportunity despite a block lies in asking yourself the following questions:

- What can I gain if I successfully convert or challenge the person who is blocking me?
- What are the consequences if I challenge the person who is blocking me and I am not successful?

The answers to these questions will help you build a business case for making this decision.

**Time for T-chart.** The next step is to create a T-chart with the answers to these questions on either side of the chart (see Figure 9.2). On one side of the chart's top, put a plus sign, and on the other side put a minus sign. Next, brainstorm all the opportunities and risks associated with challenging this block. On the plus, or opportunities, side write down all the potential benefits. These may include:

- Winning the business
- Increased sales
- Bonus money
- Recognition
- Commissions
- Reputation
- Development of a reference account
- Future opportunities for cross-selling
- Promotion
- Opportunities with other business units and companies
- Strengthening your overall value positioning with the company

On the negative, or risk, side write down all the possible negative consequences. These may include:

- Making the gatekeeper mad
- Losing the business (current and future)
- Damage to reputation
- Alienation of the gatekeeper who might then be out to get you
- Gatekeeper moving to another company and becoming an adversary there
- Personal credibility
- Additional selling time
- Opportunity costs

Again, these are just some of the minus factors you may consider.

We cannot stress enough how important it is to take out a piece of paper and write these answers down on an actual T-chart. As anyone who has taken a goal-setting seminar or class knows, a key to successful goal achievement is writing down your goals. The same is true here. In the five minutes it takes to write out the business case analysis, the answer typically becomes very clear.

FIGURE 9.2    T-chart

| *Pros* | *Cons* |
|---|---|
| *Revenue*<br>*Commission*<br>*Quota – 100% club*<br>*Recognition*<br>*Additional*<br>    *Opportunities* | *Reputation* |

> What are your risks and opportunities? Don't just think about it, T-chart it.

Now that you have your T-chart down on paper, you probably have a much better feel for whether the pluses outweigh the minuses. This will determine whether you decide to challenge the gatekeeper or accept the block. Either conclusion may be the correct course of action. Let's take a look at some of the scenarios you likely will encounter.

**Conditions of the block.** In some situations, you may be blocked but have nothing listed on the minus side of your T-chart. In that case, going forward is all upside with no drawbacks. This situation would probably arise if you were working on a new account where you have little or nothing to lose. In that case, such factors as opportunity for revenue, commission dollars, bonus, or recognition far outweigh any potential concerns associated with being blocked—particularly if you consider this customer a stretch opportunity anyway.

> *"I miss 100 percent of the shots I don't take."—Wayne Gretzky*

Other times, you may be blocked but have a significant established customer relationship you don't wish to jeopardize. In this case, the legitimate risks may well outweigh the potential upside, and you will probably accept the block (see Figure 9.3). Again, either conclusion may be correct; it's just important to go through the process to make sure you're arriving at the right course of action.

FIGURE 9.3   T-chart

| *Pros* | *Cons* |
|---|---|
| *Revenue* | *Loss of install base* |
| *Commission* | *Delay of key project* |
| *Recognition* | *Loss of revenue stream* |
| | *Loss of the account* |

The T-chart and business case analysis will help you determine whether to give an opportunity your best shot.

## Step 2. Understand the Gatekeeper's Motivation

Think about all the times you've run into a gatekeeper. Now ask yourself, "Why was I blocked?"

To figure out "What?" ask yourself "Why?"

Undoubtedly there have been many reasons. But answering this question is critical to the four-step process for dealing with gatekeepers. To determine the best strategy, you must first try to understand the gatekeeper's motivation. How many of these different gatekeeper motivations have you run into?

- *The gatekeeper doesn't want to lose control.* For any number of reasons, the gatekeeper fears losing control of the decision-making process, which may lead to diminished power and influence within his or her company. It could also result in a final decision that the gatekeeper doesn't agree with, especially if you're selling value while your competitors are just selling products. For this reason, many gatekeepers try to maintain tight control over their spheres of influence.
- *The gatekeeper feels threatened by your contact with others in the organization.* Often, a gatekeeper doesn't know how others within an organization might feel about you, your company, and your solutions. If these key players already harbor negative perceptions about you or your company or are unimpressed by your approach, the gatekeeper runs the risk of looking bad in colleagues' eyes.

- *The gatekeeper is just "doing their job."* In some cases, gatekeepers may feel their job is to protect the decision maker's time by blocking "unimportant" people and taking care of lower-level decisions. Executive secretaries and administrators often fill this role. Consider a less obvious case, like the situation we experienced where a manager wanted to "protect" his boss and ended up trying to shield him from us and our efforts. But once we broke through and the decision maker got on board, the gatekeeper became one of our best coaches.

- *The gatekeeper fears that you will make a bad impression.* It's possible that the gatekeeper thinks you'll fail if given an opportunity to be in front of the decision maker. In this scenario, the gatekeeper is staking his or her reputation on you and your performance, and a poor showing could make the gatekeeper look bad to upper-level management. As a result, the gatekeeper retains control by limiting your access.

- *The gatekeeper prefers the status quo.* Staying within an existing comfort zone is the simplest thing to do, especially for a gatekeeper whose motto is, "Don't rock the boat." A value-oriented decision might result in considerable change and additional work for the gatekeeper. The kind of people who avoid change at all costs make for formidable gatekeepers.

- *The gatekeeper doesn't understand the value you bring.* This is a rational situation. This gatekeeper may believe the competition has a superior solution or be uneducated about the value your company and solutions could provide.

> Like it or not, the reason most gatekeepers block you is because they want you to lose.

- *The gatekeeper wants you to lose.* It's quite possible that the gatekeeper simply wants you to lose and your competition to win. What if the gatekeeper's sister sells for your primary competitor? Chances are, no matter how good your people skills and relationship-building talents are, you'll never convert that hard-as-concrete block. Or perhaps the gatekeeper has been dealing with one of your competitors for years and has a terrific business relationship with them. Again, the gatekeeper may simply want to maintain this existing relationship. Or, unlikely as it may seem, maybe this particular gatekeeper just doesn't like you or your company.

For obvious reasons, many of these issues will strike an emotional chord with gatekeepers. In fact, emotions will frequently drive gatekeepers' decisions, not sound, rational business judgment. The most common emotion affecting gatekeepers' decisions is fear—fear of losing control, fear of creating more work, fear that you may make a poor impression, or fear that you might win when they want you to lose. Dealing with a gatekeeper may be a highly emotional situation.

### The rational versus irrational gatekeeper.

This brings us to the important distinction between a rational block and an irrational block. Let's say a gatekeeper is blocking you because she has been receiving tremendous service from a current supplier and feels good about the strong value-oriented business relationship that exists. In this case, she is being perfectly rational in blocking you. There are ways for you to deal with this situation. Perhaps you could win in another area and gain a foothold with this customer without threatening the relationship the gatekeeper has established with your competition.

Rational blocks can be dealt with through rational solutions. Irrational blocks, however, offer different challenges. What if the gatekeeper doesn't like your gender, your nationality, the color of your skin, or your religion? If you are unfortunate enough to encounter any kind of prejudice, you need to acknowledge that you're dealing with an irrational block and reevaluate your strategy accordingly.

Let's look at some examples of irrational blocks. What if you come across a gatekeeper who was once fired from the company you work for? Do you have any chance of converting that person and having him like you or your company? Probably not. What if this gatekeeper just doesn't like working with people your age? He either prefers older, more experienced people or younger, more energetic people (with Murphy's Law in effect, it will likely be whichever age you're not). Would you be able to convert this block? Not likely. Would it be worth investing your time to try? Again, probably not. Faced with an irrational block, you will generally be pressed to consider different strategies.

Sometimes, the block is emotional or irrational. It may not be worth the time to fix it.

Hopefully, you haven't found yourself in the situation one of our clients faced, dealing with a gatekeeper who was receiving illegal kickbacks from the competition. These situations are very emotionally charged and difficult to get around, because you're not willing to play the same game.

Now that you've taken the first two steps to dealing with gatekeepers— assessing the opportunity and understanding the gatekeeper's motivation— it's time to consider which strategies to apply to the different scenarios.

## Step 3. Consider Alternative Strategies

In step three, we have the opportunity to brainstorm a list of alternative strategies to deal with gatekeepers. Now it's particularly important to think outside the box. As we consider these various strategies, let's first go through the three potential gatekeeper scenarios you're likely to encounter:

1.  You are not actively blocked today.
2.  The threat of a block exists.
3.  You are actively blocked.

You may have already developed a set of favorite gatekeeper strategies. If so, that's great. Your previous experience and the lessons learned by peers and managers should always guide your decisions. Let's consider some different strategies for the first scenario.

**Scenario 1: You are not actively blocked.** If you are not actively blocked, now is the perfect time to start thinking about the possibility. By proactively dealing with a potential gatekeeper situation, we can anticipate future challenges and deal with them before they become too troublesome.

> *"If you are out of trouble, watch for danger."—Sophocles*

*Strategy 1. Get to the decision maker early.* Remember, the decision maker is the person who can say "yes" when everyone else says "no" and can say "no" when everyone else says "yes." By getting to and developing a relationship with this key executive, you've effectively neutralized almost any potential gatekeeper.

Think about times when you've had a solid relationship with senior-level management. Was anyone able to step between you and the decision maker? Probably not. That's because you had the opportunity to demonstrate the value of a business relationship between your company and the customer. This is the idea behind this strategy—get to the decision maker, establish the value of a business relationship with you and your company, and position yourself as a business resource.

If you can accomplish these goals, it will be virtually impossible for anyone to commoditize you or ensnare you in the Vendor Trap. Of course, this requires you to do a knockout job with the decision maker when you do get the opportunity. We'll talk more about that shortly.

*Strategy 2. Assume you can't be blocked*  By being assertive and assumptive, which means you assume you can't be blocked by any gatekeeper, you position yourself as a competent and confident sales professional. When you exude this confidence, it's difficult for anyone to try to block you.

Gatekeepers are often insecure—insecure about their role, their position, and their strength in the organization. When confronted by someone as secure, positive, and assumptive as you, gatekeepers may shy away and let you pass unhindered. You need to carry yourself in a way that communicates, "I can't be blocked. I sell value. I sell business solutions, and nobody can put me in a box. You can't commoditize me because you can't commoditize value." With gatekeepers, a little attitude goes a long way.

*Strategy 3. Identify potential gatekeepers ahead of time.*  In your research activities, try to determine who in the organization may benefit by blocking you and limiting your success. By proactively identifying future gatekeepers, you put yourself in a stronger position to utilize Strategy 4.

*Strategy 4. Avoid potential gatekeepers until the presentation is scheduled and presold.*  Ideally, you would like to gain access to the decision maker, schedule a business presentation meeting, and presell the meeting so that it can't or won't be canceled. Then, shortly before the presentation meeting, you can approach any potential gatekeepers and involve them in the process. By coming from a position of strength, with the presentation already scheduled, you are much more likely to get the gatekeeper on board with your solution.

In summary, if you're not actively blocked today, now is the best time to start thinking about your options and how to deal with any gatekeepers that may crop up. Too often, we take situations for granted and later regret that we didn't act sooner. Instead of being complacent, be assumptive and positive, assume you can't be blocked, and get to the decision maker. This is the best way to proceed when you're not actively blocked.

## Scenario 2. The threat of a block exists.  If you sense a gatekeeper situation looming on the horizon, consider the following strategies:

*Strategy 1. Don't assume you're blocked.*  How many of us have acted as our own worst gatekeeper, assuming that we're supposed to work with certain contacts even though no one has told us so? Don't fall into the trap of being your own gatekeeper.

*Strategy 2. Assume you can't or won't be blocked.*  As in Scenario 1, be positive and assumptive. Consider it your job and responsibility to sell the value of a business relationship with your company, one that can't be sold through normal product channels. Don't ask permission from potential gatekeepers; instead, use assumptive language like, "I must gain access to Brian Callaway, and I would appreciate your help." When you're positive and assertive, it's very difficult for others to block you.

*Strategy 3. Continue your research and work with your coach or coaches.* Leverage these relationships to understand the current threat you face. Is it real, or are you mistaken? Isolate the challenge so that you can generate some targeted solutions. You've built coach relationships for a reason—don't be afraid to leverage them.

*Strategy 4. Get to the decision maker early.* Yes, this strategy from Scenario 1 applies here as well. If you feel that the threat of a block exists, avoid that potential gatekeeper and get to the decision maker. Present the value of a business relationship between your two companies and develop that relationship. This may eliminate that potential block.

## Scenario 3. You are actively blocked.

We all know what this feels like. The words vary, but the feeling is always the same. You know you're blocked when someone says, "I make the decisions here," "Call me back in a few weeks," "I'm the only one you need to talk to in this organization," "Let me run that up the flagpole for you," or "The timing isn't right for your proposal." Whether it's said nicely and professionally or harshly and abruptly, the result is the same. The underlying message is, "You're a vendor, I'm in control, and we'll do things my way." This situation is tough for salespeople who sell value.

> Beyond Selling Value means acting differently than the gatekeeper wants you to.

Before considering which strategy to apply to the gatekeeper, it's important to determine why the gatekeeper is blocking you. Is his or her reason rational or irrational? Is it emotional? By thinking this through, you may come up with the appropriate strategy. Here are some key strategies for dealing with a gatekeeper when you're actively blocked:

*Strategy 1. Transform the gatekeeper into a coach.* If there is a best possible gatekeeper strategy, this is it. We'd like to turn every gatekeeper into a coach, and sometimes it's possible. To do so, finding the gatekeeper's win is critical. As we said before, a coach is someone who wants us to win and who wins when we win. What does the gatekeeper hope to accomplish, and how can you help? Show how a relationship with your company and your presentation to the decision maker will help solve the gatekeeper's issues, gain recognition for the gatekeeper, or make his or her job easier. By finding this win, you may turn the gatekeeper into a coach.

The following example, excerpted from an article in the *Globe and Mail*, illustrates the power of turning a gatekeeper into a coach:

### Scheme to Tap Lake's Big Chill Not Just a Pipe Dream
### By John Barber

Once considered a pipe dream and attacked by environmentalists as an irresponsible megaproject, an ambitious plan to cool downtown buildings with cold water drawn from the depths of Lake Ontario inched closer to reality last week.

Despite the environmental benefits of cooling buildings with inexpensive water as opposed to expensive electricity coupled with hazardous chlorofluorocarbons, the scheme was roundly attacked by local environmental groups when it was proposed two years ago.

Subsequently, *the committee charged with studying deep lake water cooling enlisted its opponents to help shape its strategy and, in the process, earned their support.*

With a broad-based consensus now formed in support of the concept, the City of Toronto last week officially gave its blessing and agreed to enlist the Metro government in helping to develop the massive new system, which carries an estimated price tag of $700 million.

Ideally, your relationship with gatekeepers will not be adversarial. As the City of Toronto learned, converting opponents into partners will often both resolve conflicts and deliver the best possible solution.

*Strategy 2. Involve the gatekeeper in the process.*   Depending on the style of the individual gatekeeper, involving them may be an effective strategy. If the gatekeeper is very outspoken and aggressive, this strategy is probably not appropriate. But for typical gatekeepers, involving them in the process is often more powerful than asking for their permission to execute the process.

For instance, try inviting the gatekeeper to review the business presentation you'll be making to the decision maker. Use wording such as, "George, I'll be making the presentation to Mr. Spacely, and frankly, it would be much more on target with the insights you might share. Would you mind reviewing my presentation?"

Another effective method is to schedule a research call with a gatekeeper just to involve him or her in the process. This often works because many gatekeepers see their relationship to suppliers in the same simplistic terms in which Tarzan viewed Jane: "Me gatekeeper; you vendor." As a result, both parties wind up assuming these roles, doing the Vendor Trap dance. But by using this process, it's sometimes possible to introduce a new paradigm to the relationship and break out of those rigid roles. That's what happened for a client of ours, Becky Igo, an insurance industry rep who was selling to a large bank. Here's how she tells the story:

> I was trying to gain access to an executive vice president to make a business presentation, but I knew I had to deal with an evaluator who stood in my way. This gatekeeper had a fair amount of influence on the decision maker, so I decided to try to leverage the strategy of involving the gatekeeper. I already knew this woman pretty well, so I conducted a research call with her and began the meeting with some high-impact questions.
>
> My philosophy was, "Let me treat this gatekeeper like she's not used to being treated." I knew she was used to being looked upon by other vendors as a gatekeeper. So I did the opposite, involving her in the process and going beyond the usual product questions she was used to fielding.
>
> Relatively soon after we began, I could tell that she was getting really involved in the process and excited. She said that she had never had anyone come in and call on her and ask questions like that before. Then she went on and voluntarily gave me some great coaching on how to gain access to the decision maker. I wound up presenting to her boss and closing on an opportunity that beforehand had been totally unavailable to me.

No, you won't be able to convert your gatekeepers into coaches every time, but Becky's experience shows that you can sometimes leverage this strategy to achieve results you could never expect from tying yourself to traditional gatekeeper-vendor roles.

Another possibility is to jointly include the gatekeeper as you conduct research calls. This strategy worked for a client of ours selling in the high-tech sector. He came face-to-face with a gatekeeper, who was blocking him from conducting any research meetings. The gatekeeper apparently feared that the rep was going to try to sell on the research calls.

To involve the gatekeeper in the process and reassure him, the rep invited the gatekeeper to join in on the calls. The rep promised not to do any selling and that his only goal was to learn more about the company's business and develop a more effective business solution. The gatekeeper agreed, attending the first of three scheduled calls. After the first, however, he expressed admiration for what the rep was doing and said he didn't feel the need to attend the next two research meetings. By participating in the process, the gatekeeper did a 180-degree turnaround, going from opponent to advocate for what the rep was trying to accomplish.

*Strategy 3. Neutralize the gatekeeper.* Sometimes gatekeepers aren't as powerful as you think. Frequently, you can find ways to neutralize a gatekeeper. One method is to ask a coach or the decision maker (assuming you have the relationship to do so) to intervene on your behalf. By using a coach who has some influence over the gatekeeper or who has the confidence of the decision maker, you can frequently neutralize the block and proceed with your strategy.

*Strategy 4. Sidestep the block.* Again, when gatekeepers are not as powerful as they initially seem, you may be able to sidestep them with ease. Move outside the area they control and begin doing your research, developing relationships in related departments or divisions. Begin to build your coach network outside their areas of influence.

*Strategy 5. Win in another area.* When you're faced with a strong gatekeeper, a great strategy is often to win in another related organization and bring your success story to the appropriate decision maker, leveraging your win. This can often be done in the context of a cross-selling strategy, where you leverage executive relationships across organizational lines.

*Strategy 6. Be persistent.* Often you can simply wear down a block, and with a reasonably rational gatekeeper, this strategy may be sound. You may be familiar with the "rule of 40"—that no one can say no to you 40 times. We hope you won't have to face 39 nos with every opportunity before you get to yes. But be persistent—it pays off.

*Strategy 7. Utilize someone else in your company.* Often, you can leverage your manager or a senior-level executive at your company to gain access to like-ranked executives in the customer's organization. This way, you're not positioned as the "bad guy." Instead, you're merely following direction from above. Sometimes this strategy is a bit transparent, but it can shield you from a gatekeeper's anger.

An interesting variation on this theme was carried out by a client who found his path to the decision maker, a corporate VP of finance, blocked by the company's comptroller. Approaching the comptroller, the rep said, "This opportunity is very important to our organization, and it makes sense for me to work with you to develop a strategy for presenting to the VP of finance. Otherwise, my manager will just call on the VP himself. But I would much rather work with you, and you probably would, too, rather than to be taken out of the loop." In some cases, just the suggestion that you will introduce more senior-level people into the process can overcome a gatekeeper's objection.

*Strategy 8. Leverage your company direction or mandate.*  Think about it this way: your job is to sell value and to provide business solutions to your customers. Whatever you sell, your success comes down to how well you can affect your customer's business.

If you think about your job this way, you can leverage what your own organization expects from you. You can say to a gatekeeper, "My job is to sell business solutions to my customers. I need to understand their business and proactively present opportunities to address business issues and concerns. My company evaluates and pays me based on how well I deal with people at different levels of the customer's organization. I also need to understand my customers' businesses, their issues, their objectives, and their challenges. With this for a directive, it's difficult for me simply to respond to a bid."

By saying this, you communicate clearly and in a very personal way that your job, reputation, and success are on the line, determined by how well you deal with all levels in the customer's organization.

*Strategy 9. Leverage your coach.*  In dealing with a gatekeeper, there are many ways to leverage coach relationships. As mentioned above, you might be able to ask the coach to intercede on your behalf and neutralize the gatekeeper. In addition, you can often involve the coach by explaining the situation and soliciting his or her insight and advice. In many cases, you'll find that coaches have the best ideas and strategies to help you move forward.

*Strategy 10. Create a personal meeting with the decision maker.*  You can do this in many ways. For instance, you might create an event like a golf outing or a boat cruise or attend an association meeting or some other function where you know the decision maker will be present. Given the opportunity to talk to a decision maker, you may find an area of common interest and create for yourself an obligation to follow up with additional ideas, thoughts, or information.

Let's say you're in an association meeting with the decision maker, talking about some of the new quality developments in your industry. The decision maker shows interest in what your company is doing around these changes, and you offer to provide follow-up information. You then gather the answers and appropriate information, schedule a presentation meeting with the decision maker, and inform the gatekeeper of this impending meeting. This is your opportunity to leverage the commitment you made to the decision maker while in a different personal setting.

*Strategy 11. Accept the block.*   Based on your T-chart and business case analysis, sometimes the appropriate strategy is to accept the block. This will be the case if the existing relationship you are risking is greater than the potential opportunity. If so, accept the block and move on. Come back and revisit the opportunity at a later date. But when you do come back, bring a sound business case analysis with you. In other circumstances, you may decide to walk away because an opportunity presents more work for you than it's worth. In that situation, you should consider focusing your efforts elsewhere.

*Strategy 12. Go over or around the block.*   Of all the different strategies for dealing with gatekeepers, this is probably the most emotionally difficult. You may be asking yourself, "Do I really want to go over a gatekeeper's head? Won't he be angry? Won't he try to stab me in the back later?" or "What if she's mad at me?" As we discussed earlier, gatekeepers often have distinct motivations, and one of those motivations may be that they want to see you lose. If that's the case, you need not be concerned with the gatekeeper's feelings.

Think about it this way: gatekeepers want to control your strategy and may want you to lose. At best, they want to limit your effectiveness by trying to do your selling job for you. If the other strategies don't seem appropriate and you still need to get to decision makers, going over or around the gatekeeper may be the best alternative.

Now, you want to do this professionally and ethically, with good communication, but you still want to do it. And you need to make it personal. Remember that the gatekeeper wants to block you. She wants to keep you from reaching your objectives. You should take this personally and respond by challenging the block, gaining access to the decision maker, and showing the value of a business relationship between your two companies. We'll illustrate this process later in the chapter with two examples from our case files.

> Remember, the gatekeeper wants to block you. Take it personally.

Salespeople often agonize over these situations and worry about how the gatekeeper will react. We recently found ourselves in a situation where we were blocked by a gatekeeper, knew we needed to elevate our access to his boss, and were worried about the gatekeeper's reaction. As we learned in retrospect, he wasn't angry at all—in fact, he didn't have the time to worry about it.

These are some of the best strategies for dealing with gatekeepers. Of course, there are many others. Depending on the specific scenario you face, one or more of the strategies listed here should prove highly effective.

## Step 4. Select and Execute the Right Strategy

Each gatekeeper scenario you face is unique and deserves special consideration. As you use this four-step process, you assess the opportunity, guess at what the gatekeeper's motivation might be, brainstorm different alternative situations that might be appropriate, and then select and execute the right strategy. These steps assume that it is essential not to ignore gatekeepers. The longer you put off dealing with a gatekeeper, the more difficult you will find gaining access to the decision maker. By doing nothing, you are choosing an alternative strategy. You are accepting that you'll remain shut out from access to higher levels in the account.

One additional note to consider: salespeople often act as their own most powerful gatekeepers. We get so concerned that our primary contact will become angry if we talk to others within a target organization, that we don't even try. In most cases, these contacts don't mind. Instead, out of a sense of misplaced loyalty or a disproportionate respect for the customer's reporting channels, we assume this burden unnecessarily and block ourselves. Even though the contact or contacts haven't told us not to talk to anyone else, we act as if they have. Remember apologizing for approaching the decision maker is much easier if you were never told not to.

## FINAL THOUGHTS

Here are some additional points to consider when selecting your strategy and executing it.

- *Solicit insight and advice.* Review the scenario with your peers, managers, and other sales professionals. Share with them the process you've gone through, and ask for their insights regarding your strategy.
- *Utilize your coaches.* Leverage these critical relationships. Review your process with them. Present the alternative strategies you've considered, and ask for their reactions and advice.
- *Implement your strategy by being strong, assertive, and assumptive.* A strong stance will make it hard for anyone to block you.
- *Consider the timing of your strategy.* Will any additional factors make your strategy less effective? Are there other operational or organizational priorities that may cloud the issue?

- *Develop a Plan B.* If your primary strategy doesn't work and, for example, all of your attempts to neutralize or develop a gatekeeper into a coach don't work, you need to create and execute another strategy.
- *Emphasize professionalism.* Regardless of your strategy, be professional and clear in your communication. Timing is critical of course, but when the time is right, you may consider informing the gatekeeper of your strategy.

*"Don't ever slam the door; you might want to go back."—Don Herold*

A key question you have to face is, "Do I communicate my strategy to the gatekeeper?" In some cases it makes sense, such as when:

- You have your presentation presold.
- The gatekeeper isn't powerful enough to cancel your meeting.
- You feel that by involving the gatekeeper, you may be able to get him or her on board.

In other cases, you should avoid gatekeepers entirely and keep them out of the loop on your strategy, such as when they are powerful enough to have your meeting canceled or they may use your strategy against you by helping to formulate your competitor's strategy.

Remember, you miss 100 percent of the shots you don't take.

This was the motivating concern for the executive we discussed earlier. His people were not taking any shots. They were walking away just because a gatekeeper told them to and, as a result, were missing out on significant opportunities. Remember, by executing this four-step process, you are doing more than the vast majority of your competitors.

In the words of Dave Fraser, an executive with IBM Canada, "We don't have a choice. We have to sell value. A going-out-of-business-strategy for us is to ignore the fact that gatekeepers don't buy value. We have to take it personally every time."

This subject reinforces something we all know and believe—that both art and science are involved in selling effectively. The science is having a process to follow and some good ideas to implement. The art is leveraging your experience and using the process appropriately in each situation.

# CASES IN POINT

To give you some idea how a few of our clients dealing with flesh-and-blood gatekeepers have handled them, we've included the following three gatekeeper case studies from our files.

## Gatekeeper Case Study #326B: "The Case of the Obstinate AVP"

Scenario Overview:

- Industry: High-tech
- Product: Communications systems
- Gatekeeper title: Assistant Vice President - Information Systems
- Decision maker title: Executive Vice President
- Block status: Severe

One of our clients faced a difficult challenge when he sought to expand the scope of his relationship with an existing customer. Bear in mind that this sales rep was on 100 percent commission and that he was a very ethical salesperson wanting the best possible solution for his customer. He and this customer had already established an outstanding relationship in one product area. He had four additional product families to offer and felt they could really make a difference.

He knew he had an outstanding opportunity to continue the impact of this customer's business, so he approached the assistant vice president, with whom he worked closely. He explained that he believed an opportunity existed to increase the benefits to both organizations by expanding the scope of the relationship.

Following the process, the rep had constructed an organizational chart indicating the other key players he would need to contact in the account. He mentioned to his contact that he needed to approach other AVPs to determine the appropriate fit. At this suggestion, the AVP bristled, responding with, "The timing's not right." The rep turned around and asked many of the same questions that you would ask, including, "Why is the timing not right?" and "What can I do to help improve the timing?" To these questions, however, he received curt, unhelpful replies.

Although he was disappointed, the rep nonetheless decided to wait until the timing improved. He recognized the value of the existing relationship with the customer, which was significant. As he did his T-chart, he came to the conclusion that it was worth it for him to wait and work with the AVP to determine when the timing might be better. He recognized the strong business relationship but never lost sight of the significant potential opportunities he would have to affect the customer's business—and also to pocket the appropriate commissions.

After a three-month delay, the rep approached the AVP again. After reviewing the idea, the AVP offered the same objection: "The timing's not right." The rep asked the same follow-up questions but, receiving the same responses, walked away and decided to wait some more. A few weeks later, he approached the AVP for a third time. Following the third "The timing's not right," the rep decided to change his strategy.

Questions:

- What would you do if you were this rep?
- Why do you think the gatekeeper was blocking the rep?
- From the information given, what do you think the rep's T-chart looked like?

**The path forward.**  After doing the initial T-chart, the rep decided to accept the block until the timing might be more appropriate. But after three times, he became convinced that there was more to the story than this gatekeeper was letting on. After several months, the rep faced a decision—either live with the block, or go over the AVP's head. What did you say the rep should do? He decided to go for it. He knew he needed to gain access to the true, senior-level decision maker, so he wrote a high-impact Access Letter to the AVP's boss, the executive vice president. The EVP was the decision maker, with five AVPs reporting to him. The rep's strategy was to get to the decision maker, develop a business relationship, and hope that he could minimize the damage to the current relationship.

In reviewing his T-chart, the rep determined that his solution had become too critical to the customer's organization for the AVP to consider deinstalling it. The rep decided that the worst thing that could happen was that they could have him removed from the account. In reality, the way things stood, he wasn't acting in the best interest of his customer or his company anyway, so that alternative didn't seem so bad.

Before writing the Access Letter to the EVP, the rep refreshed his research. Then he wrote the letter, reviewed it with a coach, and presold the letter with the decision maker's administrator. The day the letter was sent, the rep met once more with the AVP. Yet again the AVP responded to the idea of expanding the relationship between the two companies with, "Absolutely not. It's not appropriate and the timing is wrong."

At this point, the rep made his intentions clear, saying he valued the existing business relationship but felt strongly that both companies could benefit from an expanded relationship. He shared that, given this belief, he had written a letter to the EVP requesting the opportunity to make a brief, professional business presentation. As he said this, he stressed the important role the AVP had played in the success of the relationship and voiced a commitment to highlight this as part of the presentation. In closing, the rep made it clear that he would give the AVP credit for the relationship's success. You can imagine how thick the air in the office must have been during this intense conversation. In fact, the rep left the meeting not knowing whether the gatekeeper was accepting of, indifferent to, or furious at the news.

The Access Letter worked beautifully (see Appendix B for a sample letter) and the decision maker agreed to host the presentation. The rep executed the rest of the process by finalizing his research, drafting a presentation, reviewing it with a coach, and rehearsing it. When he arrived, ready to present, he found that all five AVPs were in the conference room, including the gatekeeper. At the start of the presentation, the gatekeeper exhibited negative body language, but the rep pressed on, delivering an outstanding presentation. By the close of the presentation, the AVP had become a visible advocate and supporter. When faced with the decision either to be a gatekeeper or to take credit for the success of the existing relationship, he chose the latter. He saw the opportunity, executed a 180-degree turnaround, and became an outstanding coach.

**Results.**  This strategy worked very well. The rep gained access to the decision maker, neutralized the gatekeeper, and in the process succeeded in turning the gatekeeper into a coach. More importantly, he was able to expand the business relationship from one product family to three, strengthen his overall value both to the customer and to his own company, and take home a healthy commission as a reward.

**The moral of the story.**  In reviewing this situation, it's easy to respect what this rep accomplished. Note the following critical lessons from the way this rep faced an imposing gatekeeper challenge:

- *He didn't accept the block blindly.* Instead, he formulated a business case analysis and decided that his first appropriate strategy was to accept the block and wait for a more advantageous time.
- *He revised his strategy based on changing conditions.* When he saw that his original strategy wasn't effective, he reassessed the situation and picked a new strategy.
- *He was professional and persistent.* He repeatedly asked for the opportunity and dug deeper whenever the gatekeeper said no.
- *He continually emphasized the gatekeeper's potential win.* Each time he discussed the opportunity to strengthen and expand the relationship, he committed to positioning the strength of the gatekeeper and giving the gatekeeper credit for the current success.

- *He communicated effectively and professionally.* Even after he made the difficult decision to send an Access Letter to the EVP, he communicated his decision to the AVP—intelligently. He waited until the letter had been sent and presold so as not to compromise its potential success.
- *He didn't take no for an answer.* In this case, recognizing the no wasn't easy. Here was a strong account with a contact who should have been positive and excited about expanding the relationship between the two companies, and yet the answer was still no. It was a veiled no, but a no nonetheless. The rep recognized this and didn't take no for an answer.

By the way, did you consider the gatekeeper's motivation in this example? What do you think it was? In fact, the gatekeeper was one of five direct reports to the EVP. He was achieving his objectives, and the rep and the rep's company were partially responsible for his success. In essence, he considered the relationship with this rep a part of his competitive advantage that he didn't want to share with anyone else. As is often the case, to work hard for the good of your client and your employer, you must challenge these gatekeeper scenarios.

## Gatekeeper Case Study #219A: "The Power of Conversion"

Scenario Overview:

- Industry: Transportation
- Product: Consulting
- Gatekeeper title: Purchasing Manager
- Decision maker title: Vice President
- Block status: Moderate

When faced with gatekeepers, many of our clients feel that the best way to deal with the challenge is to convert that gatekeeper into a coach. If achievable, this is clearly a positive outcome.

One client we worked with in the transportation industry faced a difficult gatekeeper who did not support the rep's desire to gain access to senior-level management. Although the sales rep wasn't sure whether the gatekeeper had the power to block him, he did know that the gatekeeper could make his life miserable if the situation wasn't handled well.

**The path forward.** After creating a T-chart, the rep determined that the opportunity definitely warranted additional effort. He asked himself, "Why is the gatekeeper blocking me?" His best guess was that the gatekeeper was worried that his credibility would be damaged if the rep presented poorly to senior-level management. As a result, the rep decided to include the gate-keeper in the process. This he accomplished in two ways. First, he conducted a research meeting with the gatekeeper. This research meeting was one of several, and the rep made it clear that he would be doing additional research with others in the organization. Second, when he scheduled a presentation with the senior-level decision maker, the rep approached the gatekeeper and said, "As we prepare for our upcoming presentation"—to which the gatekeeper was invited—"I realize that I would really benefit from some additional coaching. I feel that if you would review my presentation, it would be much more appropriate and on target."

The rep then conducted a typical coach review of a presentation with the gatekeeper, giving the gatekeeper the opportunity to have some influence and put his own stamp of approval on the presentation. The review session also supplied the gatekeeper with an opportunity to see that this wasn't a typical product pitch—that the sales rep's organization was going to deliver a highly polished, professional presentation to the decision maker. Not only did this approach eliminate the gatekeeper's risk, it also helped the gate-keeper see that if the presentation went well, it could strengthen his credibility within his own company. This is exactly what happened, and the gatekeeper became one of the rep's strongest advocates within the customer's organization.

## Gatekeeper Case Study #498D: "Permanent Vacation"

Scenario Overview:

- Industry: High-tech
- Product: Database management services
- Gatekeeper title: Assistant Vice President - Information Systems
- Decision maker title: Chief Financial Officer
- Block status: Most severe

Another client in the IT business faced a similar challenge in an opportunity with a multinational consumer goods corporation. In this case, his selling cycle lasted about six months and required frequent meetings with product evaluators, users, and all types of gatekeepers. The sales rep had no established relationship with the ultimate decision maker—the CFO—and was communicating primarily with the company's VP for information services.

In the midst of the sales cycle, the VP abruptly, with no explanation, cut short the sales cycle, telling the rep to, "Get the hell out." This was an unexpected turn of events, and the VP gave no reason for his actions. Assessing the situation, the rep could only conclude that the VP was a jerk who felt compelled to put up an irrational block.

**The path forward.**   After creating a T-chart, the rep decided that the potential benefits of the opportunity outweighed the risks. Circumventing the VP-IS, the rep conducted four research meetings with disparate people in the organization. While the first three went reasonably well, the fourth represented a real breakthrough in the opportunity. This contact became a valuable coach, and even without knowing the specifics of the proposed solution, helped the rep gain access to the CFO. Later the rep found out that the coach had been waiting for a proposed solution that the VP-IS hadn't been delivering on.

With a presentation scheduled, the rep asked the CFO for a list of appropriate attendees. Notably, the CFO asked that the VP-IS not attend. Coincidentally, the VP-IS was soon leaving on a fishing vacation, so the rep took this opportunity to schedule the meeting.

As expected, the presentation went well. The CFO was impressed with the rep's knowledge of the corporation's business and what the company could accomplish with a new information system. At the close of the meeting, the rep obtained the go-ahead on all his proposed action steps and the guarantee of continued access to the decision maker.

In a few days, the VP-IS returned from vacation and called the sales rep in to see him. Predictably, the VP chewed him out, screaming, "I'm trying to build a highway here. When I need a jackhammer, I'll call you!" Anticipating the VP's anger, the rep calmly replied, "When you need a jackhammer, don't call me. I don't sell jackhammers. I help my clients build highways."

Shortly thereafter, the VP-IS was fired, eliminating the only remaining obstacle to the development of a mutually rewarding business relationship between the two organizations.

# CONCLUSION

Despite what most salespeople think, gatekeepers do serve an important function. When an organization needs to make a purchase, gatekeepers are diligent about finding the product or service with the most appropriate specifications, the best service plan, and the lowest price. In addition, gatekeepers safeguard the valuable time of upper-level executives who can't afford to assess the offerings of every vendor who walks in the door.

But you're not just any vendor, and you don't merely sell a product. Because you sell business solutions and long-term business relationships, you are worthy of requesting some of that decision maker's precious time. In some cases, you will be able to convince gatekeepers that the decision maker will want to meet with you. Others will never see the light. In either case, you must resist gatekeeper blocks. This four-step process will help you accomplish that goal and contribute to your increased success.

> *"Never let the fear of striking out get in your way."—Babe Ruth*

Remember, when you're positive and assertive, it's very difficult for anyone to block you.

# The Power of
# PRESENTATION

On any given workday, millions of presentations are delivered. That's a lot of presenting. Frequently, the recipients of these presentations are senior-level executives. Today's business executives spend an average of 80 to 85 percent of their working time in meetings. This deluge of meetings and presentations represents a real challenge for sales professionals trying to break out of the vendor-trapped pack and differentiate themselves from the competition.

> *"Do not follow where the path may lead. Go instead where there is no path and leave a trail."—Unknown*
>
> The business presentation will provide you with a visible opportunity to blaze your own trail and break out of the vendor pack.

Yet this is precisely why we say that your business presentation is the single most important event in the sales cycle. Here you make your case to the decision maker—not that your products or services are better or priced lower than anyone else's—but that you're a capable, polished, insightful professional and a potentially powerful business resource.

This business presentation is a high-impact strategy. It has to be, because getting in front of the decision maker once is not enough. The key is to be so good that you get invited back, again and again.

## PRESENTATION PLUSES

Let's take a closer look at some of the advantages the business presentation offers and why it's so powerful.

The first advantage of the business presentation is inherent in the title—to establish the basis for a *business relationship* versus that of a vendor or supplier.

*"The best way to predict the future . . . is to create it."—Unknown*

Next, the business presentation is *flexible*. It can be used in many different selling environments, from closing a deal on the spot to moving a strategic opportunity forward to managing and expanding current customer relationships.

This presentation is also valuable because it helps establish an *objective-driven* atmosphere, designed to close on agreed-upon action steps. Everyone who walks out of this meeting should understand precisely how the relationship should move forward.

This presentation also *differentiates* you from competing sales reps, who typically conduct discussions or present facts and figures about their business instead of talking about the customer's business. After you've begun making high-impact business presentations, the way you do business and the way you sell to your customers will become one of your strongest selling points.

Unquestionably, this type of presentation delivers an impression of *professionalism*. By allowing you to set the tone and control the direction of the meeting, you gain a functional advantage over your competitors, who are busy conducting discussions or fumbling through product demos.

Understanding that most decision makers have dozens of plates spinning at once, when you stand up and present this way, you establish your company and your solution as a *priority* in the customer's mind. This presentation effectively elevates the priority of your project.

Another benefit is that the business presentation acts as a form of *qualification*. At the end of this presentation, you will know whether this account is worth spending any more time on. Honestly, what better way to qualify an opportunity than presenting to the decision maker as early in the process as possible?

Finally, another reason to use this style of presentation is to make an impression that nearly guarantees your *continued access* to senior-level management. As we said, it's not good enough to get there once; you have to be so good that you get invited back.

Beyond Selling Value means that a presentation to senior-level management is not an alternative strategy or a backup strategy—it's central to the primary strategy. The presentation isn't something you do when nothing else works or when you can't close a deal any other way.

In this section, we'll focus on three critical elements of the presentation process:

1. How to prepare for your presentation and manage the discussion that follows
2. How to gain priority and commitment from the decision maker
3. The value of continuing to apply this selling process to your accounts

As you move forward with the sales process and compile your research into a high-impact business presentation, take a moment to sympathize with those hard working, upper-level executives as they sit through meeting after meeting, day in and day out. Commit yourself to standing up and delivering a presentation that's unlike so many they see, a presentation that offers genuine solutions to the issues that keep the decision maker up at night; a presentation that drives the type of experience Andy Ayers, Regional Manager, and Kevin Martchek, Account Manager, with pharmaceutical giant Eli Lilly, had when they presented to the CEO of a large hospital system. Here's how Andy describes that meeting:

> We had been calling on this health system for about nine months, and we had developed some mid-level relationships that were pretty strong. One of the relationships was with a vice president of the health system. Through his relationship with this VP, Kevin had arranged an appointment with the CEO of the entire health system. We wanted to talk about the bigger picture things we could be doing across the multiple hospitals they owned instead of just each individual hospital. We viewed this as a critical relationship to build with someone who had a hand in the entire organization.
>
> Having just been exposed to the IMPAX® process, Kevin decided to apply it to this opportunity. In preparation for the meeting, Kevin conducted his research with a broad base of people—in fact, he even reached out to a former CEO of a different hospital, who was now doing consulting work with other hospitals. This consultant knew the decision maker Kevin would be meeting with and provided some valuable additional background. The portrait of the CEO that emerged from his research was that this was a real bottom-line guy, known for his reluctance to meet with people and develop relationships. Some people even said, "Are you sure you want to meet with this guy?"
>
> But we knew we had to get to him to move our relationship forward, so we went ahead. On the morning of the meeting, as the CEO came into the room for the presentation, he looked a little perplexed. It became apparent that he had expected a discussion and he didn't seem too pleased that this was going to be a presentation.

But as Kevin got into his business presentation and started talking about the customer's critical issues, the CEO changed his tune quickly and became very excited. He even stopped Kevin after about ten minutes and said, "You understand our organization better than the employees who work here. Would you be available to come to one of our employee meetings? I'd really like to talk about how a supplier of ours knows our business better than we do."

At that point, we all sort of exhaled in relief. Kevin continued and succeeded in impressing the CEO so much that during the dialogue after the presentation he said, "It's just a no-brainer for us to start working together on these two critical areas." So at the end of the meeting, Kevin asked, "How would you like me to follow up with you?" and the CEO responded by saying, "I'd like to meet quarterly with you to address these items and the business relationship."

At that point, the VP, who had helped set up the meeting, stepped in and asked him, "Are you sure you want to do that? You don't meet with anyone quarterly—this was just supposed to be a one-time meeting." The idea of meeting with a "vendor" on a quarterly basis was so out of character, that she clearly was trying to give him an opportunity to think about what he was saying and back out.

But he said, "No, anyone who knows this much about our organization—we need to be meeting with them quarterly."

Two weeks later, Kevin received a letter from the CEO saying, "I really want to make sure we're working together on these two issues. If there's anything that I need to do, let me know. I look forward to our next meeting."

Without this presentation, I would have given us about a 10 percent chance of having any projects develop or anything substantial come out of the meeting besides just getting to meet with someone at that high level. I would have been happy if he had said, "Hey, here are the names of a couple of people in our organization you should be meeting with." I certainly didn't expect that he would take a personal interest in the relationship.

# CHAPTER TEN

# Your Moment in the Sun
## THE BUSINESS PRESENTATION

As the premise below underscores, no other element in the sales process is as important as your meeting with the decision maker and convincing him or her of the value of a business relationship with you. Those of your competitors who even make it in to see the decision maker may prefer just to sit down and have a chat or a discussion. Many people—not just salespeople—feel uncomfortable standing in front of a group and delivering a presentation.

> *"In the middle of difficulty lies opportunity."—Albert Einstein*

In his best-selling book *Seinlanguage,* comedian Jerry Seinfeld noted a peculiar aspect of this fear. He said: "According to most studies, people's number one fear is public speaking. Number two is death. Death is number two? Does that seem right? To the average person, that means that if they have to go to a funeral, they'd be better off in the casket than giving the eulogy."

But you don't need to be afraid to present. You've got the best information, you've built up a network of great coaches, you've handled the gatekeepers who tried to block you, and you're ready to put together a killer presentation that blows away the decision maker. There's no need to be talking about eulogies at all.

But we're focusing on the negatives. Let's think for a minute about the positives. By now, you've had a chance to do your research and follow the 95-5 rule. You're fully prepared, and the time has come to present. Here's a phenomenal opportunity to have some fun and really shine. Imagine delivering a presentation and hearing these comments made by executive-level decision makers after business presentations:

- "I could take these slides and put them into my own presentations. I'm sold on this—just tell me what you want to do."

- "You know more about the company than we do. May I use this presentation to give to my chairman?"
- "Yours is the kind of company we like to do business with."
- "It's really nice to be treated like a customer."
- "This is the best presentation I've seen a supplier make. Why wouldn't we want to do business together?"
- "This is the best presentation I've ever seen about our company. I've been CEO for six months, and I haven't been able to find this type of information. I want this presentation to be used in our new employee orientation session."

## PREMISES, PREMISES

Before we jump in, however, let's step back for a moment to review the six core premises we talked about in Chapter 2. They are:

1. Senior-level management is more likely to buy from or form a relationship with you because of what you know about them and their business concerns than because of what they know about your company and your products and services.
2. No single event in the process is as important as a meeting with the decision maker.
3. You only get one chance to make a good first impression, especially with senior-level management.
4. Early and continued access to the decision maker who gives the final approval is critical to your success. You must be good enough to be invited back.
5. For effective positioning, the power of a presentation exceeds the power of a product demonstration or a discussion.
6. You need to prove the business fit before you prove the product fit.

These premises form the foundation of the entire process and should be in the front of your mind as you move ahead into the presentation stage of the sales cycle.

## PRESENT AND ACCOUNTED FOR

So what does the business presentation process involve? In this chapter, we'll take you through each of the following steps:

- Developing your presentation draft
- Preselling the presentation

- Reviewing the draft with your coaches
- Rehearsing the presentation
- Managing the presentation logistics
- Delivering your presentation effectively and successfully
- Following up the presentation

Okay, that's the big picture. Now let's refocus on the matter before us and get our hands dirty drafting your presentation.

## GET YOUR ACT TOGETHER: Developing the Presentation

While gathering your data and conducting research meetings, you probably began thinking about the presentation you planned to make to the decision maker. You've covered a lot of ground and built a strong understanding about this customer. You're also probably pretty pumped up about the match between your company and this customer. That's great! Good for you. But there's still more work to do. Now is the time to channel that enthusiasm and information into a high-impact business presentation. So let's roll up our sleeves and get tactical.

As you begin to develop your presentation, here are three critical points to keep in mind.

1. *What do you want to accomplish in the presentation?* Begin with the end in mind. Once you have concluded your presentation, what action will you want the decision maker to take? By answering this question, you begin to outline the Action Steps page that will close your presentation.
2. *What have you learned about the account?* What makes this account unique? What critical business factors drive its future success? What insider perspective have you gained? What keeps the decision maker awake at night?
3. *What is the business fit between your two companies?* You need to make sure you have a firm understanding of the business fit and can explain it so that it will be clear when you present to the decision maker.

Remember, when you're drafting the presentation, always begin with the end in mind.

## What's in a Presentation?

To help you develop your own presentation, let's first go over the elements of a typical presentation. They are:

- Cover page
- Objectives
- Agenda
- Customer business overview
- Your company overview
- Business fit
- Action steps/timetable

As we've mentioned, you can use the presentation to support a number of business objectives. For the example below, we're going to outline a conceptual business presentation where your objective is to "move the ball forward" with an important prospect, building towards a specific solution presentation.

This same type of conceptual presentation can be used with an executive at an existing customer.

To the best of our ability, the sample pages that follow are generic and applicable to any such presentation. For those that could not be generic, we have used pages from an actual presentation a client of ours conducted at a large financial services organization. The rep's objective was to gain conceptual buy-in from the senior-level decision maker to a potential business relationship *before* he put in the effort to prove the product fit.

After the examples, we'll discuss minor adjustments you can make to this template for presentations where the objectives are slightly different. With that in mind, let's go through the presentation page by page.

**Page 1: Cover Page.**  The cover page should prominently feature the customer's logo with a phrase like "A Business Presentation" or "A Business Relationship Presentation." In the lower right corner, include a note saying, "Presented by [your company]" with your logo. (See Figure 10.1)

**Page 2: Presentation Objectives.**  The second page lists three typical objectives you might have for the presentation. First, confirmation of your understanding of the customer's business. Second, a statement of your company's ability to get the job done. Third, a statement that you want to do business with the customer. Depending on your existing relationship, you may modify the third objective to read, "To initiate/develop/expand/strengthen our business relationship." (See Figure 10.2)

FIGURE 10.1    Cover Page

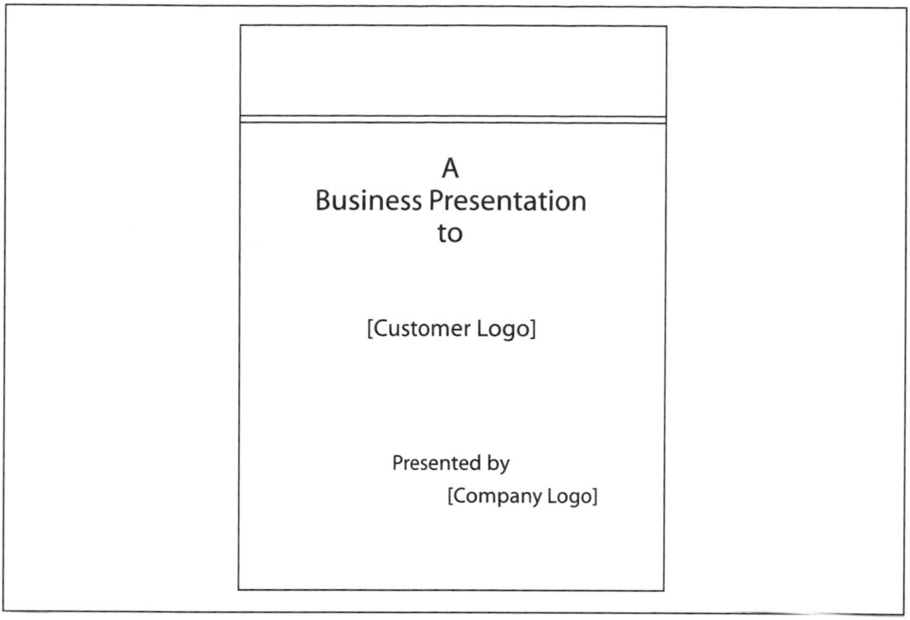

A
**Business Presentation**
to

[Customer Logo]

Presented by
[Company Logo]

FIGURE 10.2    Presentation Objectives

**Presentation Objectives**

- To confirm our understanding of [Customer's] business direction and objectives
- To present [Company] as a strategic resource
- To determine the appropriate path forward

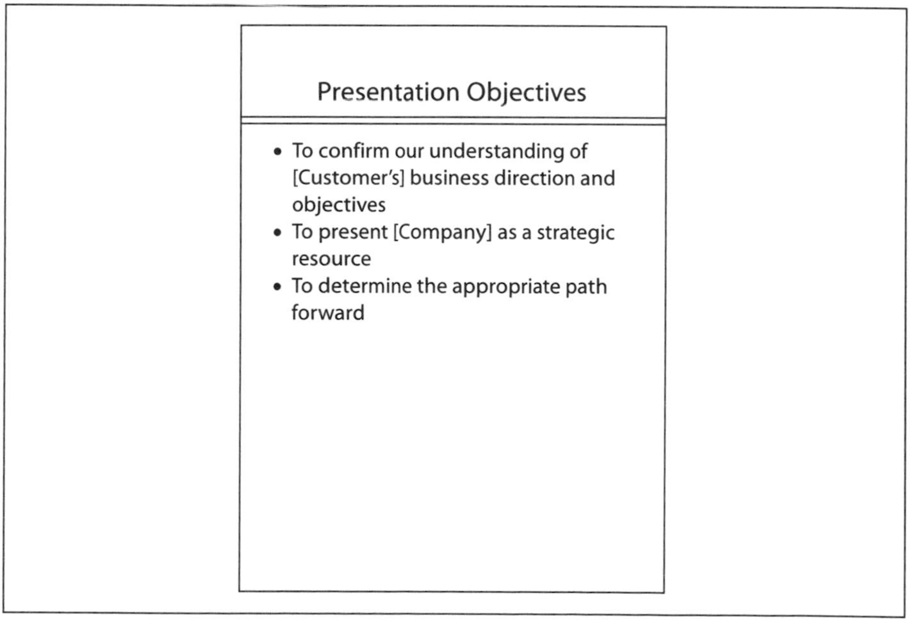

FIGURE 10.3    Agenda

```
                    ┌──────────────────────────────────┐
                    │                                  │
                    │             Agenda               │
                    │  ────────────────────────────────│
                    │  • [Customer]                    │
                    │    —A profile                    │
                    │    —Business objectives          │
                    │    —Strategies                   │
                    │    —Business issues and challenges│
                    │    —Departmental issues          │
                    │  • [Company]                     │
                    │    —A strategic resource         │
                    │  • The [Customer/Company] business fit│
                    │  • Action steps/timetable        │
                    │                                  │
                    └──────────────────────────────────┘
```

FIGURE 10.4    Customer Profile

```
                    ┌──────────────────────────────────┐
                    │                                  │
                    │       [Customer] — A Profile     │
                    │  ────────────────────────────────│
                    │  • Strong heritage               │
                    │  • Vision                        │
                    │  • Products/services             │
                    │  • Organization                  │
                    │  • Customer base                 │
                    │  • Competitive advantage         │
                    │  • Characteristics               │
                    │                                  │
                    └──────────────────────────────────┘
```

**Page 3: Agenda.** This page lists the contents of the presentation. Typically, this will be a bulleted list of page headings including a customer overview (which can include corporate profile, business objectives, strategies, business environment/issues, and departmental issues), an overview of your business, the business fit, and action steps/timetable. (See Figure 10.3)

**Page 4: Customer Profile.** This page is an overview of the customer's business, including history, markets, products, and unique positioning. In essence, you create a brief snapshot of the customer. This leads easily into talking about the rest of the customer's business in greater detail, but keep it short and succinct. (See Figure 10.4)

In some situations where you are pressed for time or are presenting to an existing customer and need to streamline the presentation, you might pull the Profile page out of the presentation and emphasize the other pages of the customer section.

**Page 5: Customer Business Objectives.** These are the customer's top priorities. They may include revenue and profit goals, cost containment, increased market share, quality improvements, etc.

Although this page may look generic, the point is to understand the detailed business objectives of the company. Your knowledge of the specifics comes through in your delivery versus the words on the page. (See Figure 10.5)

> Don't let the appearance and simplicity of the page fool you. This page will come to life when you present it.

**Page 6: Customer Strategies.** These are the plans the company has in place to attain its key objectives. Acquisitions, new markets, product development, technology investment, and training are a few of the strategies a customer may have in place already. (See Figure 10.6)

**Page 7: Business Issues.** On this page, you list the external forces affecting the customer's business such as competition, industry trends, government regulations, and new technologies, as well as the internal business issues affecting the company. (See Figure 10.7)

**Page 8: Departmental Issues.** (In this case, Branch Issues.) More specific than the previous page, this page focuses on the critical issues and challenges facing the department or departments where your solution can make an impact. (See Figure 10.8)

FIGURE 10.5    Business Objectives

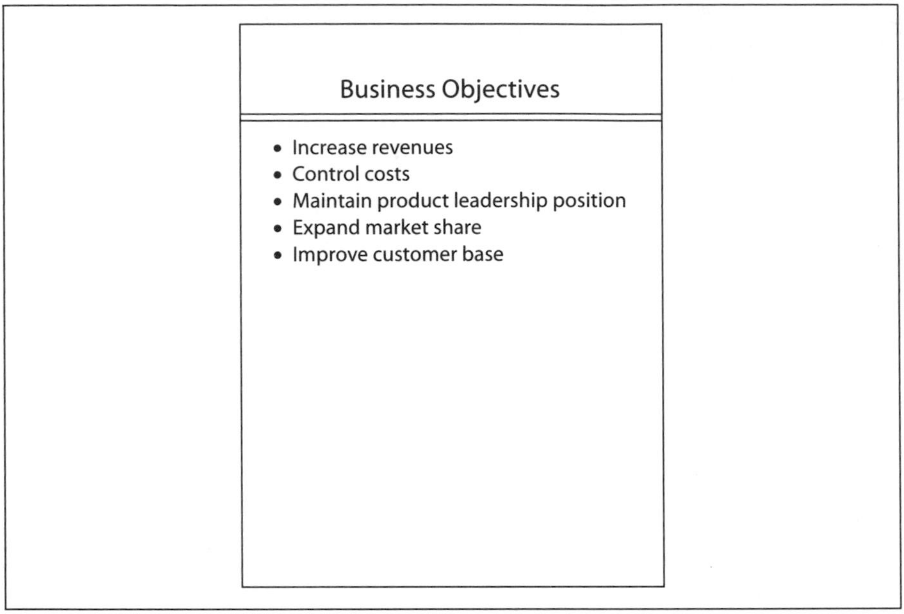

## Business Objectives

- Increase revenues
- Control costs
- Maintain product leadership position
- Expand market share
- Improve customer base

FIGURE 10.6    Strategies

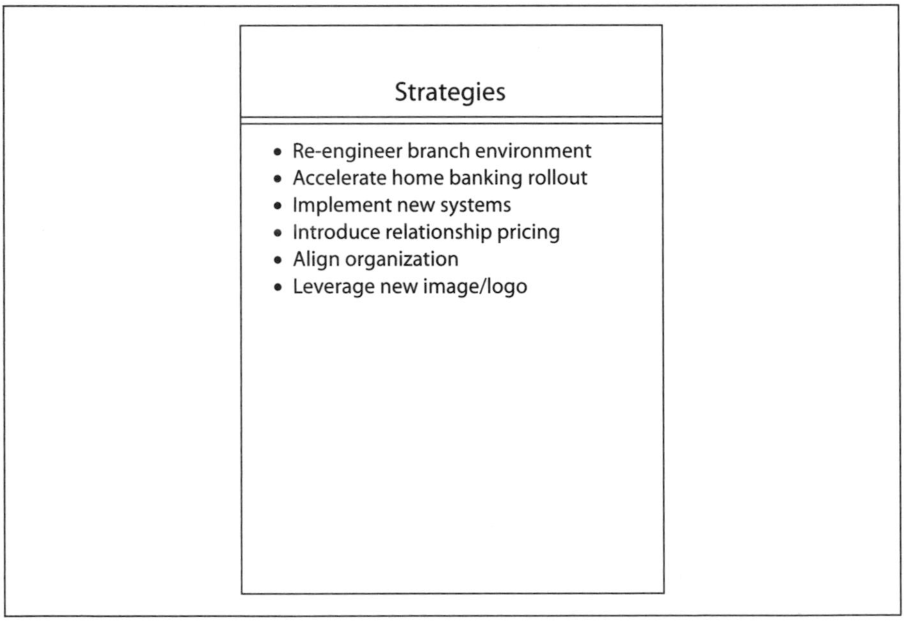

## Strategies

- Re-engineer branch environment
- Accelerate home banking rollout
- Implement new systems
- Introduce relationship pricing
- Align organization
- Leverage new image/logo

FIGURE 10.7    Business Issues and Challenges

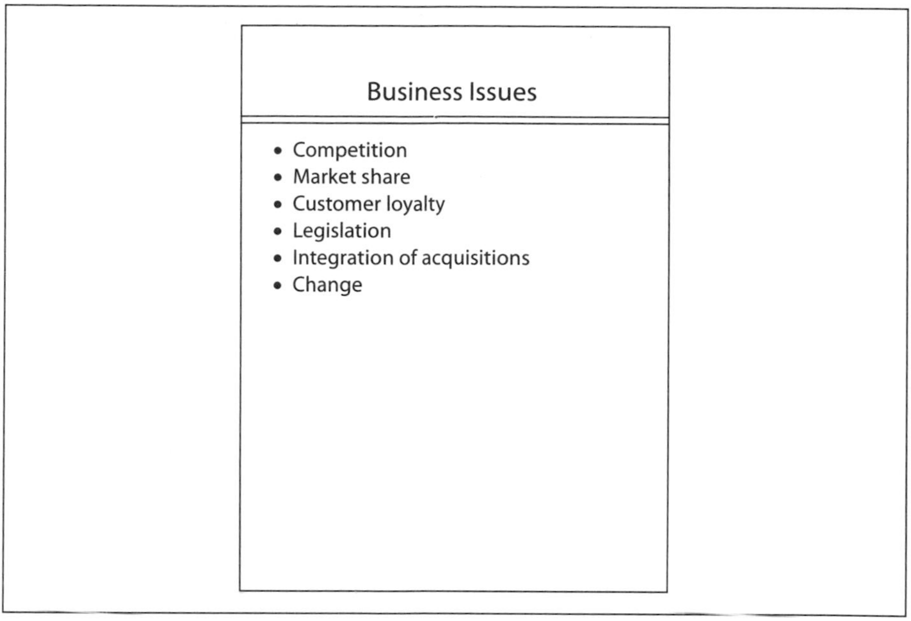

### Business Issues

- Competition
- Market share
- Customer loyalty
- Legislation
- Integration of acquisitions
- Change

FIGURE 10.8    Branch Issues

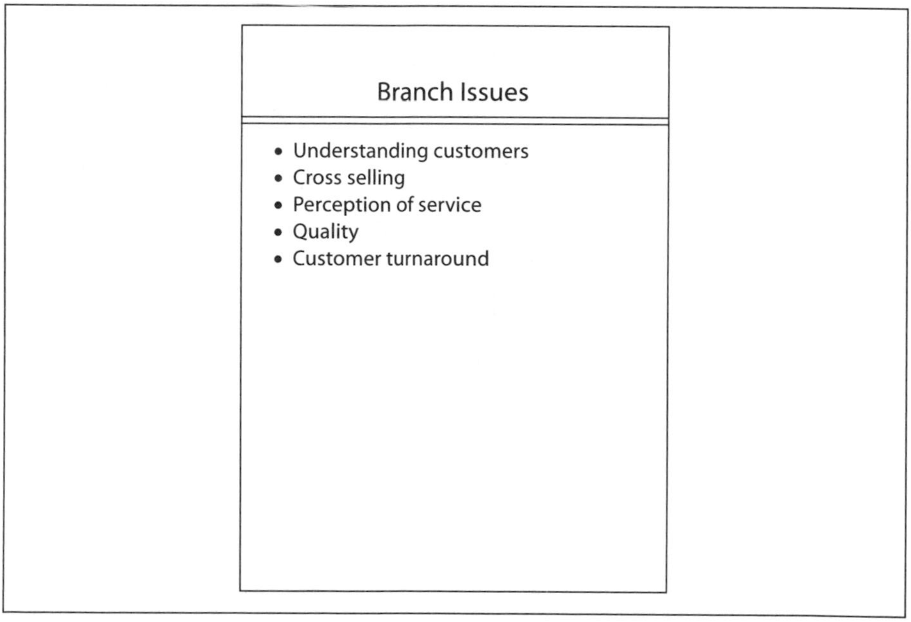

### Branch Issues

- Understanding customers
- Cross selling
- Perception of service
- Quality
- Customer turnaround

FIGURE 10.9    Your Company

> ### [Company]
> ### A Strategic Resource
>
> - Industry leadership position
> - Markets served
> - Track record of innovation
> - Service oriented
> - Flexible solutions
> - Focus on customer partnerships

FIGURE 10.10    Business Fit

> ### The [Customer/Company]
> ### Business Fit
>
> - Enhances attainment of growth objectives
> - Addresses critical branch issue
>   —Customer service
> - Impacts key strategies
>   —Home banking
>   —New systems
> - Provides broad base of resources
> - Builds foundation for a flexible, long-term, win-win business relationship

**Page 9: Your Company as a Strategic Resource.** Here you transition into talking about your company. Include points that reinforce your credibility as a business resource; for example, your company's vision and mission, track record of growth and success, strategic direction, corporate philosophy, industry recognition, etc. Choose these points based on what you think will be most compelling to the customer. (See Figure 10.9)

> Although this example uses just one page to overview your company, you may need to use a couple of pages to accomplish this. Just don't get carried away and put too much in here.

**Page 10: Business Fit.** Based on your research and phrased in the customer's terms, this page includes a statement of the business relationship opportunity between your two companies. (See Figure 10.10)

**Page 11: Action Steps/Timetable.** The final page includes your specific recommendations and the commitments needed to carry them out. Keep in mind that these bullets are very specific, unique to this presentation. Your challenge is to put in the right action steps to prove the fit following the presentation. Including dates can be a great way to drive action. (See Figure 10.11)

> Always remember to include an action requesting your next meeting with the decision maker.

## ALTERNATIVE ROUTES:
## Variations On The Business Presentation

As mentioned earlier, the previous example was a template for a conceptual or positioning presentation to a prospect or customer. But what if your goal for the presentation is different?

**Alternative scenario 1.** For example, what if you're using the presentation to expand your relationship with an existing customer? If so, you will want to add a page to your presentation that highlights the current relationship between your two organizations. This page, titled "[Customer/Company] Current Relationship," should be placed between pages nine and ten above and cover topics such as: the background of the relationship, current projects underway, issues and challenges that either are being addressed or need to be addressed, and any successes you want to highlight. This page can be used to help you leverage the positive aspects of your current relationship to close on your objectives for this meeting. (See Figure 10.12.)

**Alternative scenario 2.**  Here's another example. What if you're using the presentation to close on a specific solution? You may want to add a few pages between "Business Fit" and "Action Steps/Timetable" to describe your solution. (See Figures 10.13 to 10.15.)

These pages may include:

- *Success Criteria.* Presents your understanding of the customer's success criteria for the specific opportunity.
- *Solution Overview.* Provides an overview of your specific solution. Keep your solution overview at the technical level of the decision maker.
- *Solution Fit.* States the fit between your solution and the customer's success criteria.

These variants are just two of the most common. As you become more comfortable with making these types of presentations, you will gain confidence to adapt this template to the needs and objectives of each opportunity.

Another example of a business presentation, this one oriented toward closing on a solution, is included in Appendix C.

## WHERE INK MEETS PAPER:
### Developing Your Presentation Draft

You're almost ready to write your draft. Before you begin, consider the following points:

- *Develop a fresh draft for every customer.* Leverage other presentations for ideas and flow, but make sure each presentation is unique to that customer.
- *Weave a story.* Each page should reveal a portion of that story. To tell the story most effectively, maintain a logical order throughout the presentation.
- *Be prepared to elaborate on and support each bulleted point.* The depth and quality of your presentation comes from the quality of your research.
- *No draft is a final version.* In consultation with your coach, you may revise the draft. If there is time, reviewing a draft with your coach is always a good idea. You may also wish to solicit input from peers or your manager.
- *Differentiate yourself and your company from your competitors.* Give the decision maker an incentive to buy from you. Keep this goal in mind as you decide what to include in and what to omit from the presentation.

Above all, stay focused on the first question of this section and ask yourself, "When the meeting is over, what action do I want the decision maker to take?" The answer to this question should be the driving force behind developing a presentation draft.

> This is your opportunity to bring your presentation to life: make sure it tells a story.

## A Developing Situation

Now that you've done all the preliminary work, you're ready to begin writing your presentation draft. The following step-by-step guide will help you compile all your far-flung notes and research materials into a comprehensive presentation draft.

Step 1. Gather all your available resources. Get together all your notes, research information and data, and sample presentation materials.

Step 2. Organize your data and research notes into the following groups:

- Corporate profile/direction (subdivide into profile, objectives, strategies, trends, and issues)
- Departmental profile/direction
- Product fit
- Business fit

Step 3. Go over your notes in each group from Step 2 and circle or highlight everything that is relevant and significant to describing the target account's business.

Step 4. Categorize each circled item according to the agenda page headings.

Step 5. Determine your presentation goal. Remember, begin with the end in mind.

Step 6. Develop specific action steps and set a date for completion, including scheduling the next meeting.

Step 7. Using a separate page for each heading, convert the highlighted, categorized information into crisp, concise phrases.

**Step 8.** Describe the key points of the customer's business. Begin by casting a wide net, addressing the profile and broad business direction first, then narrow your discussion to cover the departmental objectives, strategies, and issues.

**Step 9.** To keep your presentation crisp and concise, follow these rules of thumb:

- Four to eight bullets per page
- Two to six words per bullet
- Two to five indents under each bullet, if applicable

This is where you follow that well-worn acronym, KICS—"Keep it concise, stupid."

**Step 10.** Create an entire story in logical order for each page. Remember, part of what makes your presentation compelling is that each page tells a small story.

**Step 11.** Prepare to elaborate and support each bullet presented. Annotate the background and thoughts behind each bulleted item for the presentation rehearsal.

**Step 12.** Use consistent verb tense on every page.

**Step 13.** Provide a pertinent overview of your company. Transition from this overview into describing your solution and how it fills a need (if applicable).

**Step 14.** Highlight aspects of your current relationship (if applicable).

**Step 15.** Describe the business fit specific to the customer and in the customer's terminology.

**Step 16.** Transition into an overview of your solution and how it fills a need (if applicable).

**Step 17.** Determine the appropriate presentation medium.

FIGURE 10.11    Action Steps/Timetable

## Action Steps/Timetable

- Conduct corporate visit—May 15
- Consider additional business opportunities—May 15
- Complete branch surveys—April 15
- Determine appropriate decision cycle—today
- Develop rollout implementation strategies—June 1
- Schedule management team meeting—July 15

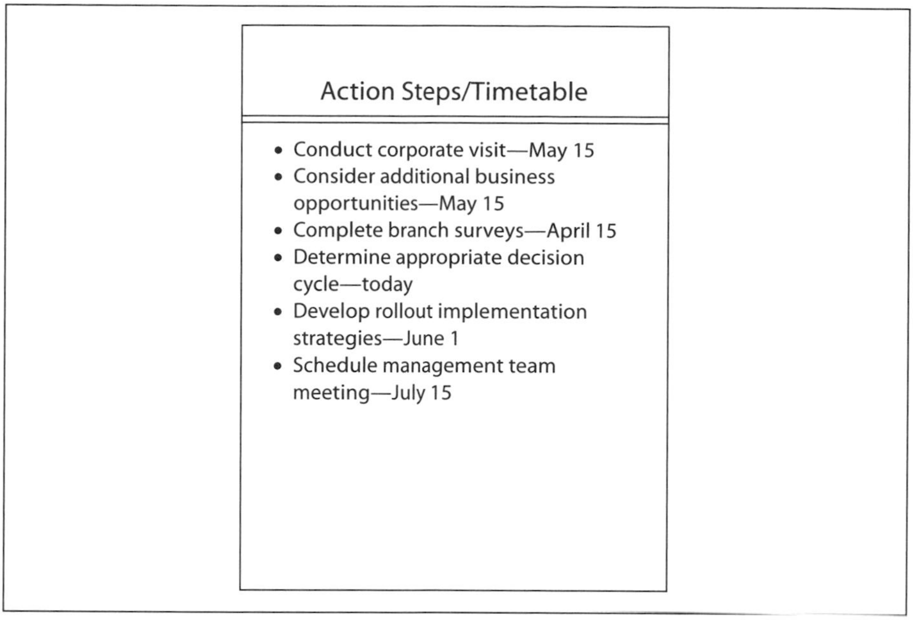

FIGURE 10.12    Current Relationship

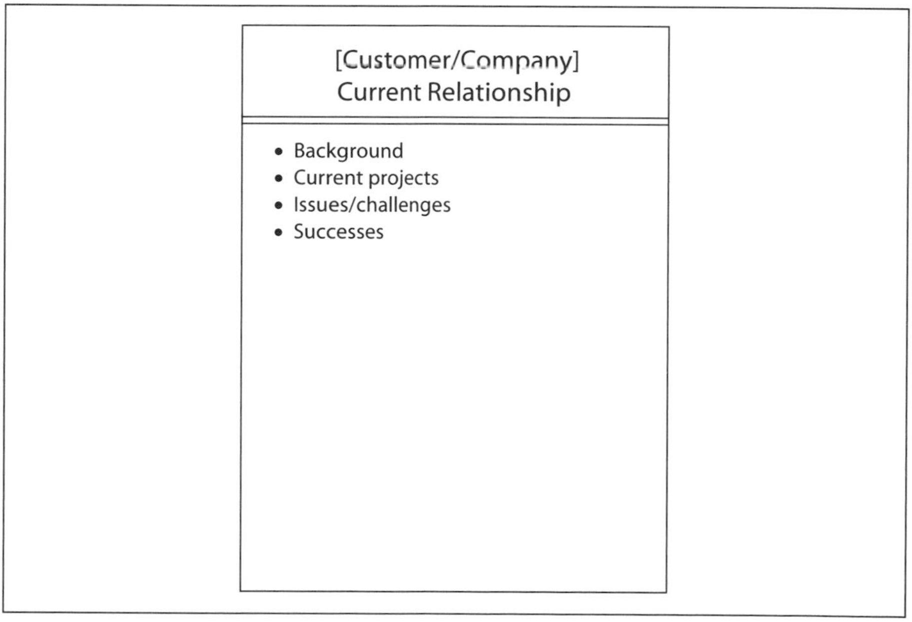

## [Customer/Company] Current Relationship

- Background
- Current projects
- Issues/challenges
- Successes

FIGURE 10.13    Success Criteria

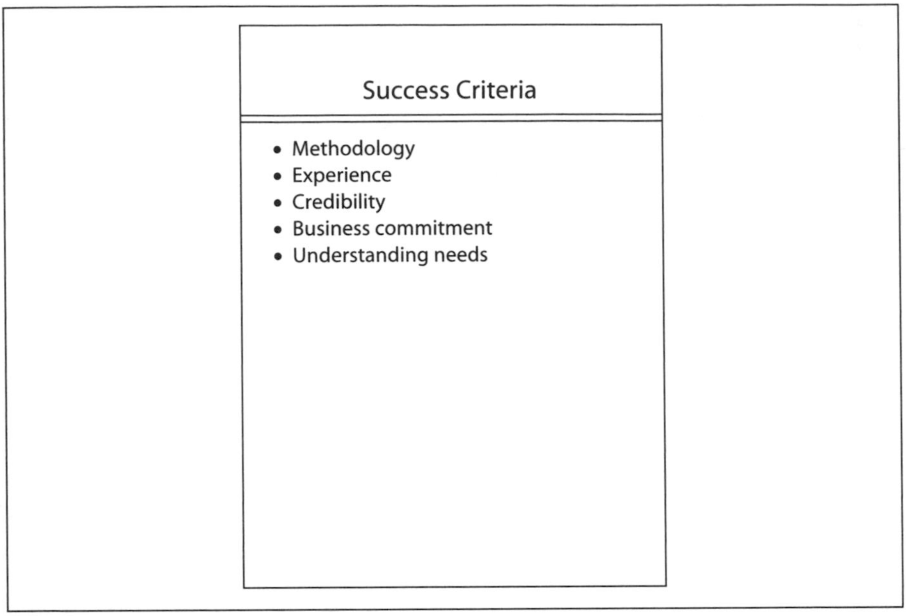

**Success Criteria**

- Methodology
- Experience
- Credibility
- Business commitment
- Understanding needs

FIGURE 10.14    Solution Overview

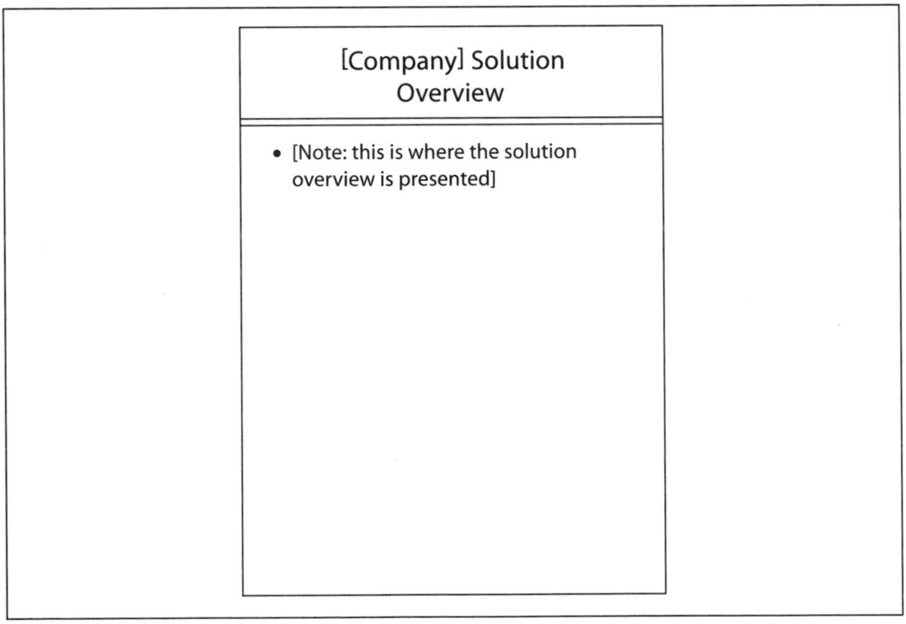

**[Company] Solution Overview**

- [Note: this is where the solution overview is presented]

FIGURE 10.15     Solution Fit

### Solution Fit

- Proven methodology
- Experienced staff
- References
- Business unit focus
- Strong business fit

FIGURE 10.16     Action Steps

### Action Steps

- Confirm the solution and business fit
- Gain authorization to proceed
- Perform quality assessment
- Develop and implement communication plan to employees
- Implement facilitator training
- Conduct periodic management update presentations

## Action Verbs

In Step 12 you were instructed to make sure to use a consistent verb tense throughout your presentation. This is one of a few key points about your use of language. The language you use should support and enhance the content. Your word choices can be especially critical in developing the customer's objectives and strategies, business fit, and action step pages. Here is a list of strong, effective action verbs.

Feel free to add verbs to this list. You may want to consider, in particular, language specific to your customer or industry.

- Accelerate
- Affect
- Build
- Capitalize
- Demonstrate
- Elevate
- Employ
- Encourage
- Enhance
- Facilitate
- Focus
- Generate
- Implement
- Incorporate
- Increase
- Leverage
- Maintain
- Penetrate

Here is a sample action steps page from a closing-oriented presentation that incorporates effective and appropriate action verbs. (See Figure 10.16)

## LOOKING GOOD: Media Selection

As with every other aspect of your presentation, the medium you use and how you use it reflects on you and your company and has a bearing on the overall effectiveness of the presentation. Ideally, your comfort presenting with the medium should contribute to the customer's perception of you as a powerful resource and competent potential business partner.

With this in mind, let's look at the factors that will help guide your choice of medium for each presentation. First, you must feel comfortable with whatever medium you choose. We've all seen presenters who foul up the order of slides, don't know how to use their high-tech presentation products, or fumble with an unwieldy projector. You may even cringe to think of the impression you've made in past presentations when something similar happened to you. Once you decide on the right medium, practice giving your presentation using that medium until you feel comfortable with it. Eventually, you will develop a familiarity with a range of media so that future presentations will require less preparation time.

As Roger Ailes says in his book, You Are the Message, it isn't the medium that's important; it's you and how you deliver the message.

Other points to consider include:

- *How much time do you have for the presentation?* What impact do time considerations have on which medium you use?
- *How significant is the opportunity?* If you stand to win a great deal of business from this opportunity and want to make the best possible impression, regardless of cost, you may want to spend extra money on professionally developed flip charts.
- *Comfort zones.* Positioning "What's most effective?" versus "What am I comfortable with?"

Don't let your comfort zones determine which medium you'll use. Pick the right medium for the situation, then practice until you're comfortable with it.

Remember, no matter what the medium is, you are the message. The selected medium should provide support for your message. You are not making a product presentation; you are making a formal business relationship presentation. The decision maker should focus on you and your words.

The following charts provide some additional guidelines for selecting an appropriate medium to suit your presentation needs:

Medium: Technology-based; e.g., a PowerPoint Presentation

| *Advantages* | *Disadvantages* |
|---|---|
| • Especially effective for presentations to large groups.<br>• Looks professional.<br>• Can be changed easily for last-minute updates. | • Requires turning down the lights, making rapport and eye contact with the audience difficult.<br>• Equipment can malfunction.<br>• Can distract the audience from the "focal point" of the meeting—you.<br>• Less effective with a small audience. |

Medium: Overhead Transparencies

| *Advantages* | *Disadvantages* |
|---|---|
| • Can be effective for presentations to large groups. | • Requires turning down the lights, making rapport and eye contact with the audience difficult.<br>• Equipment can malfunction.<br>• Commonplace, can seem dated.<br>• Less effective with very small audience.<br>• Less effective with a technology-savvy audience. |

Medium: Flip Chart

| *Advantages* | *Disadvantages* |
|---|---|
| • Easy to work with.<br>• Highly personalized.<br>• Looks professional.<br>• Shows effort.<br>• Gives you control.<br>• Lets you keep the lights on while you talk.<br>• Keeps you as the focus of the meeting.<br>• Differentiates you from other presenters. | • Requires more lead time for preparation.<br>• Has low-tech appearance.<br>• Not effective for large audience.<br>• Difficult to make last minute changes. |

## HEAR YE, HEAR YE!: Preselling the Presentation

Now that you've prepared your presentation, you want to prepare the client to receive it. This means building a groundswell of interest among the people you expect to attend the meeting.

### Divide and Confirm

One great way to build groundswell is to let each prospective attendee know about the upcoming presentation. Your options include contacting people by phone, in person, or by writing presentation confirmation letters. Your objectives are to:

- Introduce yourself, if necessary.
- Let everyone know the date, time, and location of the presentation.
- Provide an overview of the issues to be addressed during the meeting.
- Express your hope of seeing them there on the appointed day.

Writing presentation confirmation letters is a powerful tool for building groundswell. In this letter, you should focus on the date, time, and place of the meeting; what you plan to discuss during the presentation; and references to the other invitees (see Appendix D for sample letter).

Throughout the preselling stage, your objective should be to build a groundswell of interest and create excitement about your presentation. An important part of this process is defining the presentation as an event, not just another vendor sales call. One reason this perception is so important is that you can't afford to have your presentations postponed or canceled. Our experience shows that a high percentage of "postponed" presentations eventually become canceled presentations.

> Preselling may seem like a minor detail, but it's not. It creates groundswell, which is critical in turning your presentation into an event.

## FOR YOUR EYES ONLY:
### Reviewing the Presentation with a Coach

Before you break out the hammer and chisel to start carving that presentation in stone, it's a good idea to review your draft with coaches and any other people who might offer appropriate input. This step will help improve your base of support, while providing your coaches with the opportunity to gain a greater sense of ownership over your presentation.

The next question to ask is, "What part or parts of the presentation should we review with our coach?" You don't necessarily want to review the whole presentation. Typically, you'll only want to cover the section on the target company, as the coach may not appreciate what you're presenting about your company, the business fit, or the action steps. That said, the extent to which you review the rest of the presentation depends on the situation. With a strong coach, you may indeed want to review the entire presentation.

Ideally, your coach reviews should take place in person, and you should meet one-on-one whenever possible. Your coach's job is to verify that your presentation is on target.

One of our clients with a corporate services organization was calling into a mortgage services company. The rep was conducting a coach review on Friday afternoon for a presentation scheduled for the following Monday morning. As he and the coach went over the presentation, the coach became excited about it. He liked the direction the presentation was going, and he helped fill in some of the gaps. As the two of them reflected on the business fit, the executive who was to be the target of the presentation walked by the office. The coach was so excited that he called the decision maker into the room. The coach was so pumped, he was about to invite the executive to look over the presentation, forcing the rep to step in and say, "We're really looking forward to meeting with you on Monday to make this business presentation."

Luckily, this rep had the presence of mind to take charge of the situation and avoid having to present right there, before he was ready. But the point is that your coaches can get very excited, even about the coach review. In this case, the excitement almost proved to be too much, but in the end it set up the rep well and built more momentum for his presentation on Monday.

Here's a step-by-step plan for reviewing a presentation draft with a coach.

**Have a draft handy.** As the coach suggests changes, write them right there on your copy of the draft. As the coach sees that you are actually taking the advice and incorporating it into the presentation, he or she will be encouraged to make additional suggestions. People love giving advice; they love it even better when you actually accept it. Remember, you can use any, all, or none of your coach's suggested changes. That's up to you.

**Be insistent and specific.** To encourage feedback, ask the coach which trends, issues, and strategies the decision maker views as most important and in what order.

> Remember, when soliciting input from coaches on your presentation, do not accept, "It looks fine," as a response. No first draft is ever fine. Make it clear that you want honest, constructive criticism.

**Encourage changes.** In addition to asking about changes to existing content, ask, "What's missing?"

**Ask specific questions.**  This is a specific meeting, and answers to certain questions will be helpful. They can make it easier on your coach as well. Some good questions to ask during the coach review include:

- "What points are missing from this page?"
- "If you had to remove a bullet from this page, what would it be? Why?"
- "If you had to add a bullet to this page, what would it be?"
- "How would you resequence this page to make it more effective?"

> If you haven't had a chance to do as much research as you would like, a coach review provides a great way to fill in the blanks.

**Fill them in.**  Conclude the meeting by sharing with the coach how you plan to move forward, incorporating, if appropriate, the coach's suggestions for changes to your presentation.

Sometimes circumstances may require that you do your coach review over the phone. These steps apply to that environment as well. At other times, you may not be able to conduct a coach review at all. In this case, you will need to assume an extra humble tone in your presentation when you talk about the decision maker's company.

A client of ours, Terry Grill, former VP and Regional Sales Manager with Deluxe Corporation, was reviewing a presentation to a major bank. Logistics required that he conduct the coach review over the phone. He and the coach verbally reviewed the customer section of the presentation. After sharing the objectives he'd listed, he asked, "Are these right? How would you reorder them to give them more impact?" and so forth.

In retrospect, Terry says that this brief phone conversation wound up making a world of difference. He says:

> We were just about to go to press with the presentation, and we are so lucky we didn't. The coach review, even though it was done over the phone, made the presentation 100 percent better. Our coach was so good, we were able to get into the business fit with her. She helped us rework the business fit so we could really connect with the decision maker. It worked, and the decision maker committed on the spot to initiate a relationship between our two companies.

Bottom line: A coach review can be invaluable. You can even conduct a great coach review over the phone.

## Your Draft and You

When you're reviewing a draft with a coach, make it clear from the beginning that you'll be taking the review copy with you after the meeting. You can add that at the actual presentation, you will make copies available for anyone who wants one.

It's important that your presentation be fresh when you stand up in front of the decision maker. If a coach, even one with the best intentions, passes around your draft, then the power of your presentation could be diminished when you deliver. You want to take control of the presentation from the start, and if an earlier draft is floating around the customer's office, you've already lost some of that control.

Of course, sometimes a face-to-face coach review session will be impossible, and you may have to conduct the review over the phone or the Internet. But you don't want the draft to "get legs" and wind up circulated among the presentation attendees. The presentation is just a series of bullets that may be unimpressive on their own. You don't want someone to prejudge it before you get the chance to bring it to life with your delivery. For this reason, if you conduct your review over the phone, you may need to do it verbally. An Internet meeting may even be preferable, because that way you can show the coach the presentation draft without leaving a copy behind that may fall into others' hands.

## GETTING TO CARNEGIE HALL: Rehearsing the Presentation

How important is rehearsal? It probably depends on a number of factors—how much time you have, just how important the presentation is, how well you know the material already, etc. But we believe that for this type of business presentation, diligent rehearsal can make a world of difference in guaranteeing that you communicate the right message when you actually stand up in front of the decision maker.

> *"The harder I practice, the luckier I get."*—Gary Player

Some people have to learn the hard way the value of rehearsal. Take the example of a certain U.S. senator. As the story has it, this senator employed one of the finest speechwriters in Washington. He had written many fine speeches for the senator, and the senator had developed a reputation for powerful and insightful oratory. The senator had even begun believing his own press and came to think he, not the speechwriter, was primarily responsible for his reputation.

So one day, the speechwriter approached the senator and asked for a raise. Annoyed at the writer's audacity, the senator refused outright, sputtering, "I'll let you know when it's time for a raise!" The writer skulked out.

A few weeks later, the senator was scheduled to address a live TV audience. He began by saying that there were four critical issues facing the nation. Referring to the page in his hand, he told the audience he would cover each of the four issues individually. He then turned to the next page and all that was written on it was a terse, "You're on your own, you SOB."

Okay, you probably won't ever be faced with such a sticky situation, but the point remains the same: rehearsing is critical to the success of your presentation. And, although you don't want to memorize what you're going to say, you do want to convey that you are knowledgeable about the topic and have a firm command of the issues. Rehearsal gives you that comfort. However, if you go overboard and try to memorize every word, the delivery tends to appear canned, and you lose the effect.

One client of ours believes that, frequently, the rehearsal can be tougher than the actual presentation. He was staying in a quaint, historic hotel in Northfield, Minnesota, the night before he was scheduled to present to a large local circuit board manufacturer. The hotel's air-conditioning was out of service, and the rep had to rehearse in his sweltering hotel room. He told us:

> Here I am, rehearsing my presentation in a hotel room that's probably 85 degrees with my boss and my boss's boss sitting on the edge of my bed. As I'm going through the presentation, I'm just sweating like a pig, and I'm dying I'm so nervous. But I got through it, and after that I knew anything would be easy—presenting to the executives at my customer's company couldn't be half as nerve-wracking as presenting to my own. The next day, I presented and wasn't nervous, because I knew they were going to be nicer than my bosses. Plus, they had air-conditioning.

*"Luck is what happens when preparation meets opportunity."*
*—Elmer Letterman*

## Rehearsal Guidelines

Here are some of the points to consider as you rehearse the presentation.

- *Focus on content.* Start by focusing on communicating the information and message. You can work on style and delivery once you have the content down pat.
- *Start with a hard copy.* The first step is annotating your presentation— write out or type your "talk to" points on each bullet and your transitions. Then print your presentation and do your first rehearsal with just these pages to work with. For subsequent rehearsals, use your chosen presentation medium.
- *Open strong.* The first 90 seconds of your presentation typically set the tone for the whole meeting. If you rehearse the entire presentation 4 times, you should rehearse the first 90 seconds 10 or 12 times.
- *Nail the transitions.* Remember, the important transitions are from bullet point to bullet point and page to page. You're telling a story, and good storytellers don't let on when they're turning the page. Practice the transitions until they come across as smooth and polished. To give yourself a leg up on making smooth transitions from page to page, you may want to lightly pencil the heading of the next page at eye level on the page you're looking at (this only works on flip charts).
- *Do it again.* We admit that rehearsing isn't the most fun part of this process, but you must do it until you're comfortable. Rehearsal is one of the keys to leaving as little to chance as possible. There are no hard and fast rules about how many times you should rehearse a presentation. Let your comfort level and facility with the materials be your guide.

*"Better to sweat in practice than bleed in battle."—Unknown*

- *Jury of your peers.* For the final touches, you'll want to try a practice run in front of an audience that will be even more critical than the target company. If your in-laws aren't available, your coworkers will have to do. Peers can be a terribly challenging audience. If you can present effectively to them, you're more than ready for the customer. But remember: now is the time to get suggestions for improvement. If you wait until you're in front of the customer, it's too late.
- *Get a visual.* One audience is even more critical than your peers or in-laws: you. Videotape your rehearsals and watch with a critical eye. This is tough, because the tape doesn't lie. But there's no better way to iden-

tify distracting mannerisms or verbal miscues that you want to eliminate. If you can't videotape yourself, audio will suffice.

One client of ours watched a video of his rehearsal and got so disgusted with his performance that he could only watch for five minutes. So he went back to the presentation and rehearsed again. He only stopped rehearsing when he could finally stomach watching the whole thing.

If you think you're ready to deliver a presentation without rehearsing, think again. You never know what a rehearsal will expose. We heard about one rep who felt he was adequately prepared, so he didn't rehearse before presenting to a senior-level executive with GM. In the middle of the rep's LCD-projected PowerPoint presentation featuring a ghosted-back GM logo on each page, the decision maker interrupted, pointed at the screen, and asked, "What's that?" The rep turned around to see a ghosted-back Ford logo. Whoops! We never did find out whether the dry cleaner was able to get the underarm sweat stains out of the rep's shirt. The point is, rehearsing pays off. Do it.

## LET'S GET TACTICAL: Presentation Logistics

Have you ever shown up to deliver a presentation only to discover that the room you reserved was no longer available? Or that the promised projector was nowhere to be found? Or that the customer thought you said the 15th, not the 14th? Of course you have. Let's make sure none of these unanticipated snafus crop up with this presentation by taking care of all the logistics. That means running through a checklist of the following:

> "Chance favors the prepared mind."—*Louis Pasteur*

**Conference room.** Call the decision maker's administrator a few days ahead of time to make sure a conference room has been reserved for your presentation. Remember, presenting in the conference room is important because it helps to:

- Identify your presentation as an event, not just another sales call
- Build a sense of urgency and anticipation
- Establish a decision-making environment
- Minimize the likelihood of interruptions

**Internet meeting.** Although you might prefer to deliver this presentation face-to-face, leveraging an Internet meeting can still be very effective. If you're conducting your presentation via the Internet, make sure that all the participants have access to the Web meeting service that you're using—and that they have all the appropriate numbers and passwords ahead of time so that they're ready to go when the meeting starts.

**Give yourself time.** Arrange to have plenty of time before the appointed hour for setting up, as well as afterwards in case the presentation runs over. Then, on the day of the presentation, arrive early to set up the room and get comfortable with the layout, equipment, and light switches.

In his book *Instant Replay,* author Jerry Kramer, a veteran pro football player, talks about a concept developed by his coach, the legendary Vince Lombardi, called *Lombardi Time.* When Lombardi said to be somewhere at 10 AM, he really meant a quarter to ten. Lombardi Time is important for sales professionals as well, particularly when you're delivering a business presentation to a senior-level decision maker. You must never be late for a meeting. Get there early, get your bearings, collect yourself, and be ready to go before everyone else arrives.

**Tool up.** Make sure you have the necessary tools for your presentation. If you need a projector, make sure it will be there ahead of time. If you're making a flip chart presentation, you'll need a free-standing flip chart easel.

**Get graphic.** Get a high-quality copy of the customer's logo. You want to display it prominently on the cover page of your presentation, and you want it to look good.

**Hard copies.** If you plan to hand out copies of the presentation, have enough printed up so that everyone in attendance can have one. If you're going to hand them out, make sure you do so afterwards, so that people are listening to you, not reading ahead in your presentation.

**Role out.** If anyone else on your team will participate in the presentation, sit down ahead of time and review each person's role.

## THE COMPLETE PACKAGE: Delivering the Presentation

So now you've developed your compelling presentation, reviewed it with a coach, and rehearsed it—all for this moment. You're almost ready to shine when you present to the decision maker.

Yet we cannot take this presentation for granted. It is not enough to have an attractive presentation and a good strong message. We have to project a commitment, enthusiasm, and passion. This point comes out in Ralph Waldo Emerson's wisdom:

> *"What you are speaks so loudly, I can't hear what you say."*
> —*Ralph Waldo Emerson*

## Characteristics of a Successful Presentation

Certain points contribute to the likelihood that you will deliver an effective presentation. Bear these in mind from the beginning:

- *When you begin, confirm the length of time that has been scheduled for the presentation.* This ensures that you have time to accomplish your objectives. A typical presentation meeting takes between an hour and an hour-and-a-half. This includes a 30- to 45-minute presentation, followed by a roundtable discussion. Reconfirm the amount of time that's been set aside, so that expectations are set appropriately.
- *The opening sets the tone for the entire presentation.* Remember Premise #3: "You only get one chance to make a good first impression." The opening is your one chance to set the tone for the impression you want to make. You want to show that you're prepared, positive, relaxed, and ready to take control and lead the meeting.
- *The pace should be crisp.* To maintain a hold over your audience, you must keep up a crisp pace. The body language of the presentation attendees lets you know whether you're moving fast enough. Yawns, slumped over audience members, and distracted glances at newspaper racing tables indicate that your pace may have fallen off. This is especially true when you're covering the customer overview section of the presentation. Rarely will a customer ask you to slow down in this section.

  During one presentation, we quickly became concerned that we weren't crisp enough. That's because the decision maker actually fell asleep in the middle of our presentation. We later found out that the cause was a medical condition. When he woke up, we remained undaunted, thanked him for his commitment, and began a relationship with his organization.
- *Important ideas should be repeated in different pages or sections of the presentation.* To you, the repetition may seem redundant, but for people first being exposed to your ideas, it is critical that you repeat and reemphasize key points. Ask yourself, "What are the ideas that I most want people to remember after they leave the presentation?" These are the issues you need to repeat.

- *Smooth transitions are crucial.* Devote time to working out smooth, natural transitions from section to section, page to page, and point to point. For example, talk about the next page in your presentation before you show it. Peeking at the next page in front of your audience doesn't exactly inspire confidence. You are telling a story that concludes with your proposed action plan, and smooth transitions help the audience arrive there with you. We'll talk more about transitions later in the section.
- *Closing the presentation sets the tone for the discussion that follows.* To maintain a high energy level, practice your closing remarks as often as you practice the opening. Know your presentation action steps. Remember, this is why you're presenting—to close effectively and move to a productive roundtable discussion.

> The presentation may go so well that it feels like a victory. Sure, making a great presentation is a good start, but the key is closing on the action steps. That's the sale.

We hear from our clients that this is the best closing forum possible—a powerful, customer-focused presentation followed by a roundtable discussion with the decision maker. And don't feel bad if the meeting consists of just you and the decision maker. In fact, many of us consider this the ideal setting. Regardless of the size of the group, the roundtable discussion is only powerful if you use it. Close!

## Presentation Opening

Now it's time to get down to brass tacks. You're ready to get tactical and dive right into your presentation. Let's begin with the opening. At the meeting's outset, you want to take immediate control. Here are the steps to a powerful, effective opening:

- State that you appreciate the opportunity.
- Confirm the length of time available for the presentation.
- Indicate that you have done some homework.
- Make an easy transition to the presentation objectives.
- Present the agenda as the presentation road map.

Here is a sample opening to a presentation:

Thank you for the opportunity to present today. We've really been looking forward to this. We did some homework prior to our meeting, and we're excited about sharing with you some of what we've learned. I believe you had an hour set aside on your calendar—is that still accurate? Terrific. Well let's jump in, then.

We'd like to begin by sharing with you the objectives that we've set for today. And there really are three basic objectives. The first is we'd like to confirm our understanding of your business. Not that we're the experts, but we've tried to step back and learn some things—and we'd like to confirm what we've learned with you. Second, we'd then like to position ourselves as a strategic resource for your consideration. And last, if we've done those things well, we'd love to (initiate/strengthen/expand) a business relationship with you.

To help accomplish this, we've put an agenda in place, and we'd like to share that with you. Again, we'll begin by sharing our understanding of your business, starting broadly and then narrowing our focus to some of the departmental (e.g., Information Systems, Engineering, etc.) issues you might be facing. Then we'll switch gears and talk about our organization, who we are, where we are today, where we're going, and how we think we could be a strategic resource for your consideration. And then we'll get to what we feel is the highlight of the presentation, and that's the very strong business fit we see between our two organizations.

If we do all that well, as you'd expect, we'd like to present an action plan, identify the right path forward, and move ahead. Should we jump in?

Another important point about your opening: Don't waste a lot of time on chitchat. Fifteen minutes at the beginning of your presentation dedicated to the prospects of rain or whether the local professional lacrosse team is going to make the playoffs is just 15 minutes you now don't have for your presentation.

## Talking to the Customer about the Customer

After taking charge of the meeting, transition into your discussion of the customer and the results of your research. Now you share your insights into the customer's business that you've gained from the data you've collected and the research meetings you've conducted. When talking to the customer about the customer, follow a few guidelines:

This is one of the places where Beyond Selling Value comes to life most visibly.

- *Confirm versus inform.* Because you've done your homework and have gotten to know this account better than ever before, you want to share that knowledge with the customer. But if you come across as a know-it-all, you will turn off your audience. Rather than simply telling the customer how much you know (informing), present your understanding in a humble way (confirming). Use the subtle but critical difference between the two to your advantage.
- *State that you want to confirm your perceptions.* Let the customer know that you are seeking to confirm that what you determined during your research is correct. You establish this up front in your objectives by stating that you'd like to confirm your understanding of their business.
- *Be crisp and concise.* When talking to the customer about the customer, you're riding a fine line. On the one hand, you want the decision maker to recognize how well you understand his or her business, but on the other hand, you don't want to go into excruciating detail. You should determine where that line is and, if anything, err on the side of brevity.
- *Maintain a humble tone.* Contrasted with the take-charge tone you used to open the meeting, your tone during this stage should be humble. When talking about the customer, you should be deferential, respectful, and unassuming. Always defer to customers' greater understanding of their business.

By *humble,* we don't mean you should deliver the entire presentation on your knees with your eyes on the floor or beg to kiss the decision maker's ring before starting. For our purposes, *humble* means that your tone should be deferential.

As Mac Davis put it in song, "Oh Lord, it's hard to be humble when you're perfect in every way." This sentiment is particularly true for salespeople who've been trained to be the experts. Humility training is a class most of us missed. That's why, to pull this off, you have to practice. But remember, you only have to assume this humble tone during the customer section of the presentation.

- *Use "wiggle words."* In keeping with this humble, deferential tone, position your confirmation statements with indefinite words and phrases that allow for clarification and greater interpretation from the customer. Following is a list of common wiggle words and phrases to use during this stage of the presentation:
  - About
  - A few
  - Approximately
  - Maybe
  - Perhaps
  - It's my understanding that . . .
  - One perception that I have is that . . .
  - If I'm not mistaken . . .
  - One observation we've made is . . .
  - Isn't it so that . . .
  - I sense that these are some of your objectives . . .
  - These might be some of the projects and initiatives (or strategies) that . . .

On a typical presentation, using wiggle words to talk about the customer's business might go something like this:

> In talking to people, what really came through is that you seem to have several key objectives, although I'm sure there are others. One of the key objectives seems to be a focus on driving new business opportunities. As a matter of fact, I believe you're looking for a 20 percent increase in the coming year. Closely linked to that seemed to be profitability, as you focus not only on the top line but also on the bottom line of trying to grow profitability approximately 12 percent year to year.

Notice that by using the wiggle words and confirming, instead of informing, you can't be wrong. This way, if you miss the mark—maybe because you could only conduct one or two research calls and didn't get a complete picture—you can't be boxed into anything. The customer might say, "That's interesting, because we just changed that goal this week. Now we're shooting for 13 percent." And you can respond, "That's great, thank you," and move on. You didn't say, "X is true," and force the customer to say, "No, you're wrong." You give the customer a chance to share a perspective and hone your understanding. This is what you accomplish by being humble, confirming, and using wiggle words.

By the way, as you practice your presentation, determine which of the wiggle words and phrases you are most comfortable using. Then keep practicing until they flow off your tongue smoothly and naturally.

We understand that being humble may go against the grain of everything you've been taught as a sales professional. It's like telling a boxer to step into the ring to play pat-a-cake. As one client of ours, Dan Servos, an America Online sales executive, told us, "This is the tricky part of the process, because I teach my people to be strong, powerful, confident, hard-charging, and compelling. I've never taught them how to be humble. And yet, this is one of the most important things we can learn. We'll never get the chance to be compelling if we can't master how to be humble."

## Talking to the Customer about Your Company

As you switch gears and begin talking about your company, your tone changes again. Instead of being humble and deferential, you are firm and confident, conveying an air of self-assurance. Follow these steps:

- *Inform versus confirm.* Now you're talking about a subject (your company) that you clearly know more about than your customers do. Instead of confirming your understanding with the customer, you are informing them.
- *Select and present only pertinent information.* Avoid going overboard and sharing too much with the customer. Your company's recent partnership with a deep-sea exploration company to harvest kelp off the coast of Borneo may be a fascinating topic, but if it has no bearing on the presentation objectives, leave it out.
- *Use a confident tone.* Your confidence is inspiring and puts the customer at ease. It contributes to a more encouraging closing environment later.
- *Be crisp and concise.* Again, if you get the sense that the audience's attention is wandering, pick up the pace and minimize the level of detail you're going into.

## Presenting the Business Fit

The next stage in the presentation is the business fit. This is your sale. It's when you focus on the business relationship and working together. Keep the following points in mind:

- *The business fit is the highlight of your presentation.* Make sure the audience is aware that this is the conclusion you have drawn from all your research. Remember that you're speaking to business-oriented benefits.
- *Promote the business relationship as a win-win opportunity,* not a one-way street where you say "Here's what we'll do for you" or "This is what you need." Instead, emphasize that you will be working together to accomplish the customer's objectives and address key issues.
- *State each key idea and support it with an example.*

- *Use an enthusiastic tone.* From the confident tone of the previous section, ratchet up the enthusiasm a notch. This shouldn't be too difficult, because you will probably be pretty excited to share your ideas about this opportunity.

> The business fit is the highlight of your presentation—it's the sale, it's where you're truly selling value.

## Business Fit in the Real World, Revisited

Here's the business fit script the DuPont rep used during his presentation to the multinational grain producer in the case study we described in Chapter 4:

As we mentioned before, we believe that the highlight of this presentation is the outstanding business fit that exists between our two companies. There are many reasons why we believe this. One is that our business relationship capitalizes on a very strong foundation. For instance, last month our joint marketing campaign won the Best of Class award in a national industry conference. In addition to that, our Web-based distribution system went live three months ago, and the feedback has been outstanding. Your management team intends to use our work together as a model for other supplier relationships.

We also believe that the business fit between our two companies is so strong, because our relationship builds on a set of common values. As an example, we understand the importance you place on maintaining high standards of safety in the grain elevator environment. Safety has always been important to us as well. We believe we can learn a lot from your Superior Safety program, and we would love the opportunity to discuss it further. Similarly, your emphasis on environmental issues is well regarded throughout the industry, and we believe that there's also a great deal we can learn from you in this area. Of course, if we can bring you any value by sharing our safety and environmental initiatives, you know we'd love to do so.

A third reason we believe the fit is so strong between our two companies focuses on some of the business objectives and issues you're facing. For instance, we believe that our relationship complements your emphasis on improving profitability in your organization. We believe this can be done in a number of ways—for example, in areas such as distribution—but also in more tangible ways, including the resale of products to your customers. Here's another example: you may not be aware that even though you pay a premium for DuPont products that you resell to your customers, your customers also pay a premium. Through our research, we've discovered that your customers are willing to pay more for our products and that the highest gross margins you realize on products resold to customers are all on DuPont products. So again, this is just one way we believe we can help support your profitability emphasis.

Other business issues that we can support include your desire to improve customer satisfaction through smoother inventory management and stronger just-in-time delivery. How do we propose to accomplish this? In a number of ways, including leveraging the capabilities of some of our new products. For example, your customers are concerned about inventory management and handling of chemicals, as well as the shipment, storage, and educational requirements around chemical handling, and we recognize that they put pressure on you in a number of ways to ease their burden. One possible solution is to increase emphasis on the DuPont products, which have a granular, not liquid, consistency. As a result, they can be shipped on any common carrier across the country, not just on expensive, certified haulers.

## Presenting the Action Steps

Once you've gone through each key idea of the business fit between your two companies, make a simple transition into the action steps you recommend, based on the strength of that business fit. Overview the action steps at a high level, and as you're sitting down to begin the roundtable discussion, lock eyes with the decision maker and say, "These are our recommendations. How do you feel we should proceed from here?" By the way, don't flinch, don't look at anyone else in the room, don't turn away from the decision maker. Wait for the answer. Then drive the roundtable discussion to solidify your action plan.

> Remember, this is your opportunity to close on the value you're presenting. Close!

## Closing: The Roundtable Discussion

At this point, you have completed the prepared portion of the presentation and can move on to the critical roundtable discussion. During this discussion, you work to gain commitment on your recommendations or action steps. Topics to discuss in the roundtable include:

- *What action is to be taken?* Is there a consensus on the appropriate course of action? If not, what details need to be addressed?
- *Who is responsible for the action?* Because everyone in attendance will likely have some interest or involvement in the course of action, this is the perfect time to start allocating responsibility for each agreed-upon step.
- *Success criteria.* Identify what it will take to be considered successful in pursuing the action steps. For instance, driving a 21 percent ROI sounds great, doesn't it? Sure, unless the customer's ROI target is 22 percent or more.
- *When is the action scheduled for completion?* To measure the progress of your agreed upon action steps, you will want to set clear, agreeable deadlines for completion.

When you present and close effectively, the meeting will give you the momentum necessary to gain buy-in from the decision maker on the objectives or action steps you have established for the account.

Make it easy for decision makers to get into the roundtable discussion. Use action steps you really want to accomplish and that you think will engage them. Given your closing question, decision makers really only have three options. They can terminate the meeting and shut you down, which is very rare. They can suggest moving forward but offer their own set of action steps (again, very rare). Or they can agree to move the relationship forward using your proposed action steps.

Because the roundtable discussion is an essential part of your close, the transition into it is particularly important. To make the transition as smooth as possible, ask the decision maker directly what to do next. Ways to phrase this question include, "These are our recommended action steps. How do you think we should proceed?" and "These are our recommended action steps. Is there any reason we shouldn't move forward?"

When you make the transition into the roundtable discussion, focus your energy, attention, and closing question on the decision maker. When you ask the decision maker, "How do you feel we should proceed?" this is not a general question you pose to the group. You don't want a product evaluator or gatekeeper to take over and assert control over the roundtable discussion. By directing your question to the decision maker, you allow him or her to drive the conversation that follows.

Remember to thoroughly document the action plan during or after the roundtable discussion. You want to avoid confusion later about who was supposed to do what or when something was to be completed. Get it all down on paper while it's still fresh in your mind and include this information in your presentation follow-up letter.

Often, one of the last action steps is scheduling a follow-up meeting with the decision maker. Your goals for this follow-up meeting will depend upon the specific situation, but it's always valuable to maintain access to the decision maker and review agreed upon action plans and accomplishments.

## ATTENTION, PLEASE! EFFECTIVE PRESENTATION DELIVERY

Now let's take a moment to review the tone you should take during each element of your presentation. The following chart will provide a handy guide to refresh your memory at a glance:

| Presentation Element | Presenter's Tone |
|---|---|
| Introduction | Taking control |
| Objectives and Agenda | Prepared |
| Customer Overview | Humble |
| Your Company Overview | Confident |
| Business Fit | Enthusiastic |
| Action Steps | Assertive |

As you rehearse your presentation, you should become so familiar with the appropriate tones for each section that you know them without having to refer to this page.

## Transitions Fluid

It is important to prepare smooth, seamless transitions from section to section, page to page, and point to point in your presentation. Smooth transitions turn your presentation into a well-crafted story. Here are some suggestions for where you should make key transitions:

| Following . . . | Make the transition by . . . |
|---|---|
| Each point | Linking the points |
| Each page | Linking the topics |
| The customer section | Confirming your understanding |
| The section on your company | Recapping and introducing the business fit |
| The business fit | Summarizing and introducing the action steps |
| The action steps | Moving to the roundtable discussion |

## Sample Key Transitions

To ensure that you will be comfortable during the presentation, prepare and rehearse your planned transitions. Here are some sample transitions between the pages of your presentation you may wish to use.

**From Cover page to Presentation Objectives page.** Open by thanking the audience for the chance to present. Say, "Thank you for the opportunity to be here today." Then briefly describe what you plan to present. Depending on your goals for the presentation, you might say either of the following:

- "We're very excited to present to you the role that we feel we could play in impacting your strategic direction."
- "We're very excited to present to you the strong business fit that we see between [customer's company] and [your company]."

**From Presentation Objectives page to Agenda page (2 to 3).** "Now I'd like to share with you the road map we hope to follow to accomplish these objectives." [Turn page]

**From Agenda page to Customer Profile page (3 to 4).** "As we mentioned, we would like to start by sharing with you a little bit about what we've learned about your organization. Not that we're the experts, but we have been doing some homework and want to confirm that we're on target. As we began trying to understand a general profile of your company, we quickly discovered that there's an awful lot to learn. For instance. . . ." [Turn page]

**From Customer Profile page to Customer Business Objectives page (4 to 5).** "As we built this profile, we certainly wanted to understand where you are today, but we also wanted to understand where you're going in the future. We've tried to understand some of the critical objectives. Clearly, this isn't an all-inclusive list, but it contains a few of the things that jumped out at us." [Turn page]

**From Customer Business Objectives page to Customer Strategies page (5 to 6).** "It was interesting to learn about some of the strategies you've put in place to help achieve these objectives." [Turn page]

**From Customer Strategies page to Business Issues page (6 to 7).** "As we worked to understand these strategies and initiatives, we began to realize that these things aren't being addressed in a vacuum but that you may be facing a number of business issues as well. These may be a few of those challenges. . . ." [Turn page]

**From Business/Issues page to Departmental Issues page (7 to 8).** "Given these issues and concerns, we also wanted to boil down our research to a more focused level. We wanted to understand your [departmental] environment as well. Some of the things that came through were. . . ." [Turn page]

**Concluding the section on the customer.** After you finish confirming your understanding of the customer's departmental issues, say, "Before I move on to talk about my organization, I would like to pose one question: do you feel, based on my presentation up to this point, that we have at least a fair understanding of your business?"

If you've done your homework and presented an accurate portrait of the customer's business, the customer will typically respond positively. You then continue. "Thank you for that confirmation. It's very important to us, because the rest of the presentation is built on this understanding. What I would like to do now is move on to share with you a little about who we are and what we do." [Turn page]

**Between Your Company as a Strategic Resource page and Business Fit page (9 to 10).** "At this point, we'd like to take another step back. We shared with you a bit about what we've learned about your organization, and thank you again for your confirmation that we're on target. We've also shared with you a bit about who we are and what we do and why we feel we may be a strategic resource for your consideration. We'd now like to share with you what we consider to be the highlight of this presentation, and that is the very strong business fit that we see between our two organizations." [Turn page]

**Between Business Fit page and Action Steps/Timetable page (10 to 11).** "As a result of this business fit, I'd like to present and discuss the following preliminary action plan and path forward." [Turn page]

**Transition to the roundtable discussion.** After you have completed the action steps element of the presentation, make the transition to the roundtable discussion by doing the following:

- Conclude your presentation so that the action steps remain in full view, and say, "[Decision Maker], these are our recommendations. How do you feel we should proceed from here?"
- As you say this, move to sit down and join the roundtable.

Note that the tone of the transitions conforms to the appropriate tone you should exhibit during the different stages of the presentation (humble when talking to the customer about the customer, confident when talking to the customer about your company, etc.).

You have to be able to deliver these transitioning lines while moving from one page to the next. You can't peek or fake it.

### Effective Delivery Style

The following are some additional skills to focus on to make sure you deliver a polished, professional business presentation:

### Pace.

- Move crisply through the presentation.
- Err on the side of caution—don't go too slowly.
- Rehearse so that you know the length of the presentation ahead of time.
- Leave time for the action steps.

### Handling questions.

- During the presentation, defer questions to the roundtable discussion after the presentation.
- During the roundtable, address any questions succinctly.
- On technical questions or questions that require a highly detailed answer, try to stay at the technical level of the decision maker and defer a more detailed discussion to a later time.

### Tone.

- Remember to tell a story through every page.
- Don't read the material—the customer can do that perfectly well. You want to use the bulleted points to guide your storytelling.
- Use natural voice inflection and avoid a monotone delivery.
- Avoid hesitating nonwords; e.g., *um, er, ah.*
- Avoid overusing extra words or phrases; e.g., *you know* or *like.*
- Use silence to your advantage.

### Eye contact.

Eye contact is considered one of the most effective ways of communicating sincerity. One study indicated that 38 percent of all meaning that an audience receives comes solely from eye contact with the presenter. No question—eye contact is key to holding your audience's attention and getting feedback:

- In a small group, look at each individual.

- In a large group, look at individuals in each section.
- Focus on the decision maker.
- Duration of eye contact should be 2 to 3 seconds.

We don't know if it's true, but we've heard a story that illustrates the power of eye contact. According to the story, a professor in the communications department at a major university was renowned for pacing back and forth all the way across the stage as he delivered lectures in the auditorium classrooms.

At the beginning of a semester, one of his classes conspired to conduct an experiment on the professor. They agreed to limit their eye contact in the next class meeting so that they would stop looking at him when he walked a certain distance away from the center of the stage. Each class period, the range where they would keep their eyes on him was then shortened. By the end of the course, although he was unaware of what the students were doing, the professor was lecturing exclusively from behind the podium.

## Body movement.

- Be smooth and natural.
- Avoid fiddling with small items; e.g., keys, pens, pointers.
- Be comfortable with the medium you have selected.
- Refer to your medium for reminders and emphasis.
- Stand erect and maintain good posture.
- Avoid excessive or exaggerated gesturing.
- Avoid signs of insecurity.
- Remember, the medium is not the message; you are.

Here's an important point worth repeating: don't distract the audience by fiddling with pens, glasses, coins, rings, butterfly knives, etc. During a presentation, one associate of ours was fiddling with a rubber band and he inadvertently launched it. Of course it landed right in the decision maker's lap.

## LETTER RIP: Following Up the Presentation

During your presentation, you communicated some critical points about you and your company. First, that you understand the customer's business and second, that your company can be a resource in helping the customer achieve objectives, implement critical strategies, and address key challenges.

You did a great deal of work to accomplish these two goals, so as you walk out of the customer's office, it's okay if you want to exhale deeply for the first time in weeks. But don't think that your job is over. Effective follow-up is important in maintaining momentum and achieving results.

Depending on the nature of your presentation, the action steps you established may include some sort of acceptance analysis, financial comparison, or development of an implementation plan. If so, you'll want to confirm all these activities in a follow-up letter that hits these points:

- Thank the decision maker and other attendees for their time and the opportunity to present.
- Review the action steps.
- Reiterate the agreed-upon success criteria and timetable.
- Schedule a follow-up meeting with management.

See Appendix E for a typical follow-up letter.

## CONCLUSION

As you were reading through this chapter, did you imagine yourself preparing for and delivering a presentation? Just thinking about it can be invigorating. And doing it is even more so. Standing in front of a powerful decision maker—the kind of person who may wield a multi-million-dollar budget—and weaving a powerful tale that describes how your two organizations, working together, can help the decision maker achieve key objectives—this is precisely the reason many of us became sales professionals in the first place.

Sadly, most salespeople never get the chance. Most of the time, they're stuck in the Vendor Trap, trying to explain to product evaluators why, even though their product is a little more expensive than the other guy's, it really is worth it for the value. But trying to sell value to evaluators is like trying to sell a slide rule to a young child. He won't understand what it is, and even if he did, he wouldn't know what to do with it.

In the off chance they do stumble into an opportunity to meet with a true decision maker, most salespeople wind up pitching features and benefits, interrupting when the customer tries to talk, and accomplishing little more than reinforcing the decision maker's mindset never to speak to another sales rep. Here's a message to that rep from all the rest of the hardworking sales professionals who are still trying to get in to meet that executive: "Thanks a lot, pal."

But the business presentation takes you away from all that. You get the chance to talk about something that matters to you—the high-level, long-term business solutions you and your company offer—and decision makers get to listen to a presentation about something they care about—solving the pressing business concerns that keep them tossing and turning at night.

We're confident that once you start delivering business presentations to decision makers who can actually buy the value you offer, you'll cringe to think you ever tolerated trying to sell to gatekeepers or sitting down and "chatting" with a decision maker. But don't worry about the gatekeepers getting lonely in their little offices without your company. Your competitors will keep them plenty busy selling their margins down the river, while you present in the corner office upstairs.

# CHAPTER ELEVEN

# Seal the Deal
## THE CLOSING PRESENTATION

Depending on your specific situation and account, you may have concluded the business presentation described in the previous chapter by closing on a deal with the decision maker. But that won't always be the case. One of the great strengths of this process is its flexibility—in other situations, you will close by gaining agreement from the decision maker to advance the process and meet again at a later date. This later meeting, where you will assess your progress and move forward from that point, becomes your close.

*"You win not by chance, but by preparation."—Roger Maris*

Just as you prepared your business presentation to the decision maker, you'll also want to plan your closing presentation. Remember, early and continued access to the decision maker is critical to your success. This is your first chance to get back in front of the decision maker, and with this presentation you'll want to maintain the momentum you've built up, while moving the process forward. The last thing you want to do in this meeting is to disappoint the decision maker. You made a terrific impression last time and set a lofty bar. Don't stumble now.

Dave Luby, Vice President of Sales for G&K Services, feels strongly about this. He says, "At this point, we've done all the right things, and it seems like the table is set. For many, it would be easy now to fall back to old ways and simply deliver a quote or have a chat. We won't let that happen. We take the closing presentation as seriously as the business presentation."

# REMEMBER THE PREMISES

Before you get started on developing the closing presentation, it's important to revisit a couple of the underlying premises that we described back in Chapter 2. Remember these?

Senior-level management is more likely to buy from you because of what you know about them and their business concerns than what they know about you and your company.

As you put together this presentation, remember to keep in mind the decision maker's big-picture business objectives and issues, not just how terrific your solution and company are. Focus on what has gotten you this far in the process and don't undermine all the work you've done by falling back on old Vendor Trap habits like closing on price or features.

For effective positioning, the power of a presentation exceeds the power of a product demonstration or a discussion.

Beyond Selling Value means you don't fall back. You know what works with senior-level decision makers, and you stick with it.

Because you've already made a formal presentation to the decision maker, you may wonder why you should come back a few weeks later and do so again. Why not just sit down and chat about where to go from here, right? The reason is that a chat does not carry the same weight as when you stand up and present. At this stage in the process, you're asking for a substantial commitment from the decision maker. By standing up and making another presentation, you ride the momentum you've generated while creating a decision making environment.

# PRESENTATION BREAKDOWN

So what is a closing presentation, exactly? One way to understand the objectives of this meeting is to make a distinction between the elements of the business presentation we covered in Chapter 10 and this closing presentation.

| Business Presentation | Closing Presentation |
|---|---|
| Is conceptual and strategic | Is targeted and specific |
| Typically, is the first presentation | Is usually a follow-up to the business presentation |
| Emphasizes the business fit | Emphasizes the action plan, accomplishments, and solution fit |
| Closes on advancing the process | Closes on the sale |

Essentially, the purpose of this meeting is to focus on the progress of the action steps you agreed on in the first presentation and close on a final agreement. Typically, the presentation consists of the following elements:

- Cover Page
- Presentation Objectives
- Agenda
- Background Review (this includes customer business review and business fit)
- Action Steps Summary
- Success Criteria
- Solution Overview
- Solution Fit
- Recommendations/Action Steps

As you look at this list of elements, you may be wondering: what are the differences between the two presentations? Compared to the business presentation, the closing presentation may differ by including:

- Less review of the customer's business
- A review of action steps and accomplishments
- A solution overview
- A review of the solution fit, not just the business fit
- A specific, solution-oriented recommendation and close

The actual pages from a sample presentation we've included should give you a better idea how these ideas translate onto the pages of your closing presentation. (See Figures 11.1 to 11.4.)

# AFTER THE BUSINESS PRESENTATION

You should have walked out of your business presentation with a set of action steps that you and the decision maker agreed on to move the relationship forward. Now it's your job to manage the selling process to keep that momentum going and deliver on your promises. At the same time, you should also continue working on your research. Research is not a one-shot deal that ends as soon as you get in front of the decision maker—it's an ongoing process that will continue as long as you have a relationship with this customer.

> *"It's the constant and determined effort that breaks down all resistance, sweeps away all obstacles."*—Claude M. Bristol

With that in mind, here are some of the key activities for you to consider tackling between the two presentations:

- *Talk to your coaches.* Provide your coaches with information regarding the results of the first presentation while keeping them involved and determined to help you win.
- *Get on it.* Whatever your follow-up action is, bring to bear the necessary resources to make it happen.
- *Talk to your people.* Let everyone on your team know about any deadlines and commitments, then keep their feet to the fire to make sure everything gets done.
- *Find answers.* Provide the customer organization with satisfactory answers to any questions they have about you, your company, or your solution.
- *Keep them informed.* Make sure that all the right players—coaches, contacts, and other presentation attendees—remain informed on the presentation follow-up activities.

As we move forward, we'll talk about three critical aspects of the closing presentation: development, delivery, and follow up. Bear in mind, however, that all the steps surrounding presentation covered in Chapter 10—coach review, rehearsal, logistics, etc.—still apply. But here, we're going to concentrate on the unique traits of the closing presentation.

FIGURE 11.1    Cover Page

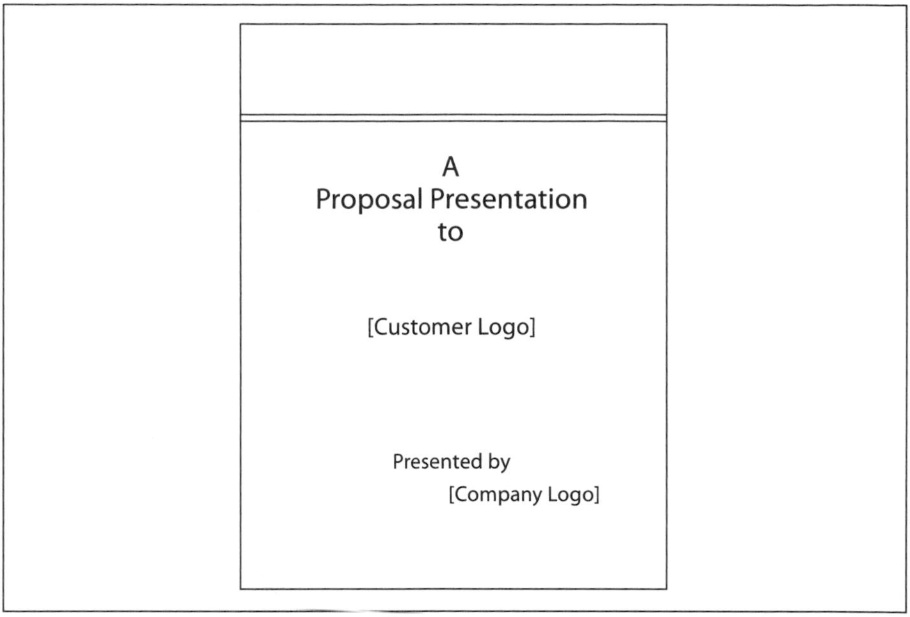

A
Proposal Presentation
to

[Customer Logo]

Presented by
[Company Logo]

FIGURE 11.2    Presentation Objectives

**Presentation Objectives**

- Review background
- Review action steps and activities
- Confirm the business fit between
  [Customer] and [Company]
- Review [Company] solution
- Solidify the business relationship

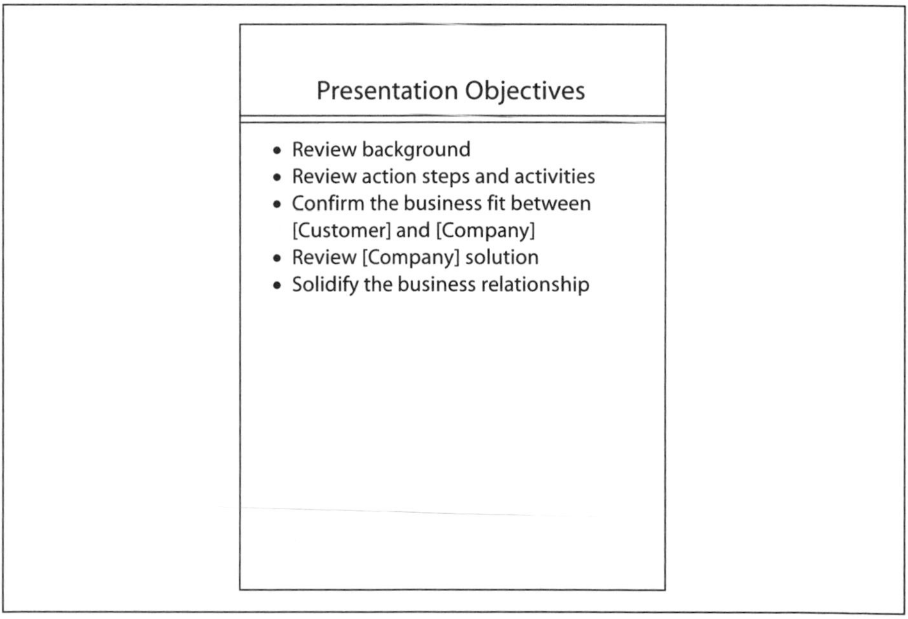

FIGURE 11.3    Agenda

**Agenda**

- Background review
  —Business initiatives
  —Business and I/S issues
  —[Customer/Company] business fit
- Action steps and activities
- Success criteria
- [Company] solution overview
- [Customer/Company] solution fit
- Action steps and timetable

FIGURE 11.4    Business Initiatives

**[Customer] Business Initiatives**

- Revenue/revenue growth
- Profitability
- Strategic direction
- Focus on efficiencies/re-engineering
- Customer service emphasis
- Value provider
- Leverage automation

# DEVELOPING THE CLOSING PRESENTATION

Although you will have to adapt your strategy to match different opportunities, the closing presentation that follows provides a general outline.

**Page 1: Cover Page.**  This page will prominently display the customer's logo along with a phrase like "A Business Solution" or "A Proposal Presentation." In the lower right corner, it should read, "Presented by [your company]." (See Figure 11.1.)

**Page 2: Presentation Objectives.**  This page includes a brief overview of what you hope to accomplish in this presentation. (See Figure 11.2.)

**Page 3: Agenda.**  Here, you include a bulleted list of the headings on successive pages. (See Figure 11.3.)

**Page 4: Customer Business Initiatives.**  Provide a brief review of the customer overview that you presented during the previous presentation. You don't need to cover this review as thoroughly as the first time you presented, just hit the highlights. (See Figure 11.4.)

**Page 5: Customer Business and I/S Issues.**  You may include either one or two pages in your review of the highlights. If one page is not sufficient, the second page will continue the brief review. (See Figure 11.5.)

**Page 6: Business Fit.**  Here you underscore once again the business fit you presented in the first presentation. (See Figure 11.6.)

**Pages 7, 8, 9: Action step summary.**  This is a summary of the action steps that you nailed down during your first business presentation. You should have set success criteria, responsibilities, and timetables, and now you're here to review your findings. The page that follows shows a summary as well as two specific pages around two specific action steps. (See Figures 11.7, 11.8, and 11.9.)

**Page 10: Success Criteria.**  These are the criteria you've identified that would make a solution successful in the customer's environment. (See Figure 11.10.)

**Page 11: Solution Overview.** Here is the specific information about your solution that you wish to present at this meeting. Remember to keep this discussion at the technical level of your decision maker. (See Figure 11.11.)

FIGURE 11.5    Business and I/S Issues

The [Customer/Company]
Business and I/S Issues

- Business
  —Economic and industry condition
  —Broad business mix
  —Inventory management
  —Labor intensive manual processes
- I/S issues
  —Systems currency
  —Logistics/distribution
  —Integration/database
  —Customer service

FIGURE 11.6    Business Fit

[Customer/Company]
Business Fit

- Builds on existing relationship
- Based on common values/
  philosophies
- Directly supports key initiatives
- Helps enhance attainment of critical
  business objectives
- Provides complementary resources
  and skills to support business and I/S
  issues

FIGURE 11.7   Action Step Summary

### Action Step Summary

- Solution presentation
- Application audit
- Financial justification
- Corporate visit
- Follow-up meeting
- Commitment

FIGURE 11.8   Action Step Pages

### Action Step:
### Application Audit

- Activity
  —Detailed study of applications/
  processes
  —Identification of strengths/
  weaknesses
- Responsibility
  —[Customer] – _____
  —[Company] – _____
- Results
  —Specific bottleneck resolution
  —Confirmed application fit

FIGURE 11.9    Action Step Pages

### Action Step: Financial Justification

- Activity
  - Detailed financial analysis
  - Review of acquisition alternatives
- Responsibility
  - [Customer] – _____
  - [Company] – _____
- Success criteria
  - Lease-purchase option
  - 18-month payback
  - 17% return on investment
- Results
  - 18-month payback
  - Est. 21% ROI
  - Intangible benefits

FIGURE 11.10    Success Criteria

### Success Criteria

- Resources
- Track record
- Teamwork
- Aggressive schedule
- Cost
- Follow through to implementation

FIGURE 11.11     Solution Overview

**[Company]**
**Solution Overview**

- [Note: a presentation of your solution follows]

FIGURE 11.12     Solution Fit

**Solution Fit**

- Resources
- Track record
- Teamwork
- Aggressive schedule
- Cost
- Follow through to implementation

- Support organization
- Industry recognition
- Joint planning
- Backlog/ availability
- ROI
- Comprehensive implementation plan

**Page 12: Solution Fit.** Review each of the decision criteria with your solution in mind to highlight the attributes of your solution and how to accomplish it. (See Figure 11.12.)

**Page 13: Recommendation.** Here is your pointed, specific recommendation that you want to close the decision maker on today. (See Figure 11.13.)

**Page 14: Action Steps.** These are the action steps that you've determined will get you to that close. (See Figure 11.14.)

Of course, when you put together your own closing presentation, you will adjust the template to match your presentation objectives, criteria, solution fit, action steps, etc.

> As you close this presentation, always end by scheduling your next meeting with the decision maker.

## DELIVERING THE CLOSING PRESENTATION

In Chapter 10, we talked about the importance of using the right tone of voice with each page as you walk through your presentation. Tone of voice is still important during the closing presentation. Use the following chart as a guide to help you develop the right tone for each page:

| Page | Tone |
|---|---|
| Cover Page | Take control |
| Presentation Objectives | Prepared |
| Agenda | Prepared |
| Customer Business Review | Humble |
| Business Fit Review | Enthusiastic |
| Action Step Summary and Activity | Confident |
| Success Criteria | Humble |
| Solution Overview | Confident |
| Solution Fit | Enthusiastic |
| Recommendations/Action Steps | Assertive |

### Transitions

Just as in your business presentation, during your closing presentation you'll want smooth, seamless transitions from page to page. Here are some suggestions for what you might want to say as you progress through this presentation:

FIGURE 11.13    Recommendation

### Recommendation

- Acquisition of solution
  —Cost: $ _____
  —Method of acquisition: _____
- Implementation
  —Schedule
  —Timeframe
- Business fit summary
  —Directly supports key initiatives
  —Helps enhance attainment of critical business objectives
  —Provides complementary resources and skills to support business and I/S issues

FIGURE 11.14    Action Steps/Timetable

### Action Steps/Timetable

- Confirm success criteria—Today
- Confirm solution fit—Today
- Gain decision to move forward —Today
- Implementation—Feb. 1
  —Confirm commitments and schedule
  —Prepare internal announcements
  —Initiate rollout
- Executive review—June 1

**From Cover Page to Presentation Objectives (1 to 2).** "Thank you all for the opportunity to be here. We're really excited about this chance to come back together again as a group and review where we were, what we've done, and where we might go from here. The objectives that we'd like to accomplish in this presentation are very straightforward. They are. . . ." [Turn page]

**From Presentation Objectives to Agenda (2 to 3).** "Like the objectives, the agenda is straightforward. Here's the road map we'd like to follow today." [Turn page]

**From Agenda to Customer Business Review (3 to 4 and 5).** "Last time we were together, we spent a little more time reviewing what we learned about your business. We started broadly and discussed what we'd learned in terms of profile, business direction, objectives and strategies, and some of the issues you faced as a business and here in your IT organization. Today, we'd like to review a little bit of that and come back to a couple of the most pressing business and IT issues that you're facing today." [Turn Page]

**From Customer Business Review to Business Fit Review (5 to 6).** "Also, last time we had the opportunity to review the business fit. Since that time, we've come to feel even stronger about it. Here's the fit that we think exists between our two companies." [Turn Page]

**From Business Fit Review to Action Step Summary and Activity (6 to 7, 8, and 9).** "As we mentioned, we really do think this is the highlight of our presentation, both the last time we were together and this time. Now let's review what we said we'd do coming out of our last presentation. These are the specific action steps we committed to pursuing, and here are the results that we realized." [Turn Page]

**From Action Step Summary and Activity to Success Criteria (9 to 10).** "Now we'd like to transition to what we understand to be the criteria that you are using as you move forward on your upcoming decision. Do we have the right understanding of your decision criteria? Great. That's important as we move forward and overview for you the solution that we're proposing." [Turn Page]

**From Success Criteria to Solution Overview (10 to 11).** "Following is an overview of our solution." [Turn page]

**From Solution Overview to Solution Fit (11 to 12).** "With that solution in mind, we'd like to share with you what we think is a great solution fit that supports the business fit we reviewed earlier. As we think about the decision criteria we presented, we believe that first. . . ." [Turn page]

In the section on success criteria, use this opportunity to confirm that your understanding of the criteria is on target. This is important, because you will use this later as you present your solution fit.

**From Solution Fit to Recommendations/Action Steps (12 to 13 and 14).** "Given the exciting solution fit we see between our two organizations and in context of the great business fit that we've discussed twice now, here is the specific recommendation that we'd like to make at this time. . . ." [Turn page]

**From Action Steps to roundtable.** "This is our recommendation. When can we get started?" [Sit down and join the roundtable.]

Succinctly outline your recommendations, then close like a cheetah chasing down a limping gazelle on the Serengeti.

## FOLLOW UP ON THE CLOSING PRESENTATION

Finally, with a wealth of research under your belt, some fancy footwork to develop your coach network and handle gatekeepers behind you, and two customized, business-oriented presentations concluded, you've closed on the relationship. Congratulations and good for you. But before you take off for your celebratory trip to Disney World, you want to make sure all your *I*'s are dotted and *T*'s are crossed. That means following up your closing presentation with a letter thanking the decision maker for his or her time and confirming the action steps.

In Appendix F, we've included an example of a typical closing presentation follow-up letter.

## CONCLUSION

As you're developing your strategy for each individual opportunity, you'll have to decide whether the situation calls for closing on a specific solution in the initial business presentation to the decision maker or if a separate closing presentation is more appropriate. As you become more familiar with the process and get a better feel for your own comfort level and what works best with your customers, you'll develop an instinct for which approach offers the most promise.

Whichever path you choose, make sure you remember to close at some point. You may find this process makes selling a lot more fun and simplifies your path to the decision maker. But the end goal isn't just to get in front of and impress senior-level executives. The whole reason you've put in all this effort is to close sales and build value-based relationships. To accomplish that goal, you still need to ask for the business.

Bob Fidler, Vice President of Sales and Marketing for Corporate Express, reflects how many of us feel about closing when he says, "This is what many of us love the most about selling—going for the close. Knowing that you're driving a decision that will impact your customer, your company, and yourself. This is where the thrill is for a lot of us, and a closing presentation can really help make it happen."

As this cartoon illustrates, sometimes the objective is staring you right in the face. For sales professionals, we're the ones in your corner yelling for you to, "Go for the close! The close!"

"Forget the body blows! Go for the head! The head!"

# CHAPTER TWELVE

# Every Shot a Bull's-Eye
## TARGET OPPORTUNITY SELECTION

Now that we've talked about the entire sales process, from research through communication and presentation, you're probably pretty enthused about getting started and applying what you've learned. That's great—you should be excited. But the question inevitably arises: which accounts or opportunities make the best candidates for applying the process?

> *"Success doesn't come to you . . . you go to it."—Marva Collins*

## Facing the Time Crunch

It's a legitimate question. Today's sales professionals are frequently racing around at top speed, and your success will often depend as much on how well you budget your time as on how you spend that time.

You may be inclined to chase after opportunities where you have a strong chance of winning. In other cases, you may want to attack accounts where your odds of success are slim but you'd still like to get into the fray and compete. And, of course, there's a great deal of room between these two. Before deciding where to prioritize your time, you'll want to analyze your accounts and opportunities to know exactly where you stand. This chapter provides a tool to help you do exactly that.

In this chapter and the next, we use the term *opportunities* to refer to individual accounts, multiple opportunities within a given account, and multiple accounts across territories. No matter which of these circumstances most accurately describes your selling environment, this selection process works effectively for each.

As Regan Hutton, Senior Vice President of Corporate Sales for US Bank, says, "It's tough out there, tougher than ever before. We just can't afford to waste our time. As a result, we're spending our time on the best opportunities we have to be successful and sell our value."

> Beyond Selling Value means consistently asking these two questions:
>
> - Which opportunities should I prioritize?
> - How well positioned am I to win?

## OPPORTUNITY CRITERIA

We use ten criteria to evaluate potential opportunities, separated into five traditional qualifying guidelines and five guidelines that focus on more strategic issues.

### Traditional Qualifying Guidelines

Consider the following criteria and circumstances to better understand each opportunity you assess:

**Product fit.** The appropriateness of your company's solutions to the customer's needs.
Circumstances:

- There's not a good product fit.
- My competitor may have a better product fit.
- My product will definitely do the job.
- My solution, whether a new program or expansion of an existing relationship, is designed with the customer's needs in mind.
- My product is clearly a superior fit, and the customer knows it.

**Relationship value.** The short-term and long-term effects of a business relationship with the account or opportunity.
Circumstances:

- The opportunity is smaller than I'd like.
- If I get this business, I will make money, and the implementation will go smoothly.
- This business is significant and is likely to lead to repeat or additional business.

- This business will represent a significant revenue contribution to the company, be nicely profitable, and lead to an ongoing revenue stream.
- The customer/prospect is a major player in its industry and an impressive reference for me with my other accounts.

*"A good system shortens the road to the goal."—Orison Swett Marden*

**Budget.**  The availability of budget at this account or for this opportunity. Circumstances:

- A budget is not in place at this time.
- The need is there, but the financial backing must be reprioritized.
- A recognized need for financial budget is identified.
- I know that the target company has earmarked funds for this project.
- I know that getting funds will not be a problem.

**Logistics.**  The ease in getting to the location at reasonable cost. Circumstances:

- Because of location, sustaining a sales and support effort can be difficult and expensive.
- Because of location, I can easily and inexpensively sustain a sales and support effort.

**Customer urgency.**  The presence or absence of an immediate need. Circumstances:

- There is no sense of urgency.
- The customer would like to act soon, but the world will not come to an end if they do nothing at all.
- The customer must act soon. The cost of doing nothing is high.

## Strategic Guidelines

*"Things which matter most must never be at the mercy of things which matter least."—Goethe*

The next five criteria are the ones that matter most.

Consider these five additional criteria and circumstances, which are more aligned with a value-based approach to selling:

**Quality of information.** These circumstances highlight what you need to know about your customer's business. The better you can understand these, the better positioned you are to compete and win on value.

Circumstances:

- I can draw a complete and accurate organization chart for the department or division I'm working with.
- I can draw a complete and accurate organization chart for all related departments and divisions.
- I can provide a general profile of the company, including primary products and services, customers, competitors, and position in the industry.
- The information that I have acquired is from an insider's perspective.
- I can articulate the mission-critical issues facing this company from the senior executive perspective.
- I can describe where the company is going, how they plan to get there, and what obstacles they have to overcome to do so.
- I know their buzz words and acronyms.
- I know what keeps the decision maker awake at night.
- I know the first three issues the decision maker might raise at a staff meeting.
- If I were to present my perception of their business to the decision maker, he or she might say, "You understand our business better than some of my own people."
- I have a clear picture of the informal organization chart; i.e., the distribution of influence in the account.
- I have a clear picture of the key players' current state/situation, objectives/priorities, and win if the solution is implemented.
- I can identify who in the organization has influence, the people who have big titles but little influence, and those who have lesser titles but substantial influence.
- I can provide a general description of the departmental profiles/direction and the relationship to corporate direction, current situation and strategies, priorities and objectives, and buying process.
- I know my competitors' differentiating messages, who is coaching the competition, and to which powerful people my competitors are connected.

> The level of knowledge you have or want to gain on your account may depend on your role and the type and size of your territory.

**Quality of coaching.** The likelihood that you'll be able to find good coach candidates—people who not only have the critical insider perspective on the account but who will be willing to share it with you.
Circumstances:

- I know no one at the account.
- I have a few contacts who are willing to share information.
- I can identify contacts either within or outside the company who can articulate the company's philosophy, objectives, strategies, obstacles, major projects and budget items, and key players.
- My contacts are generally open to sharing business information with me, but they may not be comfortable sharing the real inside story and the political organizational structure.
- I have identified the personal or business reasons that contacts are sharing information with me and not with my competitors (their win).
- I have coaches who will:
  - Admit to not knowing things and tell me who does know
  - Help me identify other opportunities for my company or create opportunities that did not exist
  - Encourage me to gain access to senior-level management and guide me to the most expedient path to them
  - Provide me with access to the people I need to see
- My coaches have significant influence with the decision maker
- I have coaches in key future areas of opportunity
- I have coaches in senior-level management

**Strength of gatekeepers.** The influence and actions of individuals within the account who can restrict access to the decision maker and block your strategy.
Circumstances:

- I have no gatekeepers within the account.
- There is a threat of potential gatekeepers.
- I currently have gatekeepers, but they are weak.
- My gatekeepers actively block me.
- My gatekeepers have significant influence with the decision maker.
- I have gatekeepers in key future areas of opportunity.
- I have gatekeepers in senior-level management.

**Alignment with influence.** The strength of your existing relationship with the decision maker and others who have influence on the decision making process.

Circumstances:

- Someone influential in the company or on the decision maker's team has had a negative experience with me or my company and still holds a grudge.
- I do not have relationships with the influential key players.
- One or more key players with the specific expertise to influence this decision is in my camp—and I can articulate why.
- I am aligned with all the critical players and can articulate why.
- I do not have access to the decision maker.
- I can gain access to the decision maker.
- I have had at least one successful business meeting with the decision maker and this person expressed support for me.
- I have ongoing access and a strong business relationship with the decision maker.

**Philosophical fit.** The similarity of feelings between your two companies on buying value and openness in building partner relationships and culture.
Circumstances:

- The company has a track record of not investing in value.
- The company is open to establishing partnerships.
- The company is extremely compatible with my company relative to:
    - Value-added selling versus price only
    - Strategic relationships versus vendor-on-demand
    - Corporate culture
    - Technical philosophy
    - Financial philosophy
    - Willingness to share information
    - Management style

> Think of these five strategic guidelines in Steven Covey terms. They are Quadrant II items—not urgent, but definitely most important.

For a more systematic approach, refer to the Target Opportunity Selection Criteria chart in Appendix G. There, you'll be able to assign numeric values to each specific criterion and come out with a total score for each account or opportunity.

As you look over your accounts and apply these criteria, you should gain a solid understanding of whether you want to pursue the opportunity and, if you do, how well positioned you are to win it. With that in mind, you can interpret the results any way you want. As we said, you may opt to go after an account or opportunity where you already stand a pretty good chance of winning, or you may prefer to chase after a long shot. The choice is yours.

Here's what Norman Schippers, a principal with Hewitt, a global leader in HR outsourcing and consulting, says:

> Like most sales reps, I was taught the traditional qualifying criteria like availability of budget or strength of the product fit. These are fine if you're selling a product or a service. But if you want to sell value, you have to go beyond these. That's what we do—we go beyond and consider more strategic criteria, like our alignment with influence and the philosophical fit between our companies.

Besides helping you size up which accounts and/or opportunities to pursue, however, this selection tool also offers a variety of other applications. You may also analyze your accounts against these criteria to do the following:

- *Begin the preliminary stages of account planning* (a topic we'll explore more thoroughly in the next chapter).
- *Evaluate your progress over time.* By asking yourself the same questions about the account at the three-month, the six-month, or the year mark, you can chart where you're making inroads and where more work remains.
- *Monitor the competition.* You can use the same criteria and guidelines to assess your competitors' chances of success with the same opportunity. With luck, your penetration will increase, while theirs stays the same or dwindles.

## CONCLUSION

Clearly, you'll consider many factors in assessing your opportunities. But almost more important than the criteria you look at is that you do get started somewhere. You've come this far, and you don't want to get so bogged down in paralysis through analysis that you never take that first step. So let's move on and plan how you should take on that next account. Let's begin applying the process.

# CHAPTER THIRTEEN

# Sweating the Details
## OPPORTUNITY PLANNING

Now that you've selected the right account or opportunity, you're ready to dig in and begin implementing this process. There's no need to be nervous—thousands of sales professionals around the globe are succeeding every day with this unique approach to the sales process. And so can you. But first you need a plan.

> *"Success or failure is often determined on the drawing board."*
> —*Robert J. McKain*

As you get started, please remember that this chapter is not meant to be a comprehensive overview of account planning. That's another book entirely. Instead, it is meant to reinforce the importance of an account or opportunity plan and to highlight some critical elements you may want to consider as you utilize this process.

## Plan It

As a professional, you probably already understand the power and value in developing a detailed plan of attack. You wouldn't begin building a house without a plan, and the same is true when you're building an important business relationship. So let's put that plan together quickly and efficiently.

> *"It's not the plan that's important, it's the planning."*—*Graeme Edwards*

The four questions you want to ask yourself while developing your opportunity plan are:

1. What do I know today about the account?
2. What do I need to know?
3. What is my objective for the account?
4. What is my action plan to accomplish this?

Here's what Dave Oulighan, Vice President, Global Customers for D&B, says about the importance of planning:

> I've been a part of planning sessions that lasted half an hour and half a week. Every situation is different, so there's no right or wrong. What is critical is that we plan.

## What Do You Know?

The first step in putting together a plan is to understand what you know today about the account. You want to get the lay of the land. Your goal is to gather all the data and information sources you can to build a preliminary profile based on what you know right now about the account.

> Beyond Selling Value means beginning the planning process by identifying what you know and, therefore, what you need to know versus how much you want to sell.

Going through the target opportunity selection process described in Chapter 12 should have given you a solid foundation for understanding what you already know about this opportunity.

## Collect Yourself

Gather all the available data you have, including any information sources that are currently in your account files. As you compile these resources, go through a mental checklist to make sure you've got all of the data you need. Refer back to Chapter 3 to remind yourself of everything you want to get your hands on. That means the annual report, the quarterly report, the 10K reports (if applicable), and brokerage reports if it's a publicly traded company. It may mean a D&B Report or recently published articles. Don't forget to look into the company's brochures, sales literature, newsletters, and company Web sites. Leverage the Internet as much as possible to gather a lot of this data quickly and efficiently. Make a list of everything you think you'll need, and put an action step in your action plan to gather those sources as soon as possible.

> *"The fool wonders, the wise man asks."*—*Benjamin Disraeli*

## Research Elements Breakdown

As you begin to piece together what you already know about the account, it's helpful to divide this thought process into manageable chunks. We recommend using the first four research elements—corporate profile/direction, organizational structure, key players/profiles, and departmental profile/direction—to guide you.

Looking over your information, think about the questions we talked about in Chapter 4. Here are some of the questions to ask yourself for each research element:

**Corporate profile/direction.** What are some key aspects of this company's profile (e.g., products, markets, customers)?

- What is their mission or vision?
- What is their culture, personality, and philosophy?
- What are the key challenges they face, both externally and internally?
- What are some of the issues facing their industry today?
- What are the top priorities and objectives of senior-level management?
- What are the company's business objectives?
- How do they measure success?
- What strategies do they have in place?

> Understand as much as you can about the big-picture direction. It's hard to help a company get where they need to go if you don't know where they're going.

## Organizational structure.

- What is the formal organizational structure?
- What is the informal or dotted-line structure?
- What are some of the key social relationships?

- Who are some people with significant influence?
- Who is the decision maker? Coaches? Evaluators? Gatekeepers? Users?
- How strong are your relationships with the key players?
- Where are your competitor's key relationships today?

## Key players/profiles.

- Who are the key players at this account?
- What are the key players' buying roles?
- What are the profiles of each of the key players—backgrounds, objectives, strategies, operating style, personal likes and dislikes, personal interests, goals, and major issues or concerns?

## Departmental profile/direction.

- Which department(s) are you trying to sell into?
- What is this department doing to support the CEO's vision?
- Who are the key players in the department?
- What are their objectives and strategies?
- What are the department's major issues, concerns, and challenges?
- How many people are in the department, and what is the trend?
- What are their frequently used acronyms and buzzwords?
- What is the department's traditional decision making process?

In some cases, the target department will be obvious, but in other opportunities, there may be multiple departments. Sales, marketing, engineering, quality, manufacturing, production, information systems, human resources —your solution might make an impact on any number of departments. If that's the case, you may want to go through these questions for each department, depending upon your scope of involvement with the account.

In Appendix H, we've included a simplified planning tool that should help you get started as you plan your individual accounts.

## Business Fit

If you have an existing relationship or experience with this account, you may have a clear idea what the product fit is. But that's usually easy for us to understand—product fit is the sales rep's bread and butter, after all. A little more difficult is the business fit. Without a complete understanding of the customer's business, understanding the business fit will be a tall order at this juncture. But it should become much clearer as you move forward with your research. So for now, put business fit on the back burner and focus on coming to grips with the other four research elements. If you do that, business fit should follow.

## What Do I Need to Know?

Categorizing what you already know about the customer's business will not only give you a sense of where you stand right now, it will also give you a feel for what you still need to find out. Looking at your information and your data and then considering the questions listed above, what gaps stand out?

> *"You can tell whether a man is clever by his answers. You can tell whether a man is wise by his questions."*—*Naguib Mahfouz*
>
> Know what questions you still have and keep asking them.

For example, maybe you know a lot about the sales department, but not much about marketing and how the two work together. Or you may have a detailed profile on your coach, but you don't even know how to spell the decision maker's name, not to mention have any idea of her top priorities. It's also possible that you don't have a clear understanding of the organizational structure.

Wherever the holes are, take these gaps in your knowledge of the customer's business and turn them into a set of unanswered questions. You should be able to generate a list of questions that, once you've answered them, will provide you with a strong understanding of this account. Use data and information to answer this list of questions.

> *"There is no achievement without goals."*—*Robert J. McKain*

## What Is My Account Objective?

Now it's time to put together an account objective. Your objectives could be focused on either opportunities or relationships. Essentially, the account objective is a statement of purpose articulating your precise goal and how you plan to achieve it. Here's an example:

> My objective with this account is to use the IMPAX Process to gain access to the senior-level decision maker, who at this time I believe is Merrill Stubing, the Captain. I want to gain access to Merrill Stubing through my coach, Gopher Smith. Working with Gopher, I will schedule a meeting with Merrill to conduct a hard-hitting business presentation to position my company as a true business resource for Merrill and his organization and to identify specific, tangible opportunities.

That's an exciting objective. Some might even say "exciting and new."

But as you move forward, the results of your research may require you to tweak your strategy. You may even modify your objective. Changing your objective is a natural result of increasing your understanding, so expect it. That said, it's best to begin with a firm foundation and then be flexible as you advance.

### What Is My Action Plan?

> *"Planning without action is futile, action without planning is fatal."*
> —*Unknown*

Here you list the key activities that you want to accomplish to achieve your objectives. Your action plan may include such items as:

- Get additional data.
- Conduct research meetings.
- Identify the decision maker.
- Gain access to the decision maker.
- Develop the presentation.
- Conduct a coach review.
- Deliver the presentation.

## CONCLUSION

With all these questions, the opportunity planning process may seem a little involved, but it's actually quite simple. It's certainly not a step that should slow you down. If anything, it should speed things up. Whether you spend an hour, a day, or a week on your plan, when you have an account plan in place, you're well positioned to hit the ground running with the process and win.

As one of our clients, Bruce Hanley, a sales executive with Nortel Networks, says:

> We all know we're supposed to plan, but how many of us don't? We may think we're too busy or that we can just wing it. What I've found is the opposite is true. Selling value is tough enough. Without a plan it's brutal.

General George S. Patton had something to say about planning, too: "A good plan today is better than a perfect plan tomorrow." So get going. Put your plan together and execute.

14

# "I See You Have Your Hand Raised . . ."

## FREQUENTLY ASKED QUESTIONS ABOUT THE IMPAX® PROCESS

The IMPAX Process does represent a significant departure from the way many salespeople have been trained to approach their accounts. So it's natural that you may have some additional questions about the process. Here are a few we tend to hear most frequently.

**Where does this process fit the best?** Let's let Charlie Burnham, the CEO of Burnham Insurance, answer this question:

> We wondered the same thing, and even made some assumptions of where we wanted to use the process—and where we didn't. Yet in one nine-month period, we sold the two biggest deals in the history of our company, used it to get acquired by a terrific parent company, and watched as one of our sales professionals made five presentations in five days and closed all five opportunities. For us, the process works everywhere!
>
> Sure, there are some variables we have to consider, like the size of the opportunity, our objective, the complexity of the situation, whether it's a customer or a prospect, whether it's publicly or privately held, how much time we have, and whether we're in a proactive or reactive position. The answers to these questions help us decide how much planning to do, how much data to get, how many research calls to make, and how high to elevate our access. In the end, we take no excuses—we use the process to sell value everywhere.

We have many clients who, like Burnham Insurance, use the process in many different situations: Travelers Express, the largest money order company in the world, sells to the neighborhood pharmacy and to Safeway; G&K Services, a supplier of uniform services, sells to the local gas stations and to Honeywell; D&B sells business information services to sole proprietors as well as to GE; Securian sells to small credit unions and the nation's largest banks. The list goes on. The best tool for determining which accounts make good candidates for using the process in your selling environment is getting some real-world experience using the process in a variety of opportunities.

**How many research calls should I make before I'm ready to schedule a presentation?**  Going into an account for the first time, it's natural to want to know how much effort you should invest and what you should expect to get out of that effort. But every situation is different, so the unsatisfying answer to this question tends to be, "It varies."

If you've got strategic accounts, you'll probably conduct several face-to-face research meetings. But if you have a particularly large territory, you may conduct only one or two research meetings, and those may take place over the phone. So there's no right or wrong answer to the question of how many research meetings to conduct. Remember, however, that in terms of scheduling the presentation to the decision maker, you should get that done as early as possible in the sales cycle.

**What do I do if I'm in the middle of a research meeting and I realize that I'm meeting with a gatekeeper?**  This can happen. You may find that as you get into a research meeting, the person across the table begins to demonstrate an interest in controlling your movements throughout the organization. Their interest might be antagonistic or just a seemingly friendly impulse. If you sense this, don't mention your plans to make a senior-level management presentation. Remember, it's easier to apologize for going over someone's head if you were never told not to do so. Generally, the longer you stay in that call, the greater your chances of being blocked. So if you sense you're in a research meeting with a gatekeeper, your best bet is to bring the meeting to a professional but quick conclusion.

**Should I always write an Access Letter to get a presentation meeting scheduled?**  The Access Letter is certainly a high-impact tool. However, the answer to the question is no. Only use an Access Letter when your relationship is not strong enough to schedule the meeting yourself or you don't have a coach with the credibility to schedule this meeting for you. These should be your first two options, but if neither is available, that's when you write an Access Letter. It's an effective tool for gaining access to decision makers, but doing it well takes some time.

**When I'm presenting to a customer, why should I bore them with a story about their own business?**  This is a good question, because if the presentation isn't delivered well, that's exactly what will happen. Or, worse than boring them, you'll wind up alienating them. This is why when you present to customers about their own business, you should use the humble tone we discussed in Chapter 10.

Bear in mind, however, that the power of the business presentation is that it's focused on the customer. This principle isn't rocket science, but when you open a presentation with the customer's logo and then transition into an overview of their business, you show that you're serious about being a true resource to the customer. Your approach also differentiates you from the competition. Your competitors probably typically focus on their own companies and products and come in talking exclusively about themselves. So remember: you won't bore customers with a story about their own business. In fact, this part may be the highlight of your presentation.

Remember, there are two tiers of people you sell to—senior level and lower level. Lower-level people typically want to learn more about your business, but senior-level people typically only want to learn more about their own business.

Here's how Rich Blakeman, a former VP of Sales for Norstan Consulting, an IT consulting firm, answers this question:

> Some of our reps wondered the same thing as they first learned the process. To some, the risk seemed big—the idea of presenting to the customer about their company was anything but second nature. Once they presented, however, everything changed. They saw that nothing was more interesting to senior-level decision makers than hearing about their own company from an outsider's perspective. It gave us the perfect platform to position ourselves as a valuable business resource.

**What happens after a business presentation? Where do I go from here?**
With your presentation, you have set the stage. Included with the presentation is a page of action steps, and now is your opportunity to prove the fit. This is the time for you and your organization to shine and show the customer why you ought to be doing business together. If proving the fit means doing a financial justification, technology assessments, needs assessments, reference visits, headquarter visits—whatever your organization does to prove the fit, that's how you move forward.

Think of the value of proving the fit now, after this presentation instead of before. Most salespeople go through these action steps before the account is truly qualified. If at the end of the presentation everybody's made a commitment to a series of action steps, this is an ideal time to carry out those steps. That's how you know you're using your resources in the best, most productive way possible.

**What are the biggest challenges associated with making a great presentation?** The biggest challenge many salespeople face is being humble enough when they present an overview of the customer's business. It's so easy to be confident and enthusiastic that you start coming across as though you're telling customers about their business instead of confirming what you learned in your research efforts. One of the keys to success is to use plenty of wiggle words and indefinite phrases such as *it seems, a few, about, approximately,* and *as we heard.* In addition, lowering your volume level and taking on more unassuming body language can support this humble positioning. Also, be sure not to use words like *clearly, obviously,* and *of course,* and avoid offering your opinion on the state of their business.

Another challenge is to make a great presentation when you're only using data. It's tough to show insight when you haven't been able to gather information and gain that critical insider perspective. Data will only get you so far.

A third challenge is not rehearsing enough to give you the confidence you need to make a great presentation.

Lastly, one of the biggest challenges is not using this business presentation with the decision maker. An evaluator isn't going to appreciate your value or the presentation the way a decision maker will.

**It sounds like this process takes a lot of time and lengthens the selling cycle. Does it?**  The answer to this question is a resounding no. This process is not intended to take time; it's intended to make time. It may seem that you have to take more time than you typically would in the front end of a selling cycle. But the reality for our clients is that you're going to be doing something anyway—it's just a question of what you're doing and how effective it is. Once you do your research, every activity that follows the research stage is done with higher probability of success.

What you won't do is chase after an account for six months only to find there's no budget or that the person you thought was the decision maker is in fact a gatekeeper. Once the process gets going, barriers start dropping and the effort you put in early in the cycle winds up saving you a great deal more time and effort as you progress toward a closed sale.

Many of our clients have answered this question by saying, "If you think you can't afford the time to implement the process, you probably can't afford the time not to."

**Do you have a visual representation of the process?**  Figure 14.1 illustrates the entire process, from opportunity identification all the way through the close.

**What advice do you have for someone using the process for the first time?**  Balance preparation with execution. Use the process and don't skip steps, but don't let yourself get so bogged down in the details that you never get to the presentation. Deliver that first presentation—once you make a business presentation, you won't want to go back.

FIGURE 14.1    The Process

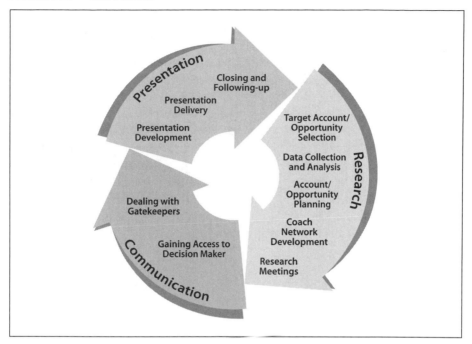

Also, don't pick Everest for your first climb. Choose an opportunity where you can practice the skills and learn the process. And remember, pick a situation that's important to you. That's the only way you'll care enough to follow through.

Don't let your comfort zones keep you from realizing the power of the process. We all have things we like to do and others we don't. Use the process as it's outlined here—focus on the customer, follow the 95-5 rule, and stand up and make a formal business presentation to senior-level decision makers (if you're feeling really adventurous, do what we do and use a flip chart!).

Tim Kelsey, an executive at Argus Insurance and a former Sales Manager for IBM, relates his first personal experience with the process:

> Like others, I had some questions about presenting to an executive about his company. I knew I needed to use the process, so I jumped in and did it. The presentation was powerful, and before I left the meeting, the president had written me a letter saying that I was his distribution management partner of choice. I got back to the office, and someone asked me what I sold. I said, "I don't know, but I'm their partner!" They then put me on retainer to show up at a couple of meetings

every month as an advisor. All because I had done my homework and shared with them what I learned.

**If we want to use a flip chart, how do we get one produced?**  We know of three ways. One, find a local graphic artist who has the capability to print a chart for you. Two, you can use your company's graphics department or internal print shop, or if that's not possible, have someone in your company buy a color ink jet plotter. Or three, use a convenience print center such as Kinko's.

**Any last advice?**  Yes—get to it. Like anything new, using this process won't necessarily be easy the first couple of times you do it. But just like golfing, rollerblading, or bridge, it gets easier, and more fun, every time you do it. And it will work. Horace said, *"Carpe diem, quam minimum, credula postero."* (Seize the day, put no trust in tomorrow.) There's no better time than right now to start using the process.

# CONCLUSION

In closing, we'd like to share with you an experience one of the authors had speaking at a global sales leadership conference. Here's how he tells the story:

I was invited to speak at the conference by a client, a company that sells business forms and services. In essence, what a business forms company does is put ink on paper, right? And anyone who puts ink on paper in this era is highly commoditized, or at least their customers are going to try to commoditize them and cram them into the vendor trap.

They had asked me to speak to the topic of selling value. At the time, they were only a small client of ours, but I saw this as an opportunity to turn them into a larger client, so I was really excited. Then, when I found out more about the agenda and that the audience was going to be 175 to 200 sales managers and executives, I became really excited.

The first speaker was the brand-new president of the business forms company. The venue was a large ballroom, the kind that's divided by partitions. There was no center aisle, just classroom tables across with one aisle on the side by the doors.

Standing in the back of the room I watched the president speak. He was electrifying. He was passionate and energized. He said, "We sell value. We cannot allow ourselves to be commoditized. We're a great company, we have terrific services and wonderful people. We sell value."

And then he said, "And to sell value, you simply have to sell higher, faster." He went back to this theme over and over again. He must have said, "Sell higher, faster," 30 times in 30 minutes. Here was a guy who believed in these people, believed in their value, and believed that they could sell value if they could do one thing—sell higher, faster.

Meanwhile, I'm standing in the back of the room watching the body language. Even from the back I could see the group getting charged up. The atmosphere was electrifying. Everyone was just pumped, and I was getting excited too. I couldn't have asked for a better intro.

As he began to wind up, I walked out of the room through a back door so I could reenter through a side door beside the stage. I stood outside, waiting for my intro. The president finished, received a huge round of applause, and got handshakes and slaps on the back from everyone along the way as he passed by on his way to his seat in the front row.

Then the emcee begins the intro. I'm really feeling it. I've got my intro story ready, and I'm thinking, "This is going to be great." But then the emcee started talking about "her" qualifications and what "she" did for a living, and I realized he wasn't introducing me (I'm pretty quick that way).

So a woman in the front row stood up and came on stage. She had an overhead projector ready with some overheads, and she launched into her speech. She looked at the group, pointed to the president, and said, "You can listen to him if you want," then paused to flip on the overhead projector, "but if you're going to sell to me, you'd better fill this out better than anyone else."

On the screen was a giant grid. Across the top of the grid were written: price, features, service, and so on. Down the other side were spots for Vendors #1-20. Nowhere on the grid appeared the word value.

She then continued, alternatively scaring and boring the wits out of these people. And then she sat down. No applause, no emotion, no life, nothing. The room was just dead.

Then the emcee got back up and introduced me. By this time, I had skulked away to the back of the room. The body language had turned completely. For the first and only time in my life, I felt claustrophobic. Everyone was pushing back to get away from this woman, away from her negative message.

So I came out, and the audience had no idea what to expect. "We got pumped; we got our butts kicked—all in the same hour. What are you going to do to us?" was the general attitude.

I opened by saying, "I'd love to be able to bridge the gap here, but I can't. There's no common ground between 'Sell higher, faster.' and, 'Fill out the grid better than anyone else.' And with all due respect," I said, pausing for effect, "I'd like to talk about how you sell higher, faster!"

And the place just came alive. I felt like a rock star. I talked about selling value, about dealing with gatekeepers like the woman who had just been on stage, and I walked off the stage as pumped as I've ever felt after a speech.

Since then, I've heard that this woman has won a permanent place in the company folklore as the Gridmeister. And I think whoever booked her lost his job or got shipped off to the company's Siberia division.

The Gridmeister story underscores the same point that we talked about in the introduction: it's not enough to dream about selling to senior-level management, all the while filling out your RFP response. It's not enough to say, "Gee, I wish I could go with the president and sell higher, faster," while you're trying to cram your solution into that stinking grid. Because out of those 20 companies, only one is going to win on the grid, and most of the time, the winner won't be a value provider.

In the introduction, we also said we were taking a stand; that rather than throw in the towel and admit that the direct sales professional is dying, forever tethered to the grid, that we were going to make a commitment—a commitment not only to selling the value our companies have to offer, but to sell that value to true decision makers—the only people genuinely poised to buy the value we sell.

Hall of Fame quarterback Fran Tarkenton knows how to take a stand. When asked by a prospective client if he could reduce his speaking fee by 50 percent because their budget couldn't accommodate his normal fee, he responded, "Which half of my presentation would you like to hear?" He wasn't about to give away his value.

Now you've read the book, and you've heard our case. Not only did we tell you that you can break out of the vendor trap and move beyond the traditional notion of selling value, we've also given you all the tools you'll need.

So we're throwing down the gauntlet and calling you to action. You've spent the time to read the book; don't stop now—go ahead and do that extra 20 percent. You've got opportunities out there. Now's the time to go to Appendix H, look at the opportunity assessment criteria, and plug in your opportunities. That process will help you determine in which opportunities you have the best chance to compete and win on value. Once you pick one, apply the simplified opportunity planner that's also included in Appendix H. In only a few minutes, you'll be executing a plan rather than just selling.

Next, jump into the research process. Get on the Internet and grab some data, make a few phone calls, get the data you need, and get it quickly. Identify some contacts and coaches. Schedule and conduct a few research meetings, whether on the phone or face-to-face. Just by doing that, you'll take huge strides in what you know about your accounts as you begin to distance yourself from the competition.

Identify your decision maker. Remember to find the person who can say yes when everyone else says no, and can say no when everyone else says yes. Get to that person. Use a letter, leverage a coach—do whatever it takes, but get to that person.

Deal with your gatekeepers, don't get blocked, don't take no for an answer. Draft your presentation, rehearse it like crazy, then stand up and blow that decision maker away. Deliver that first presentation in the next 30 days. Commit that within one month, you will stand up to make your first presentation to a decision maker who can buy value.

Do this, and you'll be in the same situation as IMPAX client Phil Styrlund, Vice President of global channels for ADC, a broadband company. Phil and his team use the process over and over again. Recently he said, "We've used the process in every imaginable situation. We've closed new customers, expanded existing customers, resolved issues, and even saved relationships. We use the process every time, and every time we use it, we're successful. This process has been responsible for millions of dollars of business."

What Phil is doing, and what you can do too, is the future of selling. But defining that future is not up to us. It's up to you, the 21st-century sales professional. Right now, you have two options. One, you can close this book, put it away on a shelf with all the others, and continue doing things the way they've always been done. If that's your choice, say hello to the gatekeepers for the rest of us.

The other option is to take a stand with us and change the way you sell and to whom. This option is an exciting possibility, isn't it? It's a little scary too. Change always is. But using the tactics and strategies we share in this book, we've found that thousands of salespeople have successfully made the transition. They're selling higher, faster. And the Gridmeister? She's setting her trap for somebody else.

To reinforce the concepts in this book, feel free to leverage some of the resources we've made available. At <www.impaxcorp.com> you'll find supportive articles as well as tips for going Beyond Selling Value. For help implementing the process, you can sign up to receive our tip-of-the-month via e-mail. Have you already had success using the process in *Beyond Selling Value*? Please send your stories to info@impaxcorp.com. Beyond Selling Value goes beyond the printed word. We speak to sales groups and teams around the world. For information about our supportive services, including training, consulting, coaching, and implementation tools (CDs, planners, software, etc.), or for anything else, contact us at info@impaxcorp.com or 1-800-457-4727.

Know that we are with you as you move Beyond Selling Value!

# SAMPLE RESEARCH MEETING QUESTIONS

## Research Element—Corporate Profile/Direction

*Profile*

- Can you give me a sense of your corporate mission?
- What is your recent financial performance (revenues, profits, market share . . .)?
- To what would you attribute your recent financial performance/trends?
- Who are your major customers?
- How are you perceived by your customers? How would you describe the value you bring to them?
- Why do your best customers buy from you?

*Objectives*

- What is your company's vision?
- What are the first three priorities the CEO is likely to bring up at a staff meeting?
- What are your company's top business objectives?
- Where do you see the business in the future, both in the short term and long term?
- What strategies are in place, or being put in place, to achieve these objectives?
- What are the company's critical success factors?
- How does the company measure its success?

*Issues*

- What is the biggest issue facing your company today?
- When the CEO is losing sleep at night, what do you think the top three to four issues are that keep him awake at night?

*Industry/Marketplace*
- What are the major external influences impacting the business today?
- What are some of the key industry trends your company is facing?
- Who are some of your closest competitors?
- What is your single greatest competitive advantage?
- What differentiates your business from the competition?

*General*
- How would you describe the philosophy of the organization?
- What event would you say has had the single greatest impact on the business in the past year?
- How will the business be different two years from today?

## Research Element—Organizational Structure

*Formal Organization*
- How is your organization structured to achieve your objectives?
- What are the major business segments or units?
- How do the different departments or divisions relate and interact?
- Can you help me draw out this organizational structure?

*Informal Organization*
- What is the informal or dotted line structure?
- Who does the decision maker turn to for guidance?
- Who has responsibility for the highest visibility projects in the company?

*Competitive Relationships*
- Where are the competitors' current relationships today? How would you describe them?
- How are the competitors perceived in the organization?

*Decision-Making Process*
- In addition to the decision maker, who else is involved in making key decisions?
- Who makes the final recommendations?
- Who has to approve the recommendations?
- If someone is going to shoot down a decision at the last hour, who would that be?

## Research Element—Key Players/Profiles

*Professional Background*
- What is her current role and set of responsibilities?
- What are her major accomplishments in that position?
- What is she proudest of in her career?

*Personal*
- How does he like to spend his personal time?
- What are his special interests, such as professional associations, service clubs, community . . . ?
- What are his personal and professional objectives?

*Issues/Concerns*
- What are her key concerns?
- What is the biggest issue she's facing now?
- What are the major issues affecting her department or organization now?

*Objectives/Priorities*
- What projects is he working on today?
- What are his top priorities?
- Where would he like to take his department or organization?

*Characteristics/Style*
- What is her management style?
- Does she make decisions quickly or slowly?
- How does she like to be presented to?
- Who does she rely on most for advice?

## Research Element—Departmental Profile/Direction

- What are the department's responsibilities?
- What is its mission?
- Who are their customers?
- What are the departments frequently used acronyms and buzzwords?
- How is the department perceived in the organization?

*Objectives/Strategies*
- What is the department doing to support the company's vision?
- Is there a strategic plan for the department?
- What is the top priority of the department?

*Projects*
- What are the department's major projects?
- What is the priority of these projects?
- What factors will influence the success of the projects?

*Issues/Concerns*
- What are the department's major issues, concerns, and challenges?
- What are the most critical issues facing the department?
- If money/time were no object, what would you fix, change, or invest in today? Why?

*Product Fit/Account Qualification*
- Who is your current supplier? How would you describe the strengths and weaknesses of their company and solutions?
- What would you change about your current situation?
- Can you give me an example of an outstanding supplier? What makes them outstanding?
- What is the payback if the department's primary objective is achieved?

# ACCESS LETTER EXAMPLE

Bud Palmer
Vice President

Dear Mr. Palmer:

Congratulations on your recent promotion from Director of the ARES Project to Vice President of the Information Systems Services Department. We recognize and respect the leadership you have provided to critical projects in the past, such as the ARES Project and the Global Positioning Satellite Project, and the leadership that you bring to ISS.

Now, as you lead ISS towards the Vision of having the finest information systems organization anywhere, and to providing the best customer service possible to both your internal clients and your ultimate customers, you may be considering such basic issues as:

- Measurement and improvement of end-user response time
- Development and management of the final implementation stages of the ARES Project
- Improvement in connectivity between various computer systems
- Effective gathering, storage, and use of data
- Availability of system "tools" for use in development and management of ISS products and services

Regarding these issues and others, Global Communications Systems can make substantial contributions that are consistent with your ISS objectives. That is why we are contacting you directly. Simply stated, we believe a mutual business opportunity currently exists. The benefits of this opportunity are directly related to the broad scope of your responsibilities.

As a point of reference, Global Communications Systems is the nation's largest privately held software systems company with over twenty years of consistent growth. We are best known for our data and network management tools as well as application-specific products. We have initiated our relationship with the installation of our network management package.

It is for these reasons that we request the opportunity to meet with you to make a concise business presentation on the above issues. The purpose of this meeting is not that of a product presentation. Instead, its content is directed at our long-term business relationship.

Mr. Palmer, we are eager for this opportunity for a brief meeting with you. If you are available during the week of July 18, we would like to schedule a 45-60 minute meeting. I will telephone your office in a few days to determine your availability for our meeting.

We look forward to meeting you.

Maureen O'Donnell

## BUSINESS PRESENTATION EXAMPLE
## (ORIENTED TOWARD CLOSING)

---

### A
### Business Presentation
### to

[Customer Logo]

Presented by
[Company Logo]

---

### Presentation Objectives

- Confirm our understanding of [Customer's] objectives and direction
- Clarify [Company] as a timely and strategic resource
- Initiate a business relationship

---

### Agenda

- [Customer]
  - A profile
  - Business objectives
  - Industry trends
  - Business issues/challenges
  - Business strategies
  - TQM/business process issues
- [Company]
  - A strategic resource
  - Commitment to the industry
- [Customer/Company] business fit
- [Company] proposal
  - Success criteria
  - Solution overview
  - Solution fit
- Action steps

---

### [Customer] Profile

- Founded 1951
- Mechanical engineering specialization
- Approximately 450 employees
- Products
- Markets
- Customers
- People

### [Customer]
### Business Objectives

- New business opportunities
- Profitability
- Return on capital employed
- Market share

### Industry Trends

- Market size
- Budgets
- Specialization
- Trend to peace
- Global environment

### [Customer] Business
### Issues/Challenges

- Aggressive competition
- Cost + to fixed price
- Integration of acquisition
- Maintain and enhance engineering expertise
- Subcontract vs. prime
- Spare parts
- Visibility
- Diverse customer set

### [Customer]
### Business Strategies

- New product development
- Acquisition
- Total quality management
- Customer focus
- Organization
- Early marketing involvement
- Leverage competitive advantage
- Cost reductions

### [Customer] TQM/Business Process Issues

- Capacity
- Costs
- Responsiveness
- Quality
- Interdepartmental processes
- Consistent job management

### [Company] A Strategic Resource

- Experience
- Proven methodology
- Practical vs. academic
- Business commitment
- Understand needs
- New ideas
- Resource availability

### Commitment to the Industry

- Twelve years of industry involvement
- Significant capital investment
- Joint ventures/strategic partnerships
- Track record of innovative solutions
- Integrated system of solutions
- Emphasis on service and support

### [Customer/Company] Business Fit

- Builds on a strong foundation with [Customer]
- Based on a set of shared philosophies
- Complements [Customer] strategies
  —Leverage technology
  —Total quality management
- Enhances attainment of business objectives
- Provides additional resource in attainment of [Customer] innovative direction
- Helps to address key TQM business issues

## Success Criteria

- Methodology
- Experience
- Credibility
- Business commitment
- Understanding needs

## [Company] Solution Overview

- [Note: this is where the solution is presented]

## Solution Fit

- Proven methodology
- Experienced staff
- References
- Business unit focus
- [Customer/Company] business fit

## Action Steps

- Confirm the business fit
- Confirm the solution fit
- Gain authorization to proceed
- Perform quality assessment
- Educate executives
- Develop and implement communication plan to employees
- Conduct facilitator training
- Perform BPR on selected processes
- Report to management on an ongoing basis

# BUSINESS PRESENTATION CONFIRMATION
# LETTER EXAMPLE

Mike Davidson
Executive Vice President

Dear Mike:

We look forward to our presentation on Thursday, December 6, at 10:00 AM, to be held in Conference Room A.

We are planning a brief presentation of a mutually beneficial business opportunity. The focus of the presentation will be on such strategic issues as:

- Identifying market changes in a short enough time to allow your organization to respond well ahead of competition.
- Expanding in-house capabilities and up-stream integration in order to provide a stronger competitive advantage.
- Improving productivity to enhance responsiveness and proactively avoid service delays.

Recognizing the strategic importance of a potential business relationship between our companies, Ted Welch, the president of my company, will be attending the presentation.

I will call Shelly Marquette to confirm the details to ensure a productive meeting, and contact each of the invited attendees as we discussed. Once again, thank you for your interest.

Cordially,

Gina Wright

# BUSINESS PRESENTATION FOLLOW-UP
# LETTER EXAMPLE

Ms. Patricia Walker
Vice President

Dear Patricia:

Thank you for the opportunity to present to you on Monday. We appreciated the time you spent with us and enjoyed our meeting.

As we did our homework in preparation for this presentation, we could not help but be excited about Scott Engineering's business direction. As you know, we strongly believe in the fit between our two organizations. We hope we have an opportunity to help contribute to your direction.

As you determined following our meeting, we will send you a proposal, provide you with some references, and call you to set up a time on Friday to meet with you.

Again, thank you. If you have any questions, please call me. We would be proud to kick off a relationship with you.

Sincerely,

Kathy Petters

APPENDIX F

# CLOSING PRESENTATION FOLLOW-UP
# LETTER EXAMPLE

Chris Mercury
Chief Financial Officer
LaRue International

Dear Chris:

Thank you for your cordial reception, time, and feedback on my presentation yesterday. I appreciate the opportunity you have given PCR Consulting to confirm the business fit between our companies and am excited about your high level of interest and receptivity to move forward in this implementation.

As a result of our meeting and previous conversation with your staff, we look forward to working with your organization to contain costs and improve productivity through re-engineering current production practices.

As I understand it, the next steps are as follows:

- Work through Jan to implement throughout your plant locations in the next two months.
- Assist Geri in the development of a corporate-wide policy and procedure document.
- Explore the financial aspects of the program with Mary in Canada.

Thank you again for your time. As we agreed, Marie and I will share the results of these projects with you in mid-June. I look forward to a long and mutually beneficial relationship with LaRue International.

Cordially,

Earl Billesby

# IMPAX® TARGET OPPORTUNITY SELECTION MODEL

| Traditional Criteria | | | | | | | |
|---|---|---|---|---|---|---|---|
| 1. Product Fit (0 to +10) | | | | | | | |
| 2. Value to Your Company (0 to +10) | | | | | | | |
| 3. Budget Availability (0 to + 5) | | | | | | | |
| 4. Logistics (–5 to +5) | | | | | | | |
| 5. Customer Urgency (0 to +10) | | | | | | | |
| **Subtotal** | | | | | | | |
| Strategic Criteria | | | | | | | |
| 6. Quality of Information (–5 to +15) | | | | | | | |
| 7. Quality of Coaching (0 to +20) | | | | | | | |
| 8. Strength of Gatekeepers (–10 to 0) | | | | | | | |
| 9. Alignment with Influence (–5 to +15) | | | | | | | |
| 10. Philosophical Fit (–10 to +10) | | | | | | | |
| **Subtotal** | | | | | | | |
| **Grand Total** | | | | | | | |
| **Account Name** | | | | | | | |

## IMPAX® OPPORTUNITY PLANNER

### Account Profile

| Account:<br>Date:<br>Sales Rep:<br><br>**Background:** | **Data Sources Checklist:**<br>❑ Annual report<br>❑ Quarterly reports<br>❑ 10K Report<br>❑ D&B Report<br>❑ Recent articles<br>❑ News releases<br>❑ Co. brochures<br>❑ Prod. literature<br>❑ Co. newsletters<br>❑ Who's who<br>❑ Mgmt. bios<br>❑ Brokerage report<br>❑ Web Site<br>❑ Other | **Target Opportunity Selection:**<br>__ 0 – 10 Product Fit<br>__ 0 – 10 Value to Company<br>__ 0 – 5 Budget Availability<br>__ -5 – 5 Logistics<br>__ 0 – 10 Customer Urgency<br><br>**Total:** | __ 5 – 15 Quality of Information<br>__ 0 – 20 Quality of Coaching<br>__ -10 – 0 Strength of Gatekeepers<br>__ - 5 – 15 Alignment with influence<br>__ -10 – 10 Philosophical Fit |
|---|---|---|---|
| **Opportunities:** | | **Obstacles:** | |

### Account Objectives

| Short Term | Long Term |
|---|---|
|  |  |
|  |  |
|  |  |

### Account Knowledge

|  | Corporate Profile/Direction: Company Profile | Corporate Profile/Direction: Business Objectives | Corporate Profile/Direction: Business Strategies | Corporate Profile/Direction: Business Issues |
|---|---|---|---|---|
| What do we know? |  |  |  |  |
| What do we need to find out? |  |  |  |  |
|  | Organizational Structure | Departmental Profile/Direction: Department Profile | Departmental Profile/Direction: Objectives/ Strategies | Departmental Profile/Direction: Issues |
| What do we know? |  |  |  |  |
| What do we need to find out? |  |  |  |  |

| Key Players<br>Name, Title, Location | Key Player Type | What do we know? | What do we need<br>to find out? |
|---|---|---|---|
| | ❏ D-M ❏ Coach<br>❏ GK ❏ User<br>❏ Evaluator ❏ Contact | | |
| | ❏ D-M ❏ Coach<br>❏ GK ❏ User<br>❏ Evaluator ❏ Contact | | |
| | ❏ D-M ❏ Coach<br>❏ GK ❏ User<br>❏ Evaluator ❏ Contact | | |

| Product Fit: | Business Fit: |
|---|---|

| Access Strategy | Presentation |
|---|---|
| **Decision Maker:** | **Attendees:** |
| **Strategy:** ❏ D-M Call ❏ Coach ❏ Personal Request ❏ Access Letter | **Target Date:** |
| **Issues:** | **Desired Outcomes:** |
| | |
| | |

## Account Action Plan

| Who | What | When |
|---|---|---|
| | | |
| | | |
| | | |

# INDEX

Together, authors and IMPAX® Corporation Co-Presidents **Mark Shonka** and **Dan Kosch** have tallied more than 40 years of experience in direct sales, sales management, and sales consulting and training. IMPAX, a leading sales consulting and training company, is committed to helping clients improve their sales, account management, and sales leadership efforts. IMPAX has worked with thousands of sales professionals in the field and the classroom throughout North America and abroad.

Shonka and Kosch are highly sought-after authorities on a range of sales topics including selling value, strategic account selling, strategic account management, account planning, and sales leadership. With names like IBM, 3M, DuPont, Eli Lilly, D&B, AT&T, and Microsoft, the authors' client list reflects some of the world's leading sales organizations.

As the editor-at-large for *Selling Power* magazine, **Malcolm Fleschner** has been actively writing about professional selling for more than ten years.

If you would like more information about IMPAX and about how we can help your company go Beyond Selling Value, please contact us at:

IMPAX
252 Wilton Road
Westport, CT 06880-1908
Toll free: 800-457-4727
Office: 203-222-1900
Fax: 203-222-8445
E-mail: info@impaxcorp.com
Web site: www.impaxcorp.com

# Also Available from
# Dearborn Trade Publishing

### Getting to "Closed"
Stephan Schiffman ($17.95 paperback, 0-7931-5389-1)

### Sales Don't Just Happen
Stephan Schiffman ($15.95 paperback, 0-7931-5463-4)

### Cause Marketing
Joe Marconi ($25 hardcover, 0-7931-5258-5)

### The Market Planning Guide, Sixth Edition
David H. Bangs Jr. ($22.95 paperback, 0-7931-5971-7)

### Legendary Brands
Laurence Vincent ($27 hardcover, 0-7931-5560-6)

### Creating Customer Evangelists
Available December 2002
Ben McDonnell and Jackie Huba ($25 hardcover, 0-7931-5561-4)

### Marketing to Women
Available January 2003
Martha Barletta ($23 hardcover, 0-7931-5963-6)

A complete list of our titles is available at

# Share the message!

### Bulk discounts
Discounts start at only 10 copies. Save up to 55% off retail price.

### Custom publishing
Private label a cover with your organization's name and logo. Or, tailor information to your needs with a custom pamphlet that highlights specific chapters.

### Ancillaries
Workshop outlines, videos, and other products are available on select titles.

### Dynamic speakers
Engaging authors are available to share their expertise and insight at your event.

Call Dearborn Trade Special Sales at 1-800-245-BOOK (2665)
or e-mail trade@dearborn.com

Dearborn™
Trade Publishing
A **Kaplan Professional** Company